UNIVERSITY OF NORTH CAROLINA
STUDIES IN THE ROMANCE LANGUAGES
AND LITERATURES

PLATONISM IN DESPORTES

by

Robert M. Burgess

THE UNIVERSITY OF NORTH CAROLINA PRESS
CHAPEL HILL

NUMBER TWENTY-TWO   1954

Copyright, 1954
The University of North Carolina Press

Presses of
The Orange Printshop
Chapel Hill, N. C.

TABLE OF CONTENTS

	Introduction	vii
Chapter One	The Era of Desportes and its Platonic Manifestations	1
Chapter Two	The Creation	24
Chapter Three	The Soul	40
Chapter Four	The Ideas	52
Chapter Five	Love	59
Chapter Six	The God Love	88
Chapter Seven	Beauty	97
Chapter Eight	The Lover and the Beloved	106
Chapter Nine	The Poet and Poetry	119
Chapter Ten	The Virtues	133
Chapter Eleven	Fear: A Passion of the Soul	141
Chapter Twelve	Concluding Remarks	145
	De La Crainte	149-150
	Appendix	
	Notes	157
	General Bibliography	180

ACKNOWLEDGEMENTS

Numerous persons have contributed generously toward making this study a *fait accompli*, and to them a debt of gratitude is herein acknowledged. They are too numerous to be mentioned in every case but the following have been particularly helpful. Professor Robert V. Merrill of the University of California at Los Angeles first interested me in literary Platonism and then supervised the beginnings of this study, giving invaluable counsel until his untimely death. Others of his colleagues at UCLA, Professors A. G. Fite, Charles Speroni, E. H. Templin and F. M. Carey, read the manuscript, made corrections and offered additional helpful suggestions. The work could not have been completed without the guiding hand of Professor Paul Friedlander through the period of classical antiquity, and without his intimate knowledge of basic Platonic concepts, nor would it have been possible but for the friendship and encouragement over a long period of years of Professor C. C. Humiston, under whose immediate supervision it was completed.

Certain of my colleagues at Montana State University have also been consulted on matters relating to their specific fields and have been most kind in lending their help. Professor Mary B. Clapp, who is thoroughly acquainted with Church history and doctrine, was called upon repeatedly to aid in determining the influence of Platonic concepts on the writings of Churchmen and on Church doctrine; Professor W. P. Clark was helpful in clarifying certain points having to do with Greek and Latin literatures; Professors Nan C. Carpenter and Robert T. Turner read the text and made corrections; Professor Emeritus Louise Arnoldson did valuable research for me at the Bibliothèque Nationale, bought and sent microfilms and books from France and aided in the final proofreading. The whole staff of the Library at MSU cooperated in every possible way in securing works, not in our library, through inter-library loan, and in running down other materials.

Several friends abroad have shown a friendly disposition toward my efforts. For biographical information concerning Philippe Desportes I have leaned heavily on the work of Prof. Jacques Lavaud of the U. of Poitiers, with whom I established relations through a pleasant correspondence. Professor Fernand Baldensperger of the Sorbonne, a former professor of mine, was helpful with recommendations on numerous occasions. Dr. Ian F. Fraser, Director of the American Library in Paris, very kindly unearthed needed books long out of print and sent them to me, along with microfilms of books in various French libraries.

Finally, I should like to acknowledge my debt to Prof. Urban T. Holmes, Jr. of the U. of North Carolina, who permitted me to send my manuscript to him for his examination, who confessed to finding something worthwhile in it, and who encouraged its publication. It is due to his influence that the study is now appearing in published form.

INTRODUCTION

In his essay entitled *The Agony of Christianity* Miguel de Unamuno says: "The state of being Christian is the state of being Christ. The Christian makes himself Christ. . . . Not only with Christ but with all power, human and divine, with every man, living and eternal, whom one knows with a mystic knowledge through the compenetration of the vitals, as it were, it is the same: in knowing, the lover ultimately becomes the thing known, becomes the beloved. . . . In order to be a Pascalian it does not suffice to accept his thoughts: one must *be* Pascal, become a Pascal."[1] If one were to accept such conditions as the necessary criterion for being a Platonist it would be impossible to say that Philippe Desportes, or any other person, ever fitted the pattern. The term Platonist is almost impossible of definition. No one knows just how much of the philosophic thought we designate as Platonic originated with the great Athenian. We do know that much of it did not. Plato profited by all the rich heritage of speculative thought before his day, subjecting everything to the scrutiny of reason and drawing new conclusions. His inquiries entered not only into those things which are purely philosophical but also into those which are theological, metaphysical, ethical, aesthetic, political, and scientific in nature. He owed something to ancient Oriental and Egyptian speculations concerning the nature of the gods and of man's soul, to the myth of the Thracian Orpheus,[2] and to the teachings of the Greek Sophists.[3] He was more particularly indebted to such of his predecessors as Homer,[4] Heraclitus,[5] Pythagoras,[6] Parmenides,[7] Empedocles,[8] and Socrates,[9] whose thoughts concerning the true nature of things formed a background for his own. He followed a course of assimilation and of rejection, of reconciliation or of finding a midpoint acceptable to him. He could agree with neither the perpetual flux of the world of Heraclitus nor the eternal permanence of that of Parmenides. But he did conclude that there are two worlds, that of flux, which is the world of opinion, and that of permanence, which is one of true knowledge. And thus he conceived his own theory of reality, which is at the bottom of his thinking.

It has been said that Platonism *is* philosophy and that Plato was merely a recorder; that this philosophy existed before Plato and would eventually have been set down by someone had he not lived; that the philosophic speculations of the western world since his day consist simply of a series of footnotes to his dialogues. Certainly he touched upon every philosophic and metaphysical problem which has ever puzzled man. His dialectic method of approach to knowledge did not call for dogmatic conclusions. Every person taking part in the dialogues is called upon for his thoughts upon any particular subject. Sometimes the speaker is shown the fallacy of his own thoughts, while on other occasions he is permitted to believe that his conclusions are as worthy of consideration as those of anyone else. Plato's concepts are therefore not to be considered as ultimate truths. They are rather in the nature of truth. The evolution of his own thought upon certain matters can be noted. He realized that what he was setting down in his dialogues was only an image of true being.

The Platonic Academy which Plato founded in Athens in 387 B.C. continued its work until it was dissolved in A.D. 529. Therefore the direct influence of the teachings of the Athenian remained strong throughout Greece during that period and spread as well to many other parts of the Mediterranean world. With the ascendancy of Rome in that world Platonic doctrine spread to the Italian peninsula, so that many young scholars studied under its adherents, and others went to Greece to pursue their studies. Perhaps the most prominent of these latter was Cicero (106-43 B.C.). Besides his translation of the *Timaeus*—now lost—his writings which most clearly reflect the influence of the dialogues are: *De natura deorum, Tusculan Disputations, Somnium Scipionis,* and *De Amicitia.* Rome was a place of many gods and many philosophies, and, at the same time Cicero was Platonizing, Lucretius (*c.* 99-*c.* 55 B.C.) was writing his *De rerum natura* and living his life under the influence of the teachings of Epicurus. The old Roman religion had lost its hold on the educated classes, and a general skepticism prevailed. Philosophically minded Romans turned to Stoicism during the troubled times of the first century of the Christian era, while Christianity itself was becoming more and more imbued with Platonic concepts. Among the Jews Philo the Alexandrian—a contemporary of Christ—had striven to harmonize Plato's conception of mind as the cause of all things with Hebrew religious thought.[10]

Neoplatonism came into being in Alexandria in the third century of our era. Its founder, Plotinus, and his followers took Plato as their point of reference and considered themselves good Platonists. Their variations from the Platonic norm have been often corroborated, although one can find justification in the dialogues for all of their beliefs. Generally speaking, the differences between Platonism and Neoplatonism are ones of emphasis. Plato, for all his preoccupation with metaphysical matters, was primarily interested in the acquisition of knowledge and wisdom, and the transmission of these to others for the practical good of the state. The Neoplatonists emphasized his metaphysical preoccupations, divorced themselves from things of the world and affairs of state, and read into what Plato had said about God and creation the idea that man is one with God and that his mission is to find his way back to that oneness. Their teachings attracted a wide following, even among persons of importance, both in and out of the Church. The pagan revival of the emperor Julian (331-363) was Neoplatonic, and St. Augustine and others of the early Latin Church Fathers—Ambrose, Jerome, and Gregory—seem to have come under the influence of Neoplatonic teachings. In the works of St. Augustine these concepts became inseparably tied up with Christian doctrine.

The transmission of Neoplatonism through the Middle Ages is due in large part to the anonymous author whose works were long ascribed to St. Dionysius the Areopagite, and to John Scotus Erigena. As for the dialogues themselves, they were never entirely lost or completely out of view of at least a small number of scholars in the Byzantine world down to the time of the conquest of Constantinople by the Turks in 1453, but during much of this period intellectual exchange between East and West was nearly nonexistent.

The West remained in possession of the works of Cicero which embodied Platonic doctrine and also of those of the Neoplatonists. Of the dialogues of Plato there remained only a Latin translation of the *Timaeus* by Chalcidius (c. A.D. 350), to which were added much later translations in the same language of the *Meno* and the *Phaedo* by Henricus Aristippus (c. 1156). These three dialogues played an important part in the revival of interest in Platonic doctrine in certain Cathedral Schools of France—notably that of Chartres—during the twelfth century, and their teachings, along with those of the Neoplatonists and the early Church Fathers, entered into the writings of St. Thomas Aquinas and thus became an inseparable part of orthodox Catholic philosophy.

Meantime, in the eleventh and twelfth centuries, literature in the vernacular in France was devoting itself more and more to matters of love, and a new trend which owed something to Platonic doctrine was developing with respect to the poet's attitude *vis-à-vis* his lady. Later in this study we shall have occasion to develop more fully this phenomenon, but for the moment it suffices to say that the new attitude was one of idealization of both lady and love. It was first manifest among the troubadours of Provence, and was later fully rationalized at the courts of Eleanor of Poitou and of her daughter, Marie of Champagne. One will recall in particular the works of Andreas Capellanus and of Chrétien de Troyes.

In Italy, among the writers in the vernacular, it was the poets of the *dolce stil nuovo*—including Dante—and later Petrarch who refined to a high degree of perfection the Platonic, Neoplatonic, Christian, and courtly concepts and passed them on to succeeding generations of literary men. Like the poets of northern France they had come under the influence of the aristocratic verse of the Provençal poets—Arnaut Daniel, Bertrand de Born, *et al*—and it was their idealized concepts of the lady and of love, as well as their verse form, the *canso*, which attracted the attention of the Italians.

As for the complete dialogues of Plato in the original, the scholars of western Europe remained in ignorance of them until the fifteenth century, when Greek scholars began to arrive in Italy in rather large numbers, first because of increased commerce between the Italian city states and the East and then because of the threat of a Turkish invasion of Constantinople. This was perhaps the most brilliant age in the life of these states, when certain families which had become rich and powerful through trade and banking also became patrons of the arts and letters. The men of these families had their eyes opened concerning the brilliance of the thought and art of antiquity by Greek refugee scholars, among whom the greatest were Chrysoloras, Bessarion, and Gemistus Plethon.

Florence became the greatest of the Italian centers of intellectual and artistic fermentation, and the life of the city centered in the Medici family. So intrigued by the teachings of Plato was Cosimo de' Medici that he took under his protection the bright young Marsilio Ficino, son of his doctor, and had him trained and educated to lead a revival of Platonism in the city on the Arno. The young scholar learned Greek and Latin, among other languages, immersed himself in the study of the works of Plato and the Neoplatonists, established, under the protection of the Medici, an Accademia Platonica, and was soon busily engaged in translating the dialogues from Greek into the more universally understood Latin. To these he added Latin translations of many of the Neoplatonists, giving long and detailed commentaries on these works to explain away difficulties, and finally writing his own original *Theologia platonica de immortalitate animarum*, which sought to reconcile Platonic and Christian theology. The men of Ficino's academy did not then fear charges of heresy. They regularly celebrated Plato's anniversary, and his statue was a sort of shrine before which candles were kept perpetually burning. Ficino was protected by, and did his work under, three of the great Medicis—Cosimo, Piero, and Lorenzo—and when he died the tradition which he had established was carried on by the Medici pope, Leo X. The academic spirit spread throughout the Italian peninsula,[11] and its preoccupations passed on to succeeding generations through the works which Ficino left behind and through those of his disciple, Pico della Mirandola, and such men as Cardinal Bembo, Castiglione, and Leone Ebreo. In their sonnet sequences the Petrarchists of this age—including such poets as Lorenzo de' Medici and Michelangelo—were continuing the poetic traditions of Petrarch and adding to their verses the Platonic concepts newly discovered or developed by Ficino and his followers.

It was of course not long before all the above-mentioned activities of the Italians were known in France. Pico made an extended stay there and did his bit toward acquainting a few French with the work of Ficino and the Florentine Academy. The Italian campaigns of Charles VIII, Louis XII, and François I gave larger numbers of Frenchmen a close view of the enviable cultural developments among the Italian city states. The Greek refugee scholar Lascaris visited France on several occasions, under Charles VIII and Louis XII, and gave open lectures on the Greek language and literature. Among his auditors were Charles Estienne and Guillaume Budé, who were to become two of France's leading humanists. A Lyonese doctor, Symphorien Champier, less than a generation after Ficino's great work of translation, was writing treatises in Latin on the Platonic dialogues, and into the verse of the poets of the Lyonese School—Maurice Scève and Louise Labé, among others—entered frequent Platonic elements of the type current in contemporary Italian poetry.

In the greatest decades of the French Renaissance—those of François I and his sister Marguerite de Navarre—Platonic doctrine entered into the theological precepts of such men as Marguerite's spiritual advisers, Guillaume Briçonnet and Lefèvre d'Etaples and philosophers and teachers like the already mentioned Budé and Pierre de la Ramée; and into the poetic works not only of the Lyonese School but also of such protégés of Marguerite as Antoine Héroët, perhaps the most truly Platonic poet of the age. Already in 1537 Colin had translated Castiglione's *Cortegiano* into French for François I, to serve him and his courtiers as a guide for their education and conduct.[12]

On the informal side, the coteries of Scève and Pontus de Tyard in Lyon and that of Marguerite in Paris, Tusson, and Nérac carried on the academic spirit which became formalized in the Trilingue et noble academie, founded by François in 1530 and placed under the direction of Budé.[13]

Shortly after the deaths of François (1547) and of Marguerite (1549), the Italian influence received a new impetus when a descendant of the famous Medici family, Catherine, became Queen of France as the wife of Henri II. Almost immediately the Pléiade, under the encouragement of the great humanist and poet Jean Dorat, came into being, and among the first works it produced was Joachim Du Bellay's *Deffense et Illustration de la Langue Françoise* (1549), which served as the manifesto of the new school and gave the following advice to its members: "Lis donc, et relis premierement, ô poëte futur, feuillette de main nocturne et journelle les exemplaires grecs et latins...."[14] In the same year Du Bellay published his sonnet sequence *Olive*, in which Platonic doctrine played an important role.[15]

Catherine's sons, François II, Charles IX, and Henri III, who, one after the other, succeeded their father on the throne of France, were even more conscious of the Medici heritage than was their mother. They were proud of the patronage which their illustrious Florentine ancestors had given to the arts, science, and philosophy, and they sought to emulate them. They too established academies and protected men of learning, although they were living in a different age and met with opposition on every hand. Their reigns were marked by violent social upheaval and intolerance which worked against their efforts.

It is not the purpose of this study to try to prove that the poet with whom our interest lies—Philippe Desportes—was a Platonist in the Unamuno sense, but rather to point out the Platonic manifestations during the period in which he lived, his own inclinations with respect to the teachings of Plato, and more particularly the Platonic concepts which are to be found in his works. Having considered these things the reader will be able to judge the extent to which Platonic or Neoplatonic doctrine exerted its influence upon this poet from Chartres. The work does propose to show, however, that the poet's great learning rested upon a foundation of Platonism and that his major philosophical, as well as his metaphysical, beliefs, reflected in his life and works, sprang from the dialogues.

It has been maintained in certain studies concerned with literary Platonism during the French Renaissance that the authors treated were only superficially drawn toward Platonic philosophy, and that they made use of Platonic conceits only to embellish their works and because such conceits were in the atmosphere at the time. In his work on the philosophy of Marsilio Ficino and its influence on sixteenth-century French literature Jean Festugière says: "J'ai pris au sérieux les hommes qui ont rénové ce culte de l'amour platonicien: j'ai cru à leur sincérité. Et sans penser, certes, que tous les adeptes des théories du *Phèdre* et du *Banquet* ont pratiqué la vertu de chasteté, j'ai admis que, lorsqu'ils célébraient dans leurs vers la Beauté souveraine, ce n'était point la simple rhétorique, mais qu'un sentiment vrai les animait. Il est très humain de rêver un idéal de pureté céleste tout en s'abandonnant aux voluptés de la chair. Depuis qu'il existe, l'homme est double. Et je ne vois nulle invraisemblance à ce que des poètes aient adressé à telles maîtresses, qui n'étaient pas toujours insensibles, des sonnets tout inspirés de cet idéal. Ils chantaient sincèrement. Peut-être même, au moment où ils écrivaient, oubliant leur faiblesses, se figuraient-ils adorer uniquement la Beauté idéale et ne connaître que le pur amour. Pour beaucoup, sauf pour Ronsard dont le tempérament est surtout d'un voluptueux, j'inclinerais à le penser. L'âme humaine est si complexe."[16]

Festugière has nothing to say about Desportes, or about the poets after the time of Ronsard. However, in accord with his attitude "j'ai pris au sérieux" Desportes, and I have found in the poet's works repeated evidence of all the basic Platonic teachings having to do with the Creation, the Soul, the Ideas, Love and Beauty, the Lover and the Beloved, the Poet and Poetry, the Virtues and the Vices. These are the basic concerns of literary Platonism.

It should be constantly remembered that Desportes is not at the beginning of the Platonic tradition in France, but rather at its apex. Platonic concepts had become by this time a part of the general culture, and just as Racine, a century later, accepted as a matter of course the classical doctrine against which Corneille had revolted, so Desportes absorbed as a natural part of his culture the Platonism which had been an intriguing novelty to an earlier generation of Renaissance men.

Although at least two of Desportes' longer poems, *Chant d'Amour* and *Procez contre Amour*,[17] are of Platonic inspiration from beginning to end, in general his concepts drawn from the Athenian are contained in brief passages, scattered here and there throughout his works. The total of these fragments, sowed in the midst of a prolific production embodying every conceivable poetic motif, conceit, and philosophic idea within the limits of idealized love, is sufficient to show the enormous influence which the Greek philosopher was still exerting on poets and scholars who were writing under the last of the Valois.

It will be with these fragments of Platonism, for the most part, gathered together in special categories and presented in conjunction with their probable sources, that this work will deal primarily. However, since Desportes is completely representative of his age, he will be better understood if we devote some introductory consideration to Platonic manifestations at the court where he was first "poet of princes" and then "prince of poets" for at least a full generation. We can then seek out similar manifestations in the life of this remarkable man.

Platonism in France during the first half of the century under consideration has been studied by such scholars as Abel Lefranc,[18] Jean Festugière,[19] and Robert V. Merrill.[20] Nothing has been done, to my knowledge, on this subject covering the period of Henry III.

The complete poetic works of Desportes have been published

only in the edition of Alfred Michiels,[21] and it is that edition which has been used in this study and to which reference will be made. As for his prose works, they consist only of some prayers and three discourses delivered before the Académie du Palais of Henri III. There is considerable Platonic matter in the discourses. Two of them on the subject *Quelles sont les plus excellentes, les vertus intellectuelles ou les moralles* have been reproduced in Edouard Frémy's work on *l'Académie des derniers Valois*,[22] and the other on *la Crainte* has been transcribed from the manuscript in the Bibliothèque Nationale[23] and has been placed in an Appendix at the end of this work. Except for several short quotations in Jacques Lavaud's study of Desportes,[24] this discourse has never before appeared in print.

It is the hope of the author of this study that the student of French literature may find set forth in these pages a clear, simple, and complete treatment of a sixteenth-century literary influence which left its indelible mark not only on that age but on all succeeding ages. It affected not only the literature of France but also that of all western civilization. It is not too much to say that the literature of the West cannot be fully understood without a more or less intimate knowledge of the Platonic influence.

It may be objected that too much of Plato has found its way into these pages; and that words or concepts from the dialogues have been repeated upon occasion. If the first of these objections is valid it is excused on the basis of the limited knowledge of the usual student of literature with respect to concepts in the dialogues which have intrigued literary men through the ages. It has been considered worthwhile to isolate these concepts rather frequently, and to present them in the beautiful and poetic words of their author—so far as this is possible in a translation—so that by way of comparison our own poet's words and thoughts may be better understood. Thus the reader may acquire a better background for an understanding of the influence of those concepts on literature in general. As for the second objection, any repetition of words from the dialogues will not annoy too much someone who is thoroughly familiar with them, and it may be of infinite help to the novice. Such repetition is necessary because in a single context one may find in combination concepts dealing with such varied subjects as Love, Beauty, or the Ideas, which are treated elsewhere, in this study, under separate headings. It has occasionally been judged advisable, therefore, either to summarize or to repeat words which have already been quoted.

Plato's words are presented in the famous English translation by Benjamin Jowett.[25] Care has been taken to avoid straying from the main subject into controversy over the meaning of certain isolated Greek words. In short, there is nothing in these pages which cannot be understood by any student of French literature.

NOTES

INTRODUCTION
1. Trans. Pierre Loving (New York: Payson & Clarke Ltd., 1928), pp. 34-36.

2. Concerned with the dual nature of man, life after death, original sin, the concept of the soul as imprisoned in the body, the life of the soul, free will and responsibility, the cycles of the soul, and the influence of music upon it.

3. In so far as they were concerned with man's place in the universe of which he is the center, though not irrevocably bound to it nor subject to its inevitable laws; with him as a measure of all things and free to determine his own fate; with his relationships with other men; with his unrealized possibilities; with the appeal to reason; with the denial of a plurality of gods.

4. As a source of mythological and legendary matter.

5. With respect to his belief that fire was the primitive essence of matter and his theory of the universal state of flux.

6. For his elevated morality, recommendation of an austere, ascetic life, theory of numbers, and emphasis on the moral effects of music and its place in the universe.

7. He held that change is impossible; that what we see with the eyes is not real but is an illusion; that the universe is unchangeable, unmovable.

8. For his belief that the universe is composed of four elements: earth, air, fire and water; that their mingling is bought about by love, their separation, by hate.

9. For the primacy of the search for truth in his life; for his emphasis on the importance of the role of love in the soul's ascent to the realm of the ideas. Much of what Plato has to say is represented as coming from Socrates.

10. Will Durant, in his *Caesar and Christ* (New York: Simon and Schuster, 1944), pp. 501-2, says that he sometimes identified the Logos with Divine Mind and treated it as a person—the Son of God by the Virgin Wisdom. His later influence on the Fathers of the Church was great. They made use of his allegorical principles "to answer the critics of the Hebrew Scriptures and joined with Gnostics and Neo-Platonists in accepting the mystical vision of God as the crown of human enterprise."

11. The more important Italian academies were: Accademia Platonica of Ficino, Florence, fifteenth century. Orti Oricellari, Florence, early sixteenth century. Accademia Fiorentina, late fifteenth century. Accademia della Crusca, Florence, sixteenth century. Accademia degli Infiammati, Padua, sixteenth century. Accademia degli Affidati, Pavia, sixteenth century. Accademia delle Notti Vaticane, Rome, sixteenth century.

12. Abel Lefranc, in his "Marguerite de Navarre et le Platonisme de la Renaissance," *Grands écrivains français de la Renaissance* (Paris: Champion, 1914), pp. 237-38, says that among the books which Marguerite carried with her in all her travels were the Holy Bible, the translations of Ficino, the works of Boccaccio and of Dante, Boethius' *Consolation*, and Castiglione's *Cortegiano*.

13. This academy developed into what is today the Collége de France.

14. *Op cit.*, ed. Henri Chamard (Paris: Cornély et Cie, 1908), Part II, chap. IV.

15. See Robert V. Merrill, *The Platonism of Joachim Du Bellay* (Chicago: U. of Chicago Press, 1925).

16. *La Philosophie de l'amour de Marsile Ficin et son influence sur la littérature française au XVIe siècle* (Paris: Librairie Philosophique J. Vrin, 1941), pp. 1-2.

17. Philippe Desportes, *Œuvres de* . . ., ed. Alfred Michiels (Paris: Adolphe Delahays, 1858), pp. 50-57.

18. *Grands écrivains français de la Renaissance*, "Le Platonisme et la littérature en France à l'époque de la Renaissance"; "Marguerite de Navarre et le Platonisme de la Renaissance" (Paris: E. Champion, 1914).

19. *La Philosophie de l'amour de Marsile Ficin et son influence sur la littérature française au XVIe siècle* (Paris: Librairie Philosophique J. Vrin, 1941).

20. *The Platonism of Joachim Du Bellay* (Chicago: U. of Chicago Press, 1925); "Platonism in Pontus de Tyard's *Erreurs amoureuses* (1549)," *Modern Philology*, XXXV (1937), 139-58; "The Pléiade and the Androgyne," *Comparative Literature*, I (1949), 97-112.

21. Philippe Desportes, *Œuvres de* . . ., ed. Alfred Michiels (Paris: Adolphe Delahays, 1858).

22. (Paris: Ernest Leroux, 1887), pp. 231-38.

23. Nouv. acq. franç. 4655, fol. 50 et 63.

24. *Un Poète de cour au temps des derniers Valois, Philippe Desportes (1546-1606)* (Paris: Librairie E. Droz, 1936).

25. *The Dialogues of Plato* (New York: Random House, 1937).

Chapter I

THE ERA OF PHILIPPE DESPORTES
AND
ITS PLATONIC MANIFESTATIONS

Philippe Desportes was born in 1546 and died sixty years later. His rise to fame began in the reign of Charles IX (1560-1574), came to its full flower in that of Henri III (1574-1589), and continued until his death during the reign of Henri IV (1589-1610). From the position of "poète des princes" he rose to that of "prince des poètes," and went on to become one of the great courtiers and scholars of his age, never losing for a moment the favor which he had earned as the "bien aymé" poet of Henri III. Although Ronsard held the official position of "prince des poètes" until his death in 1585, Desportes had replaced him long before in the affections of the court.

The age during which he lived was a tragic one for France, full of plotting, bitterness, civil wars, and massacres. There is little wonder that the frivolities of the young Valois princes, who succeeded each other on the throne during those years, were short lived and that, once the insoluble difficulties rested on their shoulders, they should have turned from their pleasures to seek the re-establishment of harmony within their kingdom by giving attention to all sorts of ethical, philosophical, and religious activities.

The poets of the Pléiade who had begun their domination of the French literary scene at about the middle of the century were either dead or aging when the star of Desportes began to rise. Furthermore, their concern had been more with aesthetic matters than with ethical or philosophical ones. They had not fully attained the perfection they had sought and found in the works of antiquity, in spite of their insistence on classical genres and their recommendation that the poet "feuillette de main nocturne et journelle les exemplaires grecs et latins...."[1]

When Desportes made his way to Paris in 1564 from his native city of Chartres the times were ripe for something new. The young Valois princes had become aware—not without the suggestions of their courtiers—of the examples which had been set for them by their ancestors, the Florentine Medici, who had fostered the Italian Renaissance and had taken as their protégé the young Marsilio Ficino. Nor were they allowed to forget that they were the grandsons of François I, father of the French Renaissance, and nephews of Marguerite de Navarre, who had done so much to promote the new learning in France.

In her excellent book on the French academies, Frances Yates says: "One must not forget that Charles IX and Henri III were, on the maternal side, scions of the house of Medici and that in encouraging French academies they were following in the illustrious traditions of their family. Three years before the foundation of Baïf's Academy, the philosopher Ramus had reminded Catherine de' Medici of the Florentine Academy which her ancestors Cosimo and Lorenzo had fostered. He describes how, in the house at Careggi put at his disposal by the Medici, Ficino made his translation of Plato and was able to philosophise in liberty, and he urges Catherine to imitate her forbears in such wise and generous encouragement of scholarship."[2]

There was nothing in the background of the young Chartrain which gave early promise of the brilliant career which he was to enjoy, with no eclipse, over a period of many years. He came from a bourgeois family, which, however, had some well-placed connections. Practically nothing of an exact nature is known concerning his education, except that all of his formal studies were done in Chartres before he left that city; that they must have been pursued in the Cathedral school there, since he was early tonsured; that his work must have been of a broad and serious nature, for he knew Latin, Greek, Italian, and Hebrew, and in the years of his greatness was known as one of the most learned men of France.

Something more concerning the education of our poet may be conjectured if one looks for a moment into the history of the School of Chartres, which had become famous as a great center of learning as early as the eleventh century.[3] One of its early heads, Fulbert (eleventh century), declared Plato superior to all the other thinkers of antiquity.[4] The works of the Neoplatonists, the pseudo-Dionysius, Boethius, Scotus Erigena, were known and revered at an early date. Chalcidius' Latin translation of Plato's *Timaeus* (c.A.D. 350) enjoyed particular favor as early as the twelfth century, and exerted a profound influence on the teachers. In their commentaries on it they sought to reconcile Platonic and Mosaic accounts of the creation.[5] It was from Plato's work that the Chartrains derived their metaphysics and their theories concerning the cosmos. The twelfth-century teacher, Bernard of Chartres, was greatly interested in the Platonic Ideas.

and the dual nature of things as portrayed in the *Timaeus,* and was carried along the Neoplatonic path of seeing God Himself in the Ideas, and the universe in a pantheistic manner.[6]

While Chartres was overshadowed by such schools as that of Paris during the later Middle Ages and the first years of the Renaissance, it cherished its proud tradition and could look with pride upon its Platonic proclivities in an age when Plato was coming back into his own. In his *Story of Chartres,* Cecil Headlam says: "The School of Chartres had . . . long been famous. When at the end of the fifteenth century, the new movement in literature, philosophy and art began to be felt through France, the successors of Fulbert were not unaffected by it. They welcomed the new learning. The discussion of the schoolmen yielded place to the new appreciation of Greek and Latin, art and literature."[7] The school was, then, almost certainly living under this great tradition when Desportes was a scholar there, and it is perhaps not too much to suppose that it was there that he gained a more or less intimate knowledge of the Platonic doctrine which was later to find its way into his verse and into his philosophy of life.

The poet's initial stay in Paris was of short and inauspicious duration. However, since he was a young man of keen intellect seeking for a position worthy of his talents, Antoine de Senecterre, Bishop of Puy, "l'engagea sur sa belle mine"[8] as secretary and took him to Italy with him. There he remained for some three years, according to M. Emile Faguet.[9] Nothing definite is known of his stay in Italy, but again we can conjecture, with a reasonable degree of certitude, something of his activities there. From the liberal use which he made, at a later date, of the works of the Italian Petrarchists, he must have spent considerable time thoroughly familiarizing himself with them. He doubtless profited by his stay among the Italians so far as his manners were concerned, for he acquired very early the art of being the perfect courtier, which he found personified all around him and which had been so well outlined by Castiglione in his *Cortegiano.*[10] Our poet's long and brillant career under three French kings would indicate that few men, have played the role of the courtier more successfully than he did. Faguet says of him: "Desportes est un courtisan dans toute l"acceptation du mot."[11] It was while he was in Italy that he composed his *Contre une nuict trop claire,*[12] imitated from Ariosto, which was later put to music and enjoyed a great sucess in France.

When Desportes returned to Paris, probably in 1567, he had

acquired all the skills and polish needed for getting ahead in a court dominated by young lords and ladies, and he was prepared to put his knowledge to practical use. The more one studies his life and works the more one is impressed by his dual nature. On the one hand there was the serious scholar, who spent a fortune collecting one of the great libraries of the time and devoted much of his life to study—he is said to have died finally from having overtaxed his strength in study[13]—and on the other hand there was the somewhat ingratiating courtier and poet, who knew that he had to make use of his wits and render himself indispensable if he was to secure and maintain for himself the place he desired in a world to which he had not been born.

His return to France was at a most favorable moment. He almost immediately made the greatest friendship of his life—one which can be called truly Platonic—with the young Claude de Laubespine, who was very shortly to become "secrétaire d'Etat" upon the death of his father. Through Claude he was introduced into the worldly milieu of Claude's sister, the charming Madeleine, wife of Nicolas de Neufville, seigneur de Villeroy. Philippe's friendship for Claude was, however, not of long duration and the supreme sorrow of his life came when this friend died in 1570. We shall have occasion to see how Desportes honored him in his verse.

Through the Laubespines and Villeroys the fortunes of Philippe were made, so far as the *beau monde* and his official position were concerned. His next step was to establish himself as a poet. In this move fortune again smiled upon him. Ronsard was the favorite of Charles IX, a position which was too firmly held to offer any prospects to our poet. However, the king's brother, the young and brilliant duc d'Anjou,[14] had, as yet, no favorite among the aspiring poets of the age. This prince has been more maligned by the historians than any prince ever to have sat on the throne of France, and he owes this ignominy to forces largely outside himself. When he came to the throne as Henri III the St. Bartholomew Massacre was still fresh in the minds of everyone, and the civil wars between the Ligue and the Huguenots were periodically rending all France. The reigning house was being attacked from all sides by pamphleteers and writers of scabrous *pasquils*. It is largely from a collection of these latter[15] and from the works of the embittered Agrippa d'Aubigné[16] that the historians have obtained their information concerning this prince. The great men of letters and the scholars of his own period saw him in quite another light, and if one looks at the serious preoccupations of his reign one can only conclude that he used every possible conciliatory means to bring peace again to his realm, but without success. A strong hand was needed rather than a philosopher king. We shall say more about this later. It suffices here to say that when Desportes began his career in Paris and his first poems were circulating in manuscript, he made the friendship and served as poetic mouthpiece of such high-born youths as Brantôme, Bussy d'Amboise, Le Guast, and finally the young duc d'Anjou himself. In one of his early works he predicted for the prince a brilliant military career[17] which seemed to have been partially realized in his victories at Jarnac and Montcontour in 1569. At any rate the poetic fortunes of the poet did not suffer because of having compared the prince to Achilles, and his position at court was becoming firmly fixed.

In 1570 three of Philippe's poems were set to music by one of the most celebrated musicians of the age, Nicolas de La Grotte, and they appeared in a published collection.[18] Only a very promising youth could have had such attention paid to his early efforts by so distinguished a musician.

Desportes' fortunes were still further promoted in the brilliant salon of the maréchale de Retz, where he became one of the reigning favorites. Whereas a "franche gaité" reigned at the home of the Villeroys, in the salon of the maréchale—the greatest in France prior to that of the marquise de Rambouillet—"plus de plaisanteries sur les femmes et le mariage, les épouses infidéles et le maris, mais un respect de la femme poussé jusqu'à l'adulation, une sorte de sanctuaire du néo-pétrarquisme; plus de satires, d'épigrammes ou de quartrains; mais des élégies, des complaintes, et des sonnets. Nous allons pénétrer dans le plus illustre des salons littéraires de l'époque, celui dont sortit vraisemblablement, au siècle suivant, le salon de la marquise de Rambouillet, en un mot dans le salon de la maréchale de Retz."[19] Mme de Retz' salon began to flourish in 1570, and soon thereafter a new wave[20] of Petrarchism and Platonism, fostered in its midst, was manifest in such works as Pontus de Tyard's *Nouvelles œuvres poétiques* (1573), Desporte's own *Premières œuvres* (1573), and Amadis Jamyn's *Œuvres Poétiques* (1575). The favor of Albert de Gondi, the wealthy Italian second husband of the maréchale, grew rapidly at the Italianate court of the sons of Catherine de' Medici, so that by 1573 he had become one of the great men of the realm. His wife was a reigning beauty, and all the poets of the age celebrated her in their verse. Her intellectual attainments rivalled her beauty. She was to be distinguished for her discourses before the Académie of Henri III a few years later. Lavaud says: "... se réunissait chez la maréchale tout ce que Paris comptait de plus brilliant."[21]

The début of Desportes is contemporary with that of Mme de Retz' "salon vert," and soon his verse—much of which was in imitation of the Italian Petrarchists—became so popular that the aging Ronsard felt himself obliged to write and publish a new sonnet sequence, *Sonnets à Hélène,* also in the Italianate manner, in order not to be forgotten.

In 1571 Desportes collected his poems into a beautifully bound manuscript volume which he presented to Charles IX. The following year his *Imitations d'Arioste* were published along with those of other French poets and were very favorably received. In 1573 he published the first collection of his own poetry, and the *privilège* bears witness to the fact that he was already "secrétaire de la chambre du roi."[22] The salon of the maréchale de Retz was furnishing a perfect setting for his verse. Whether he was writing for himself, for his prince, or for one of the other young lords of the court, the sentiments which he expressed were pure, the ladies whose beauties and virtues he extolled were chaste, the love he professed was idealized, and through this love and the beauty of the lady the poet was inspired to cultivate nobility of thought and conduct, although at the same time he might suffer from the coldness of the lady. The whole tone of his first collection of poems, addressed to a lady represented under the fictitious name of Diane, chaste goddess of the hunt, was basically Platonic, and there was a liberal scattering of precise Platonic concepts to be found even among the very first of these poems.

Scarcely had Desportes established himself at court and become the envy of many another young, aspiring poet, when Henri, duc d'Anjou, was elected to the throne of Poland, and Desportes was among the lords and courtiers who accompanied him into the land which seemed so forbidding to them. Most of the lords soon found pretexts to return to France, but the faithful Chartrain stayed on with his royal protector, as did another great man—Guy Du Faur de Pibrac—of his entourage. The latter was one of the truly fine intellects of the age, and Henri now began to use him to help repair his deficiencies in rhetoric and philosophy.[23] The first months of his reign were difficult and did not go well. Things were beginning to improve just at the moment when Charles IX died and Henri was called back to the throne of France. Pibrac advised him that he owed his first allegiance to France and should return.[24] Historians since his day have severely criticized him for abandoning his new kingdom and subjects.

Although they had been gone from France for less than a year (January to July, 1574) both Henri and his favorite poet returned to their native soil older and wiser. En route back to "la douce France" the new monarch made a triumphant detour through northern Italy, in every city of which he received all the honors of a mighty prince. In Venice he gave Desportes funds with which to enrich his own library, which was to become one of the greatest in France. "At Monza, in the Milanese, he heard Mass said by Carlo Borromeo, the future saint, with whom he had several conversations and who gave him at parting a golden crucifix containing wood from the true cross."[25] This archbishop of Milan had a great influence on Henri. He believed that the Counter-Reformation was to be effected through penitence and good works, two methods which Henri was to institute afterward, in France, along with numerous others, in his attempt to restore peace within his realm. Pierre Champion says in this connection: "Oui, Henri apportait en France une grande espérance. Mais son projet des mœurs et de la religion unique, non pas par la force, mais par la douceur, n'était qu'une utopie. Elle peut faire honneur aux sentiments d'humanité et à la foi religieuse d'Henri, à sa manière un mystique et un platonicien .... L'adolescent efféminé et courageux, le jeune homme secret mais décidé et passionné que fut le roi de Pologne, se retrouveront chez le roi, adonné à la grande chimère de la réforme des mœurs et de la foi, aux côtés d'une épouse, Louise de Vaudemont, qui fut la sainteté elle-même. Henri, de même que Catherine de' Medici, a le sentiment du beau et se montre connaisseur. Comme sa mère, il semble avoir eu, sinon le goût des sciences, du moins celui de la connaissance philosophique."[26]

The poets were naturally warm and expansive in their welcome of Henri back to France. They were no less so in their welcome of his protégé, and the great scholar-humanist-poet, Jean Dorat, father of the Pléiade and now an old man, celebrated the return in a Latin poem, making of Desportes the Orpheus of Argonaut fame returning to his homeland with Jason, who was the king.[27] It is significant that Desportes was made the counterpart of Orpheus, not only by Dorat but by numerous other poets of the age, for Orpheus was the legendary Greek musician so frequently mentioned by Plato himself, to whom the Greeks are believed to be indebted for many of their ideas on theological and metaphysical matters, and whose sweet music could charm animals and the very rocks themselves.

No distinction was made between music and poetry by the Greeks, who placed great emphasis upon their moral effects. Following the example of the Greeks this emphasis was being introduced into France by Antoine de Baïf in the form of *musique mesurée*. In his efforts Desportes played an important role, for already the sweet music of his verse was being extolled. As for Henri himself, Baïf had dared to express in verse what France was expecting of her new king and had suggested:

> Si veux te bien régler, en la royale vie,
> Conjoin l'expérience à la Philosophie;
> Par bon enseignemens apprendras le chemin
> Et, par l'effect, tes faicts conduiras à leur fin.[28]

Thus we see the important consideration being given philosophy and the moral effects of music and poetry by the men of this age, and the role which was being assigned them during the reign of the new king.

Henri was inclined to take his new duties seriously. His first concern was to surround himself with men whom he could trust and to relegate the others to places of little importance. As Desportes had been his favorite poet, addressing sonnets for him to Françoise d'Estrées, Renée de Rieux (Mlle de Chateauneuf), and the princesse de Clèves (Marie de Clèves), now he became a reader to the king—a position of great importance in this age—as well as counselor. M. Michiels, in his introduction to the collected works of the poet, says that it appears evident that Desportes took part in the "escapades nocturnes" of the prince.[29] This may be true but there is no evidence to prove that it is so. Nor does one have reliable evidence as to what those escapades of the king were, for Michiels relies too much on the words of d'Aubigné and of L'Estoile, both of whom are suspect. Furthermore, it scarcely seems reasonable that the king should have chosen as a companion for such pleasures his reader and counselor, upon whom he was to heap so many distinctions as the years passed. Accusations brought against the poet himself by the men of his age are practically non-existent, for he was highly respected in his time. Henri must have found in him a perfect courtier, discreet and trustworthy.

Many other men were to serve Henri as loyally as did Desportes. Pontus de Tyard, one of his readers, has already been mentioned. The particular subjects on which he kept the king informed were astronomy, mathematics, geography, and philosophy.[30] It was he who had translated Leone Ebreo's *Dialoghi d'amore* into French (1551) and had thus made available to all French readers one of the most purely Platonic treatises to come out of Italy during this age.

The Italian scholar, Bartolomeo Delbene, was a favorite of the king and wrote for him a long Latin poem on the *Civitas veri sive morum*, which was an allegory based on Aristotle's *Ethics*. He took a prominent part in Henri's Académie and seems to have had something to do with advising the king as to the selection of subjects on which discourses were to be made before it.[31] The moral and contemplative virtues in which he was interested became subjects of prime importance in the Académie, as we shall see when Desportes' own discourses before that body are discussed in a later section of this work.

Another distinguished man who moved in Henri's intellectual circle was Jean Bodin, who opened his *Six livres de la république* (1576) with a discussion of the active and contemplative virtues.[32] The famous and learned Italian philosopher, Giordano Bruno, spent about five years in Paris and was also a reader to the king during a part of that time. The poet Vauquelin de la Fresnaie wrote his *Art poétique* (1574) at the request of Henri. Frémy has the following to say about the friendship of the prince for Henri Estienne, of the great family of printers and scholars: "Des relations d'étroite amitié unissaient également Henri III à l'illustre imprimeur Henri Estienne. Traducteur de Plato, latiniste et grammarien, Estienne qui fut l'un des hommes dont le prince goûtait le plus la conversation, nous montre le dernier des Valois non plus, ainsi que l'ont tant de fois dépeint les auteurs d'écrits satiriques et séditieux, plongé dans les plus honteux excès, mais entouré de livres qu'il annote, de savants dont il dirige les recherches et dont il inspire souvent les travaux."[33]

Champion says of the king: "Sa libéralité envers les gens de lettres était reconnue" and, quoting Antoine du Verdier, he continues: "Il ne fust jamais présenté un livre qu'il ne donnast quelque chose à l'auteur; il aymoit ouyr discourir les savans sur quelque beau sujet. . .et estoit bien disant."[34] Even the king's Huguenot enemy, d'Aubigné, attested to his skill in the composition of verse,[35] and Ronsard, in a long poem,[36] spoke of his great thirst for knowledge. Scaliger said of him that he had more intelligence and more royal virtues than did his successor, Henri IV,[37] and a century after his death, Henri Bayle, author of the famous *Dictionnaire historique,* wrote that: "Ce prince aima les sciences et se plaisoit beaucoup à entendre discourir les personnes doctes."[38] Many other famous men of the age, such as Pibrac, Du Perron, and Jamyn, could be mentioned as having been favorably received by the king.

Although our interest is not primarily in the king nor in his numerous associates, we must have some idea concerning the milieu in which Desportes moved if we are to draw any conclusions as to whether a philosophy as transcendent and serious as Platonism could find nourishment there. As to that milieu something must be said concerning Henri and his *mignons,* for they have received much attention in commentaries on the period and they figure prominently in the verses of Philippe.

The pamphleteers of Henri's age delighted in intimating all sorts of debaucheries on the part of this prince, and Desportes himself is responsible for having recorded, as a very young poet, one of his youthful adventures, which is anything but Platonic in nature, and is one of his few erotic poems.[39] The episode might be paralleled by a thousand similar affairs in that or any other age, but, having to do with a detested prince, son of a detested mother, in an age of bitter hatreds when any pretext was used to slander the name of an enemy, it contributed toward Henri's being branded as "l'un des pires rois de France,"[40] and as a result of this poem Desportes has sometimes been accused of recording the shameful loves of his prince.

Far more serious charges were brought against the king and his young favorites, the *mignons*—Quélus, Maugiron, Entragues, Saint-Luc, Le Guast, Saint-Mégrin, Epernon, and Joyeuse. Certain facts concerning these close friends of the monarch are known. Many others have been guessed, and the worst interpretation has been put on the king's relations with them. It is known that he raised some of them from relative obscurity to dukes of the realm,[41] and that he gave them preferences over men of the ancient nobility by showering titles and responsibilities upon them. Perhaps he showed these youths the favor that he did because he could trust them, as he could not trust any among the old warring factions, and because he wanted to form around himself an élite guard for protection against his numerous enemies who would have gone—and did eventually go—to the lengths of murdering him or having him murdered. He did not choose his guard too badly. The fact that most of them died violent deaths, because of their attachment to the king or in his services on the field of battle, is evidence that they were not cowards.

The king promoted their interests for another reason of greater importance so far as we are concerned. They were his friends, and as with his ancestors, the Medici who had sponsored the Platonic Academy of Marsilio Ficino, the word "friend" carried a special significance and denoted particular responsibilities. Some have intimated that they were much more than the king's friends.[42] However, we have seen that Henri was a brilliant student and a youth of great sensitiveness. He was thoroughly acquainted with the philosophy of Plato as reflected in the works of Ficino and as seen in the dialogues. Perhaps the best-known work of Ficino is his *Commentary* on Plato's *Symposium*. The emphasis here is on the role of love—that human love for one's companions leading eventually to divine love—which was for him in reality the close bond of friendship that he sought to establish between himself and the members of his Platonic Academy. "Our Soul exists in the bodies of several friends as the result of Platonic Love," he says.[43] According to Paul Kristeller, Ficino was the first to use the term "Platonic Love," and by that term he meant intellectual love between friends, uniting them into a close community. Such a love is based upon the individual's love for God.[44]

There is nothing unlikely in the probability that Henri saw himself playing a Socratic role in surrounding himself with his young favorites, at the same time handsome and brilliant, skilled in arms and ready to die for their sovereign. There is evidence that he believed he was fashioning deserving and receptive youths into worthy statesmen, as Socrates had hoped to do, for he gave them as instructors the most learned men of the day. Desportes himself, having earned through ceaseless study the reputation of being such a man, was entrusted with the education of the duc d'Epernon. The fact that there were always a number of these favorites at any one time in the entourage of the king, that their relations were harmonious, and that the king seems to have been very much in love with his pious queen, tends to rule out any questionable relations between him and them. His dearest hope was for an heir to succeed him on the throne.

Strangely enough Desportes does not seem to figure in any of the scandals surrounding the king and his favorites, as related by the king's enemies, except that he celebrated some of the favorites in his verse. Although in some of his works he had been the *porte-parole* of the king, the poems which he had addressed to the ladies of his prince were of a highly refined and chaste nature. The king looked upon him with great respect, entrusting to him responsibilities which called for honesty, dependability, and integrity. He never had occasion, so far as we know, to be disappointed with the services of this subject who was a trusted secretary and member of his privy council.

Having examined the milieu in which Desportes moved and the nature of the king who was his protector, we have prepared the way for a more comprehensive understanding of the poet himself and the possible authenticity of his Platonic loves, friendships, and literary conceits. Here again little of an exact nature is known of the objects of his nobler affections, of the ladies who inspired the verse which he wrote to express his own sentiments rather than those of some protector. We do know, so far as his love poetry is concerned, that: "Par rapport à Ronsard, les Amours de Desportes offrent une autre particularité qui mérite d'être signalée: la parfaite convenance, la chasteté, pourrait-on dire, de l'expression. . . .Toute cette mise en scéne de sensualité est scrupuleusement bannie de *Diane* et *d'Hippolyte*.[45]. . . . Les poésies de Desportes ont assurément été écrites dans le goût de cette impérieuse grande dame[46] qui voulait réagir contre la brutalité des mœurs et la grossièreté du language des camps."[47]

Whatever the loves of this poet may have been, they had to be pursued with a certain degree of circumspection even in this age, for, as we have said, he was tonsured and destined for the Church while still a student at Chartres. This fact did not prevent him from pursuing loves of a more profane nature. For medieval and Renaissance man there was no inconsistency in seeking satisfaction for one's sensual nature with one woman, allying oneself through marriage with another to insure the continuity of one's line, and idealizing still another. Nor was it unusual for churchmen to pursue at least the first and last mentioned of such loves. It was the chaplain of Marie de Champagne who wrote for her a famous treatise on profane and sacred love. In an age nearer our poet's own the celebrated Cardinal Bembo wrote most beautifully of Platonic love in his *Gli Asolani* and was the *porte-parole* of Castiglione's ideas on sacred love in the fourth book of the *Cortegiano*. Perhaps it should be mentioned also that our poet, like the monk Rabelais a generation earlier, fathered a son—out of wedlock of course, since such was forbidden to him—whom he adopted legally, but there is no evidence that the mother of his son was among the objects of his higher aspirations.

The close and valued friend of Philippe's first years in Paris, Claude de Laubespine, had died in 1570, and his death was one of the great sorrows of the poet's life. He lamented his friend's passing in these verses:

> J'avois un seul amy, sage, heureux et parfait,
> La mort en son printans sans pitié l'a desfait,
> Comblant mes yeux de pleurs et mon ame de rage.[48]

For Desportes, as for Ficino, deep friendship and love seem to have represented the same things, and Lavaud says[49] of the following sonnet, also in memory of Claude, that it "...prenait presque...l'allure d'une complainte amoureuse":

> Autour de mon esprit, qui jamais ne repose,
> Jour et nuit vont errant effroyables tombeaux,
> Convois, habits de deuil, mortuaires flambeaux;
> La porte de mes sens ne recoit autre chose.
> Helas! que le destin injustement dispose
> Des ouvrages mortels plus parfaits et plus beaux!
> Tuant les rossignols, il laisse les corbeaux;
> Espargnant les buissons, il moissonne la rose.
> Entre tant de milliers son coup malicieux
> A bien sceu remarquer ce chef-d'œuvre des cieux,
> Et ravir tout l'honneur de ce monde où nous sommes.
> Ce qu'est l'herbe à la terre, à l'herbage les fleurs,
> L'or aux autres metaux, la blancheur aux couleurs,
> Cher amy, tu l'estois à la race des hommes.[50]

In an age when poets were accustomed to praise their friends in verse, Laubespine was the only man who received more than passing attention in Desportes' verse, other than the king himself, and he had nothing to say about the king after his death. In another sonnet Philippe laments the passing of Claude and connects his sorrow with an idealized love which he has conceived for Claude's sister:

> Sur le tombeau sacré d'un que j'ay tant aimé,
> Et dont la souvenance est en vous si bien painte,

> J'asseure et vay jurant, plein d'amour et de crainte,
> Que, sans plus, de vos yeux mon cœur est enflamé.[51]

There is no reason to believe that this love was reciprocated. Madeleine and her husband, the seigneur de Villeroy, had been among the early protectors of Philippe, and he was playing the role of the earlier troubadour when he declared himself inflamed with love for the lady. Save for the Platonic lover he was aiming far above his station in life.

The affection which Desportes had for his protector and friend was not unusual during this age, for youths were associated only with other youths of their own sex through their years in school. There they studied the classics together, and read together the treatises from antiquity on friendship, such as that of Cicero. It was natural that they sought to emulate the great ideals which they found portrayed in their readings. We know of no other friendship in the life of our poet like that he enjoyed in his youth with Claude, but as he grew older intellectual friendships took the place of close personal ones, and he became something of a Maecenas. When he had attained the position and wealth to permit him to do so, Desportes assumed the role of protector, and many a promising youth owed his advancement, in intellectual matters as well as in worldly ones, to his good offices. One of Desportes' first protégés, whom he met at Blois in 1576, was Jacques Davy Du Perron. He was to become one of the great men of France and to wear the robes of a cardinal. From the moment of their first meeting these two men became fast friends and spent their days together conferring on their studies and seeking new ornaments for French poetry and eloquence. Du Perron was of the reformed religion, and it was through the efforts of Desportes that he was converted to Catholicism.[52] Soon after that our poet was successfully recommending him to the king as a reader to replace himself.[53] Du Perron dedicated to Desportes, the published edition of his funeral oration for Ronsard, in which he said: "...vous recueillirez le fruict de ce que j'ay appris en vostre conversation."[54]

On the subject of Desportes' patronage of men of letters in general, Michiels says: "Obligeant et affectueux, Desportes se servit de son influence pour améliorer le sort des écrivains; il leur faisait obtenir des places lucratives, des bénéfices, des pensions, des avantages de toute nature. Vauquelin de la Fresnaie lui dut l'intendance des côtes de la mer, qui lui fut octroyée par le due de Joyeuse, nommé grand amiral de France."⁵⁵ In 1584 he gave shelter for a time to Robert III Estienne, son of Robert II and nephew of the great Henri, of the family of humanists and printers which we have already had occasion to mention. In 1586 he obtained for the future historian, de Thou, the position of "président au Parlement de Paris" to succeed his uncle, Augustin de Thou, and when the young man came to thank him for his services, the poet replied: "...on se fait honneur quand on rend service à un homme de mérite."⁵⁶

After the civil war which resulted in the succession of Henri IV to the throne, Guillaume de Baïf, son of Desportes' once faithful friend Antoine, found himself without means or friends in Paris. Desportes was himself in Rouen at the time, and when Guillaume came to him there he was made welcome. Guillaume later showed his gratitude by writing thus of his benefactor:

>   Si tost que j'arrive il m'embrasse,
>   A sa table il me donne place,
>   M'engage à luy, je vous promets,
>   Si fort que j'y suis pour jamais,
>   Tenant pour souveraine gloire
>   De rendre honneur à sa memoire
>   Et de servir qui l'aymera,
>   Tant que possible me sera.⁵⁷

Philippe Desportes had a younger brother Thibault. Under the protection of the poet, who had found such marked favor at court, the brother also became a man of importance there, occupying the position of counselor, notary, and secretary of the king, and carrying on important negotiations for the Ligue during the wars which followed the death of Henri III. The poet also served as protector to his nephew, Maturin Régnier, who became one of France's greatest satiric poets. He appreciated what his uncle had done for him and frequently took occasion to praise him and his household, "... où, si je sçay rien, j'appris ce que je sçay."⁵⁸ Two other young poets to whom Desportes gave his protection were Jean de Montereul and Claude Garnier. After our poet's death the former wrote in his honor a long poem which he entitled *Tombeau*.⁵⁹

When François de Malherbe appeared at the court of Henri IV, Desportes was disposed to welcome him in a friendly manner. Malherbe accepted Desportes' hospitality but caused an almost immediate breach when Régnier brought him one day to his uncle's to dinner. Desportes, who was by now better known as the abbé de Tiron, welcomed him and was about to present him with a copy of his translations of the Psalms. This kindly gesture was met on the part of Malherbe by the remark that he had already seen the translations and that Desportes' soup was better than his Psalms.[60]

Desportes owed his fame to his intimate sonnet sequences. Malherbe was to become known for the impersonal eloquence of the official ode. As M. Ferdinand Brunot says, in his excellent work on Malherbe: "Ce n'était pas en réalité, deux hommes qui se brouillaient, c'était la nouvelle poésie qui rompait avec l'ancienne."[61]

Among the great men at the court of Henri III none better exemplified *l'uomo di virtù, l'uomo universale,* than did Guy Du Faur de Pibrac (1529-86) who, as we have seen, accompanied the prince to Poland and, among other things, instructed him in rhetoric and philosophy. This man was universally respected for his learning and his selfless devotion to the crown. It was he who conceived the idea of putting new life into Baïf's Académie de poésie et de musique, which had flourished under Charles IX, and he "...résolut de lui donner un caractère conforme aux traditions philosophiques de la Compagnie florentine qui prétendait avoir religieusement conservé le dépôt des doctrines du grand philosophe athénien."[62] But let us say something more about Baïf's Académie, which, although somewhat in eclipse, seems not to have discontinued its activities at this time.

Even during the reign of Charles IX those who were concerned about the total lack of harmony in France were seeking some means of pacifying the revolting elements within the kingdom. None was more concerned or more active in trying to ameliorate conditions by some ethical means than Antoine de Baïf. His father, Lazare de Baïf, had spent much time in Italy, and Antoine, his natural son by an Italian woman, was born there. Hoping to make a great humanist of his son, Lazare brought him back to France and gave him as a tutor one of the great scholars and poets of the age, Jean Dorat. After years of study with this master, who was also the teacher of Ronsard and of Du Bellay, Baïf, like the other youths who made up the Pléiade, became interested in giving a new literature to France. His own particular preoccupations were orthographical reforms and the bringing about of a close alliance between measured verse and measured music in the manner of the Greeks, with emphasis on the ethical effects to be derived from verse and music. He was particularly impressed by the great role that music had played in early Greek civilization and by the important place which music, verse, and the dance occupied in the Platonic dialogues. In the Greek mind these three had been inseparably tied together. The Orphic and the Pythagorean traditions had combined to make of music one of the primary subjects of study in the schools. Pythagoras had treated music as a part of universal harmony, and Plato had stressed its importance in the ideal state.

The Romans, who modeled their educational system after that of the Greeks, also gave to music an important place. Marcus Fabius Quintilianus (A.D. c. 35-100), a great teacher of rhetoric at Rome, devoted considerable space in his lengthy treatise, *Institutio oratoria*, to the importance of music to the orator. He referred to Plato and the Greeks repeatedly and stressed the influences of musical effects, saying "Give me the knowledge of the principles of music, which have power to excite or assuage the emotions of mankind."[63]

The musical treatise which had the greatest influence on the Middle Ages was the *De institutione musica* of Boethius (c. 470-525). Nan Carpenter, in her Music in the Medieval and Renaissance Universities, says: "This work on music, patterned after the philosophical *protreptikos* (the hortatory introduction), is especially significant in carrying over into the Middle Ages the ancient Greek educational tradition which led through the study of music to philosophy proper. In a system culminating in philosophy, the knowledge of music was the first step toward knowledge of Being, of Truth. Here Boethius directly followed Plato, in whose system the mathematical quadrivium was preliminary to the study of dialectic or philosophy:"[64]

As time passed this emphasis which had been placed on music was shifted to other subjects, and during the early years of the Renaissance music was no longer a required subject in the quadrivium as it had been throughout the Middle Ages. With the new learning, however, it began to regain its place, and it is said of Jean Dorat, the teacher of the poets of the Pléiade, that "son logis résonne du matin au soir d'un frémissement de lyres."[65]

In his *Solitaire second* (1552) Pontus de Tyard gave ". . .a rambling treatise on musical notation and nomenclature, musical instruments, and the *effect of music* on animals and men."[66] Antoine de Baïf was therefore not proposing something new when, in collaboration with his friend, the musician Joachim Thibault de Courville, he requested and received from Charles IX permission to form an Académie de poésie et de musique (1570), for the purpose of giving instruction in *musique mesurée* and to provide for the performance of such music. *Ethos* was stressed in the ancient Greek sense, as can be seen from the opening words of the statutes of the Académie, which read as follows. "Afin de remettre en usage la musique selon sa perfection, qui est de représenter la parole en chant accomply de sons, harmonie et mélodie, qui consiste au choix, règle des voix, sons et accords bien accommodez, pour faire l'effet, selon que le sens de la lettre le requiert, ou resserrant ou desserrant ou accroissant l'esprit *renouvelant aussi l'ancienne façon de composer vers mesurez pour y accommoder le chant pareillement mesuré, selon l'art métrique,* afin aussi que, par ce moyen, les esprits des *Auditeurs,* accoustumez et dressez à la musique par forme de ses membres, se composent pour estre capables de plus haute connoissance, après qu'ils seront repurgez de ce qu'il pourroit leur rester de la barbarie, sous le bon plaisir du Roy nostre souverain seigneur, Nous avons convenu dresser une *Académie ou Compagnie composée de Musiciens et Auditeurs,* sous les loix et conditions qui ensuivent."[67] Baïf's Académie carried on its activities through the reign of Charles and must still have been in operation when Henri III came to the throne. There was nothing very positive in its attacks upon the evils of the times, since it sought to promote social harmony only through musical harmony, and in that it failed.

The men in Henri's entourage sought something more dynamic, more positive, more didactic in their approach to the ills of the times, and it was felt that greater encouragement should be given to philosophic thinkers. The above-mentioned Guy Du Faur de Pibrac set about reviving Baïf's Académie and broadening its interests to include not only poetry and music but also the discussion of philosophic matters and the consideration of grammar and philology. He wished the range of subjects to be encyclopedic, yet unified. He presented his ideas to the king, who received them with enthusiasm and agreed to act as protector of the new assembly. The exact date of its inauguration is not known, but it was already functioning in the year 1576. Concerning it Frances Yates says: "In France in the reign of Henri III, Baïf's Academy of Poetry and Music develops a branch—the Palace Academy—in which Ronsard and Desportes debate on the active and contemplative lives, Pibrac discusses righteous anger, and the aim of the debates seems to be to form Henri as the ideal philosopher king."[68] Lavaud says that this academy, "sous l'impulsion de Pibrac, tendit à se rapprocher des académies platoniciennes d'Italie."[69] Desportes occupied a very important place in it, being entrusted with the *Livre d'institution de l'Académie* and delivering learned discourses, as we have seen, in the quotation above. We shall have more to say of Desportes' discourses later in this study when we seek out the sources for his more exact philosophic thoughts.

The French had long been aware of the great place which the academies occupied in Italian life, as has been remarked many times, and it is interesting to note in passing that their own interests were soon to impress the English.[70]

One of the trends accompanying the revival of Platonism in Italy was the attempt to reconcile the world's great religions of all times and to find the truth which lay behind their teachings. Ficino had attempted to reconcile Platonism and Christianity in his *Theologia platonica,* and he and his followers had studied the Orphic hymns, the Platonic dialogues, the Hermetic writings, and the works of the Neoplatonists, as well as those of St. Augustine, the pseudo-Dionysius, and St. Thomas. It was probably under the influence of this fusion of religion and philosophy, which had been brought about in the Italian academies, that Henri passed into the next and final phase of his life. As time went on and the situation in his kingdom grew worse, and as he had still produced no heir to succeed him, Henri's interest in the Académie and its philosophical leanings was replaced by religious and metaphysical preoccupations. Mention has been made of the audiences he had had with Carlo Borromeo upon his passage through Italy at the beginning of his reign. Borromeo had kept in touch with Henri through the French ambassador in Venice and had continued to impress upon him his conviction that only by way of penitenial religious reform could the disorders in France be healed. Penitential *confréries* were numerous in Italy, and the king began the creation of a series of them in France, insisting that his courtiers take an active part in them.[71] These *confreries* kept something of the aspect of the earlier academies, still stressed the importance of music and its effects, and still served as forums for the gifted orators of the day. However, the discourses were now of a sacred nature. One of the last of these groups to be sponsored by the king was the Congrégation de Notre Dame de Vie Saine, which was established at Vincennes in 1584. This group consisted of some of the first lords of the realm and some of the most learned men. Among others were Desportes, Amyot, and Du Perron. The Palace Academy had gone into retreat in the woods of Vincennes.[72]

It is doubtful that our poet followed his king enthusiastically into this maze of mysticism. He was now a man of importance in the kingdom who seems to have enjoyed the role of mentor and protector of talented youths and who delighted in gathering around his table the great men of the times, as well as immersing himself in study in his justly famed library. He was in possession of three abbeys, which furnished him with an excellent income, and was a canon of the Cathedral of Chartres as well as of the Sainte-Chapelle in Paris. After having been invested with his first abbey (1482) he had given up the composition of love poetry and had then become known for his religious works. The last ten or fifteen years of his life were spent in translating the Psalms into French verse. One of his young protégés, Jean de Montereul, spoke of the change which took place in him thus:

> L'amour de Dieu l'assaut, et d'un divin effort,
> Entré dans ce beau cœur, se rend maistre du fort,
> Tuë le faux Amour. O heureuse victoire![73]

Almost a century (1665) later Jean de Rival, in speaking of Desportes' translation, clearly indicated that the poet's ethical purpose was understood by everyone. He said: "Et d'autre fois Philippe Desportes, abbé de Tiron et de Bonport, les a tournés en rime françoise à dessein de les faire chanter publiquement par les peuples, et mettre dans la bouche des hommes les sainctes et glorieuses louanges du Créateur, au lieu des chansons déshonestes, profanes et impudiques que l'enfer a de tout temps dictées pour le déshonorer en son visage."[74]

After the death of Henri III Desportes went over to the Ligue, since he, in his position as abbé, could scarcely have championed the cause of the heretic Henri de Navarre. He was in no wise inactive during the tragic years of war while the latter was consolidating his hold on France. However, he conducted himself with such circumspection that, when Henri finally ascended his throne in 1594, Desportes had lost none of his universal prestige.

He retained his Church holdings and added a new rich one—the abbaye de Bonport near Rouen[75]—and he continued to command a position of respect and influence. He was offered the archbishopric of Bordeaux, which he refused, but was soon "conseiller du Roi en ses Conseils d'Etat et privé,"[76] and in 1598 he was again lodged in the Enclos du Palais, quarters allocated to him as canon of the Sainte-Chapelle. At his favorite home at Vanvres he entertained and lodged his numerous friends. Henri IV brought his son, the Dauphin, to visit him there. Shortly before the poet's death in 1606 the king had decided to entrust the education of the Dauphin to him. No greater honor could have been bestowed, but it was an honor which was denied him by death. However one of his protégés did become tutor of the young prince. Desportes spent his last days at Bonport immersed in study, in the midst of his books, and Lavaud suggests that overstudy caused his death.[77]

Long before the last years of his life l'abbé de Tiron had gained a wide reputation for his erudition. In a letter to Thibault Desportes, the brother of the poet, after Philippe's death, Pomponne de Bellièvre wrote: "Il avoit faict tel et si grand progres en toutes les bonnes sciences qui embellissent l'esprit d'un homme que nous le tenions pour ung des plus rares personnages de nostre temps. Il n'avoit pas seulement le scavoir, mais aussy la science d'en scavoir bien user."[78] We have already spoken of Desportes' interest in books and of those which he bought in passing through Venice, with money given him by the king. In the years of his greatness his library was reputed to be one of the most complete in France, and Scévole de Sainte-Marthe said: "Point d'homme qui employast plus d'argent et plus de soin à dresser une ample et magnifique bibliothèque."[79] Lavaud adds: ". . .s'il lisait tous ses livres, M. de Tiron justifiait amplement sa réputation d'être plus savant qu'homme au monde."[80] Ronsard, in his familiar *carpe diem* theme, had early warned the poet against too much study in the following words:

> Des-Portes, qu'Aristote amuse tout le jour,
> Qui honores ta Dure, et les champs qu'à l'entour
> Chartres voit de son mont, et panché les regards,
> Je te donne ces vers, à fin de prendre garde
> De ne tuer ton corps, desireux d'acquerir
> Un renom journalier qui doit bien tost mourir;
> Mais happe le present d'un cœur plein d'allegresse,
> Cependant que le Prince, Amour, et la jeunesse,

> T'en donnent le loisir, sans croire au lendemain,
> Le futur est douteux, le present est certain.[81]

Ronsard also recognized in his young rival an "ecolier de Platon," although he himself disavowed Platonism. He showed a trace of jealousy and was not flattering when he wrote:

> Lecteur, je ne veux estre escolier de Platon,
> Qui la vertu nous presche, et ne fait pas de mesme:
> Ny volontaire Icare ou lourdant Phaethon
> Perdus pour attenter une sotise estreme.[82]

He could only have been speaking of Philippe, for the latter had written a famous sonnet about Icarus and his noble flight.

We have seen that Desportes' verses were a reflection of the refined atmosphere of the salon of the maréchale de Retz where he was received with so much favor as a young poet. His attitude vis-à-vis his lady is well illustrated in these lines:

> Que je suis redevable aux cieux
> De ce qu'ils m'ont ouvert les yeux
> Et si bien purgé ma poitrine,
> Que rien plus ne me satisfait
> Qui ne soit divin et parfait
> Et qui n'ait celeste origine.[83]

We shall see that sometimes—as when he defines Love—he paraphrases Plato. At other times his Platonism is more a matter of tone than of doctrine. His thoughts concerning the Creation and the Cosmos, the nature of Love and Beauty, the Soul and the Ideas, the relationship between the Lover and the Beloved, the divine inspiration of the poet and the role of poetry, the consideration given to the Virtues and "affections" of the Soul, are all Platonic and stem directly from the dialogues, although the words the poet uses to express his thoughts are not invariably traceable to some exact passage in Plato.

Speaking of the nature of Desportes' verse, Ferdinand Brunot says: "Vaugelas dit qu'il a le premier répandu le mot *pudeur*, il ne s'est pas contenté de baptiser cette vertu, il l'a respectée et le plus souvent pratiquée. Henri Estiene l'en félicitait et l'éloge est mérité."[84]

Not only was the good abbé considered among the first poets of France by the people of his own age, he was esteemed and imitated by numerous English poets as well, such as Henry Constable, Samuel Daniel, William Drummond, and Thomas Lodge. Sidney Lee, in his *The French Renaissance in England*, quotes Lodge as follows: "Few men are able to second the sweet conceits of Philippe Desportes, whose poetical writings are for the most part Englished, and ordinarily in everybody's hands."[85]

Whatever Desportes' debt to the Italian Petrarchists[86]—and anyone who has read both cannot have failed to note the similarities—one should remember that the poets of this age were living under the dispensation of the Pléiade, whose poets, in their manifestoes, had recommended going to writers of antiquity and even to the Italians for their models. As Clements says in his *Critical Theory and Practice of the Pléiade*: "In their sustained campaign for the enrichment of the vernacular language, the leaders of the Pléiade felt the value of translations so keenly that they held them to be of equal value with the creative literature . . . .considering how common the practice of *innutrition* was, there might be actually little difference between a creative work and an imitation."[87] Desportes' own contemporaries were aware of his borrowings and imitations, and since his time a number of studies have been made concerning them.[88] These studies have been devoted to a consideration of words expressed rather than to philosophic bent. They have been so exhaustive that most of the poet's debt must now be known. We shall note those borrowings of ideas and of occasional words, which occur rather frequently, but which in no wise preclude Desportes' own thorough grounding in Platonic doctrine and in the concepts to be found in the dialogues. His techniques in using this doctrine and these concepts are, for the most part, original with him and bear the stamp of sincerity.

The general opinion of the poet with whose *literary* Platonism we are to deal is summed up in these lines of Jean de Montereul:

>Dites comme à la cour des rois il fut chery,
>Aimé des grands seigneurs, des princes favory,
>Qu'à la cour ne le print des courtisans le vice,
>L'ardante ambition, l'exécrable avarice;
>Riche de la vertu, mesprisant les grandeurs,
>Aux autres, non à soy departant les honneurs,
>Il posséda son roy; des affaires de France
>Oncques homme vivant n'eut si grand' connaissance.
>L'age l'y conviant, guidé par la raison,
>Il changea doucement la cour à sa maison,
>Port de félicité aux autres non commune.
>Jamais homme n'usa des bien de la fortune
>Sagement comme luy; . . .[89]

Chapter II

THE CREATION

In a study concerned primarily with literary Platonism some pattern must be followed, and, since our interest now lies in the Platonic concepts expressed in the works of a particular author, we shall find our task facilitated if we seek out similar concepts, wherever they may be found, group them according to subject matter, and arrange them in logical sequence. Such a sequence would quite naturally begin with the Creation and the Creative Power or Powers.

Men have always been curious about the origin of things, but for Renaissance man every question concerning God and his creation had been resolved, either by the Scriptures themselves or by the interpretations of the Church Fathers. Their rationalizations, over a period of many centuries, left little or nothing unsettled. Following in the steps of the Italian, Marsilio Ficino, these men of the Renaissance sought to reconcile the teachings of the Scriptures with those to be found in the dialogues of Plato and in the writings of the Neoplatonists.[1] Plato himself had been raised by them to a level of sainthood almost equal to that of the Biblical saints, and his writings were considered by many to have been inspired as were the Scriptures. The poet Pontus de Tyard, a contemporary of Desportes, spoke of him as "digne de son surnom divin, si autre philosophe l'a jamais mérité,"[2] and put into the mouth of Hieromnine, in his *Premier Curieux*, these words: "Platon, à mon advis seroit faict Chrestien facilement, si l'on prend garde combien naifvement[3] il touche les plus secrets & beaux points de nostre religion."[4] Plato's ideas concerning God as the source of all creation resembled those to be found in the Old Testament and were of particular interest to the men of this age.

Plato had lived in a period when established beliefs in the gods and their powers were in a state of disintegration, and, following the lead of his teacher Socrates, he was bold in his insistence on the Supreme God, above all other gods, and on the moral nature of the lesser gods, his creatures.

The *Timaeus*[5] is the great Platonic dialogue having to do with the creation. It begins with a discussion of the State, but the men involved find that to treat the subject properly they must go back to original principles. Socrates says at the very beginning that this matter should not be broached until the gods have been called upon. Timaeus replies: "All men, Socrates, who have any degree of right feeling, at the beginning of every enterprise, whether small or great, always call upon God. . . . Now that which is created must, as we affirm, of necessity be created by a cause. But the father and maker of the universe is past finding out . . . I will do my best to give as probable an explanation as any other, —or rather, more probable."[6] Thus we see that the opinions concerning the creation which Plato will have his speakers express are not to be of a dogmatic nature. It is significant, however, that, in a society where the belief in a multiplicity of gods was so widespread, he should repeatedly speak of the one God, the best of causes,[7] the Creator,[8] the maker of all things.[9] Nevertheless he does not completely discard the traditional Greek deities.[10]

In the dialogue under consideration the creation of the universe is a matter of bringing order out of chaos by a Creator who is good, who has no jealousy, and who desires that all things shall be as like Himself as possible. Timaeus says: "God desired that all things should be good and nothing bad, so far as this was attainable. Wherefore also finding the whole visible sphere not at rest, but moving in an irregular and disorderly fashion, out of disorder (Chaos) he brought order."[11] Later he says: " . . . we must consider the nature of fire, and water, and air, and earth, such as they were prior to the creation of the heavens, and what was happening to them in this previous state; for no one has yet explained the manner of their generation, but we speak of fire and the rest of them whatever they mean, as though men knew their natures, and we maintain them to be the first principles and letters or elements of the whole. . . . "[12] From all this we gather that the elements existed prior to the creation in a state of disorder, and that the creation was from them.

The Scriptural account of the creation, on which the Christians base their belief, reads thus: "In the beginning God created heaven and earth. And the earth was void and empty, and darkness was upon the face of the deep; and the spirit of God moved over the waters."[13] The implication here is that nothing existed before the creation, and that the creation was from nothingness.

Desportes touches repeatedly upon aspects of the creation, for example in his *Sonnets spirituels*, which are a part of his *Œuvres chrestiennes*. In the lines appearing below, a Biblical description of the creation is followed by a Platonic one:[14]

> Sur des abysmes creux les fondemens poser
> De la terre pesante, immobile et feconde,

> Semer d'astres le ciel, *d'un mot* creer le monde,
> La mer, les vens, la foudre à son gré maistriser,
> De *contrarietez* tant *d'accords* composer,
> La matiere difforme orner de forme ronde,
> Et par ta prevoyance, en merveilles profonde,
> Voir tout, conduire tout, et de tout disposer.[15]

In bringing about this fusion of ideas Desportes is doing no more than Christian thinkers had done from time immemorial. When meditating upon their credo they compared their thoughts concerning the universe, its origin and structure, with those of Plato, and they found many pleasing similarities. In the lines above, Desportes' "abysmes" correspond to the "deep"—"abîmes" in the French translation—of Genesis. His words "d'un mot creer le monde" have particular significance. According to Plato the Demiurge created the world after a fair, perfect, and unchangeable pattern (Idea).[16] He is not clear about the relationship between the Ideas and the Demiurge. In the first chapter of Genesis, we find God using the *word* to bring about the creation—"And God *said*, Let there be light...." The personification of the *word* of God is common in the New Testament. In the first chapter of the Gospel according to Saint John, we find: "In the beginning was the Word, and the Word was with God, and the Word was God." Here we are to understand that Jesus Christ is the Word (Logos). Saint John's *Logos* doctrine is derived from the teachings of Philo the Jew. "For Philo the Logoi are thoughts in the mind of God, or phases of divine activity. They are his equivalent for the Ideas of Plato. God and the two supreme powers are a threefold appearance of one reality."[17] For Saint John the Word becomes the second member of the Trinity in Christian doctrine. Later Christians found no trouble in identifying it with the Platonic Ideas, the Aristotelian formal Cause, or the Neoplatonic Nous, or Mind.

In the quatrain following that having to do with the "abysmes" and "d'un mot" we find a completely Platonic account of the creation, for here Desportes' "contrarietez" can be nothing other than the "disorder" or Chaos, in the *Timaeus*, out of which the Demiurge brought order. And this concept is accompanied by two other Platonic ones: "tant d'accords"—reference to the harmony of the spheres when set in motion; and the "forme ronde"—concerning its perfect circular nature. Both of these we shall have occasion to consider later.

Elsewhere in the *Œuvres chrestiennes* our poet follows a more consistently Biblical account of the creation, when he speaks of

. . . . tes hautes merveilles
Quand de *rien* tu formas les cieux.¹⁸

The heavens are formed from nothingness in this ode of which Michiels says: "Il faudra plus d'un demi-siècle pour que l'on entende, dans Polyeucte, des notes équivalentes."¹⁹ And Faguet says: "Cette pièce . . . est certainement celle où Desportes s'est montré le plus véritablement poète, par l'intensité du sentiment, par la vigueur de la forme, et par ce mouvement ardent et précipité qu'il n'a guère connu que cette fois."²⁰

In the *Chant d'Amour*, Desportes' lengthiest poem to be devoted solely to Platonism, the poet repeats that the creation of the universe consisted in bringing order out of Chaos, and he introduces into the picture still another aspect of the creation which occupies a whole section of the *Timaeus* and receives a great deal of attention for varying reasons throughout the dialogues. This idea has to do with the elements—fire, water, air, and earth—and with their union, which has brought about the "body of the universe." We find Timaeus saying: "Wherefore also God in the beginning of creation made the body of the universe to consist of fire and earth . . . God placed water and air in the mean between fire and earth." He continues: "And for these reasons, and out of such elements which are in number four, the body of the world was created, and it was *harmonized* by proportion, and therefore has the spirit of friendship . . . . But when the world began to get into order, fire and water, and earth and air had only certain faint traces of themselves . . . . and God fashioned them by form and number . . . God made them as far as possible the fairest and best, out of things which were not fair and good."²¹

In Desportes' poem, mentioned above, we find that he has incorporated all of these ideas, nearly word for word, as follows:

> Durant *le grand debat* de la masse premiere,
> Que *l'air, la mer, la terre* et *la belle lumiere,*
> *Meslés confusément,* faisoient un pesant corps,
> Amour, qui fut marry de leur longue querelle,
> De la matiere lourde en bastit une belle,
> Rengeant les elemens en *paisibles accords.*²²

Again the pre-creation Chaos is described, but this time it is "le grand debat de la masse premiere" and the elements which composed this chaotic state are introduced. It is Love here which is the ordering force rather than God, an idea which again has its origin in the *Timaeus*. There we learn that the reason why the Creator made the universe was that "He was good, and the good can never have any jealousy .... he desired that all things should be as like himself as they could be."[23] The obvious implication is that the Creator brought about the creation through Love, and this contention is verified in the *Symposium*, where we find Agathon saying: "And so Love set in order the empire of the gods."[24] In Desportes' lines, however, the Platonic picture is briefly interrupted by a Biblical allusion, which our Christian poet cannot seem to avoid, or does not wish to, seeing no inconsistency. In the verse, "Amour, qui fut marry de leur longue querelle," we have another of those fusions of the Platonic and the Biblical. In Plato, Love is an emanation flowing from God and back to Him. In the New Testament God *is* Love. Now the Platonic God is not a personal God, at least in the sense that He is in both the Old and the New Testament. That is, He is not a God of wrath and vengeance, nor is he a God of sorrow and compassion. But Desportes says He was "marry—sorrowful, repentant—so that we seem to have a Platonic God, acting through Love, but because he has the sorrow of the Biblical God concerning the chaotic nature of things.

In the lines quoted above from the *Timaeus* one sees that Love not only brings order out of Chaos, it also holds the universe together, it is "harmonized by proportion, and therefore has the spirit of friendship." Desportes' universe is impregnated with love and held together by it also. The poet says:

> D'une chose sans forme il en fit une ronde,
> Que, pour son ornement, on appelle le monde,
> Entretenu d'*amour*, dont il est tout remply.[25]

Friendship and love were one and the same thing for Plato, and although such an identity may have been lost for a time in the western world it was re-established, as an ideal, at least, among the men of Ficino's Accademia Platonica.

Further evidence that our poet conformed to the Platonic concept of Love as a creative force is found in these lines:

> Car cet amour tousjours par la beauté l'attire;
> En suivant la beauté, belle forme il desire;
> Voilà comme l'*amour* rend le monde accompli.[26]

There is still another significant idea in some lines quoted above, having to do with the words, "... il en fit une ronde,/ Que, pour son ornement, on appelle le monde."[27] In the *Timaeus* we find this question and answer: "Which of the patterns had the artificer in view when he made the world,—the pattern of the unchangeable, or of that which is created? If the world be indeed fair and the artificer good, it is manifest that he must have looked to that which is eternal; for the world is the fairest of creations and he is the best of causes . . . He gave the world the figure which was suitable and also natural . . . Wherefore he made the world in the form of a globe . . . the most perfect and the most like itself of all figures."[28] When Desportes speaks of the "ronde" he is referring to the most perfect of geometrical figures, the globe, and he is adding double weight to the idea of its fairness when he uses not only the word "ornement" but also "monde" for the Latin word from which the latter comes, "mundus," embodies within it the idea of ornament or decoration. He pursues still further this insistence on the spherical shape of the world in some lines already quoted in another context:

> De contrarietez tout d'accords composer
> La matiere difforme de forme *ronde*.[29]

In these words we have an almost exact reproduction of Timaeus' words, "the body of the world . . was *harmonized* by proportion . . . . Whereas he made the world in the form of a globe. . . . "

In a sonnet more particularly devoted to the love of a lady, our poet identifies the perfection of the round shape of the world with the ring worn by his lady, a symbol of love itself, when he says of the ring:

> Tu es tout rond: parfaite est la rondeur.[30]

The men of Desportes' age were intrigued by the idea of perfection exemplified by the spherical form of the world. Pontus de Tyard says in his *Premier Curieux;* "Mais trop mieux me plaist de confesser le ciel estre parfait en sa ronde perfection."[31] In the same work he says; "Mais c'est peu, de dire que la figure ronde est premiere, si l'on ne luy donne nom de perfection, lequel vrayment elle merite, si nous descrivons bien, cela estre parfait à-quoy rien d'estranger ne peut estre adjousté, car il est trop evident que l'on peut bien adjouster aux lignes droites."[32]

Not only is the sphere the most perfect of all figures, but the revolution of the planets is circular. Timaeus says, in speaking of the world; " . . . the movement suited to his spherical form was assigned to him, being of all the seven (motions) that which is most appropriate to mind and intelligence; and he was made to move in the same manner and on the same spot, within his own limits revolving in a circle."[33] Desportes describes the *turning* of "ceste masse ronde" but he does not specifically state that it is in the path of a circle. In one of his *Œuvres chrestiennes* he says:

> C'est toy, qui d'une main puissante
> . . . .
> Fais tourner ceste masse ronde.³⁴

Elsewhere, however, he is more specific about the path of at least one important planet when he speaks of the "cercle de la lune."³⁵

We have seen that the elements, which were in existence in a chaotic state and from which the Creator made the universe, were fire, water, earth and air, and in another connection we have found our poet speaking of these elements as "la matiere lourde" from which the Creator went about "Rengeant les elemens en paisibles accords." In the lines below he speaks of them as the serfs of God:

> La flamme, l'air, la terre et l'onde
> Sont serfs de ton commandement.³⁶

He brings in another Platonic concept in connection with the elements when he says that they, like all things, seek the good:

> Tout ce que l'univers enserre
> Tend au *bien*, le cherche et le suit,
> Le feu, l'air, les eaux et la terre,
> Et tout ce qui d'eux est produit.³⁷

Plato says of the Creator that "He was good, and the good can never have any jealousy of anything. And being free from jealousy, he desired that all things should be as like himself as they could be . . ."³⁸ And elsewhere he says, speaking more particularly of man, that "we will to do that which conduces to our good, and if the act is not conducive to our good we do not will it."³⁹

Concerning the elements Plato says—doubtless owing his idea of flux to Heraclitus—that they are perpetually changing into and out of one another and have in them nothing permanent.⁴⁰ Desportes echoes this idea in one of his *Chansons*:

> Rien n'est icy de constant
> Et tout se change à un instant
> Dessous le cercle de la lune,
> Les saisons, les jours et les nuits.⁴¹

He places the earth within the circle of the moon, as had Plato— "There was the moon in the orbit nearest the earth"⁴²—but this arrangement was common in Desportes' day and he may have owed more to Aristotle, in these lines, than to Plato. This suggestion is supported by the insertion of the words "dessous le cercle de la lune," for in Aristotle's *De mundo* things are changing in the sublunary world, whereas in the Ether, the substance of the heavens and the stars, they are "free from disturbance, change and external influence."[43]

As for the heavens, Plato tells us that they were created according to a perfect and unchanging pattern (Idea), and he says of the pattern: "Now the nature of the ideal being was everlasting, but to bestow this attribute in its fullness upon a creature was impossible. Wherefore he resolved to have a moving image of eternity, and when he set in order the heaven, he made this image eternal but moving according to number, while eternity itself rests in unity; and this image, we call time ... for the pattern exists from eternity, and the created heaven has been, and will be, in all time."[44] We find an interesting poetic interpretation of these words in Desportes' *Chant d'Amour:*

> Tout ce qui vit icy recognoist sa puissance:
> Car, en entretenant ce qui est en essence,
> Fait que ce qui a fin n'est jamais finissant.[45]

This concept carries us into the realm of the unchanging, everlasting Ideas, which we shall have occasion to examine at much greater length in a chapter devoted entirely to this concept. The following quotation from our poet is one more which has to do with the eternal course of the heavens, so far as the idea of revolution is concerned:

> S'il est vray que le ciel ait sa course eternelle
> Que l'air soit inconstant, la mer sans fermeté. . . .[46]

These lines carry in them the Platonic "moving image of eternity" as well as the concept of the inconstancy of the sublunary world.

One of the most poetic aspects of the Platonic account of the creation is a further extension of the idea of bringing order out of Chaos, in which order becomes harmony. Already we have had occasion to quote the words "the body of the world was created, and it was harmonized by proportion."[47] This concept is reflected in Desportes' *Chant d'Amour:*

> S'il a formé le monde, il luy donne durée,
> Et rend par bonne *paix* sa matiere asseurée,
> En *discordans accords* toute chose unissant.[48]

The word "monde" here applies to the universe rather than to our planet, and the words "discordans accords" refer, of course, to the harmonization of the pre-creation chaos.

Besides the idea of harmony set forth here we should note the similarity between Desportes' "toute chose" and the words of Plato which follow almost immediately those quoted above: "Now the creation took up *the whole* of each of the four elements; for the Creator compounded the world out of *all* the fire and *all* the water and *all* the air and *all* the earth, leaving no part of any of them nor any power of them outside. His intention was, in the first place, that the animal should be as far as possible a perfect *whole* and of perfect parts: secondly, that it should be *one*, leaving no remnant out of which another such world might be created: and also that it should be free from old age and unaffected by disease."[49] When our poet speaks of "toute chose unissant" he is reflecting the oneness of Plato's world.

The order and harmony which went into the creation find their final poetic development in the music created by the harmonious revolution of the heavenly bodies. The idea of the music of the spheres goes back at least to Pythagoras but occurs time and again in Plato,[50] from whom many writers after his time borrowed it.[51] The most complete treatment of the concept in Plato is in the tenth book of the *Republic,* where Socrates, after explaining the arrangement and the revolution of the eight whorls representing the spheres of the heavenly bodies and likening them to a spindle, says: "The spindle turns on the knees of Necessity; and on the upper surface of each circle is a siren, who goes round with them hymning a single tone or note. The eight together form one harmony and round about, at equal intervals, there is another band, three in number, each sitting on her throne: these are the Fates ... who accompany with their voices the harmony of the sirens."[52]

Desportes never goes into such detail concerning the harmony of the spheres. Indeed the idea was so common among the poets of the Renaissance that it is doubtful that any particular passage of Plato was in his thoughts when he composed the following lines:

> Ravy de mon penser, si hautement je volle,
> Que je conte un à un les astres radieux;
> J'oy les divers *accords* du mouvement des cieux,
> Et voy ce qui se meut sous l'un et l'autre pole.[53]

This concept did not have to await the Renaissance rediscovery of the complete set of Platonic dialogues to be known to western Europe. It was used poetically in the vernacular by Dante, who could have known it through Chalcidius' translation of the *Timaeus,* or more probably through Macrobius' version of Cicero's *Somnium Scipionis.* Dante departs from his usual strict Aristotelianism[54] when he says in the *Divina Commedia:*

> Quando la rota, che Tu sempiterni
> Desiderato, a sè me fece atteso,

> Con l'armonia che temperi e discerni,
> Parvemi tanto allor del cielo acceso
> Della fiamma del sol, che pioggia o fiume
> Lago non fece mai tanto disteso.
> La novità del suono et il grande lume
> Di lor cagion m'accesaro un disio
> Mai non sentito di cotanto acume.[55]

Before proceeding to the heavenly and earthly creatures we must retrace our steps to the Creator, if we are to understand the role assigned Him by Desportes, and determine whether there was a Platonic influence in the poet's assumptions. For Plato He is the One, unchangeable God, perfect and past finding out.[56] He is worthy of the utmost reverence although he is not a personal God in the Christian sense. He created the inferior deities and to them left the creation of men and of animals, so far as their physical natures are concerned, while reserving to Himself the imparting of souls.[57] The soul of man does not long to return to a oneness with God Himself, as the Neoplatonists would have it, though the following words from the *Phaedo* seem to give ample excuse for their interpretation: "But when returning into herself she [the Soul] reflects, then she passes into the other world, the region of purity, and eternity, and immortality, and unchangeableness, which are her kindred, and with them she ever lives, when she is by herself and is not let or hindered; then she ceases from her erring ways, and being in communion with the unchanging is unchanging. And this state of the soul is called wisdom."[58] Elsewhere emphasis is placed upon the reascent of the soul toward the intellectual realm from which it fell into the body and where it had knowledge of all things. For Plato knowledge is the road to wisdom, and wisdom places man in a position where the trials of life can barely touch him, and assures the release of his soul from the evils of the flesh. Man's highest goal is the contemplation of ultimate Truth, which is one with the Good and the Beautiful. Love itself is a desire for the Beautiful, or the Good, and therefore for happiness.

Aristotle added his speculations as to the nature of God to those of his teacher, Plato. God became for him the "unmoved mover," and all the universe, every object and being in it, desires to realize itself because of God, whose existence is the ultimate cause of its striving. He is the center toward which all things are drawn, the ultimate principle of the universe. Man seeks the *summum bonum*[59] which is identified with happiness, a thing to be desired not for what it can give but for itself alone.

Since in Plato the highest goal of the philosopher, the noblest of men, is the Good, Beauty and Truth, which are one and emanate from God, Aristotle is not far removed from the Platonic ideal.

Dr. Robert V. Merrill, in his work on Pontus de Tyard, says that the term *summum bonum* passed into the theological language of the Middle Ages and became identified with God Himself.[60] From the inception of their religion Christians had looked forward to the "many mansions" in the "house" of God, of which Christ had spoken and to which He had returned, as the only goal worth striving for. In this "house" they would be in the presence of God. Everything of this earth was vanity. The Neoplatonists, like the Christians, were unconcerned with the things of this earth and unlike either Plato or Aristotle—they placed no emphasis on intellectual pursuits. Their sole concern was to reascend to a oneness with God. This was to be accomplished through contemplation. Plotinus says: "But our concern is not merely to be sinless but to be God."[61] As we have seen, there is some justification for this interpretation in words to be found in the dialogues. Later Boethius (c. 470-525), a great scholar of both Plato and Aristotle who had hoped to translate their works into Latin and to reconcile their teachings, spoke at great length of the "highest good" in his *Consolation of Philosophy*. We find him saying: "The universally accepted notion of men proves that God, the fountain-head of all things is good . . . Now reason shows us that in Him lies also the perfect good."[62] No Renaissance library was without its copy of Boethius' work, and there must have been a copy in the library of Desportes.

Petrarch, no mystic himself, but a religious man of a highly sensitive nature, seems to have been one of the first to introduce the idea of God as the "sommo Ben" into profane vernacular letters. We find the following sentiments in one of his sonnets:

> Da lei ti vien l'amoroso pensiero
> Che, mentre 'l segui, al *sommo Ben* t'invia,
> Poco prezzando quel ch'ogni uom desia.[63]

And a century later, after all of Plato's dialogues had been introduced anew into western culture, one of the great Neoplatonists, Benivieni, writes in his very mystical *Canzone dell'amore divino:*

> Io dico com'amor dal divin fonte
> Dell'*increato ben* qua aiù s'infonde.

Speaking of the seat of more perfect beauty, he says:

> Ivi non l'ombra pur ch'en terra fede
> Del *vero ben* ne dia ecorge, ma certo
> Lume et del vero sol piu ver' effige.[64]

In France, the great Renaissance patroness of letters and learning, Marguerite de Navarre, after a series of sorrows and disappointments, became deeply interested in Neoplatonic doctrine through Briçonnet and Lefèvre d'Etaples, who became her spiritual guides. They introduced to her the works of Nicolas de Cusa (1401-1464), who, before Ficino and the Florentine Academy, had sought a higher understanding of metaphysical things in the limited content of the works of Plato available to the men of his time. He taught that true happiness is to think, to know, to see truth with the eyes of the spirit; that the heart lives in reality only in so far as it loves; that God cannot be known through the reason only; that it is man's mission to raise his soul to the source of all truth and of all beauty. The supreme Being was for him a pantheistic God.[65] We find a fusion of the Aristotelian *summum bonum* and the Neoplatonic One or All in lines from Marguerite's *Prisons*, one of the most mystical books of the French Renaissance:

> *Uny* au *Tout* et au *souverain Bien*
> Pour estre fait aveques Jesus Rien.[66]

In the dialogue following the nineteenth tale of her *Heptaméron*, Marguerite says: "Car l'ame qui n'est créée que pour retourner à son *souverain bien* ne faict, tant qu'elle est dedans le corps, que desirer d'y parvenir."[67]

This emphasis on the mystic desire to be absorbed by God—the object of spiritual yearning identified with the final principle of reality in the universe—is Neoplatonic. However, it is not strange that Plato's words from the sixth book of the *Republic*—"In like manner the good may be said to be not only the author of knowledge to all things known, but of their being and essence, and yet the good is not essence, but far exceeds essence in dignity and power"[68]—should have been interpreted as identifying God and the Good. Thus we may say that the varying interpretations of God which we have passed in review and which influenced Christian thought can all find their origin in Plato. Desportes inherited all of these interpretations but seems to have leaned heavily on the Neoplatonists, so far as his concept of God is concerned, or perhaps directly on Marguerite. We find him speaking of his "bien" as Marguerite had spoken of her "souverain bien" in one of his *Complaintes:*

> O pauvre corps! jusqu'à quelle journée
> Retiendras-tu mon ame emprisonnée
> En tant de fers, la gardant qu'elle volle
> Apres son *bien*, dont l'espoir me console?[69]

In a prayer among his *Œuvres chrestiennes* he speaks of his soul as longing for its "bien" in these words:

> Ta main d'ame et de corps a mon tout façonné,
> De corps foible et mortel à la terre addonné,
> Qui retourne à la terre au soir de sa journée;
> D'ame immortelle et vive à jamais demeurant,
> Tousjours, comme à son *bien*, vers le ciel aspirant,
> Si le monde abuseur ne l'en rend destournée.[70]

Elsewhere the sovereign good of our poet becomes *souverain* happiness:

> Puis que l'*heur souverain* ailleurs se doit chercher,
> Il faut de ces gluaux ton plumage arracher
> Et voller dans le ciel d'une legère traicte.
> Là se trouve le *bien* affranchi de souci,
> La foy, l'amour sans feinte et la beauté parfaicte
> Qu'à clos yeux, sans profit, tu vas cherchant ici.[71]

The poet is certainly entertaining thoughts of the realm of the Ideas, for here in one place he brings together happiness, the good, love, and perfect beauty.

For the Greeks all material things were only acts and manifestations of divine Intelligence. Plato himself admitted a principle transcending Intelligence, which is the Good, and which may be arrived at, after exhausting the powers of reason, through the dialectic of love, when the soul is seized by desire and arrives at a sudden and ineffable intuition of the Good. The Neoplatonists placed their emphasis on love, rather than on the intellect, as the medium through which one remounts to the Good. The Good, which is the beloved, is for them identical with love itself. Emile Bréhier, in his *La Philosophie de Plotin*, quotes Plotinus thus: "La seule preuve qu'on a atteint le Bien, c'est que l'on reste auprès de lui et que l'on ne cherche plus rien."[72] Desportes' words in the lines above—"affranchi de souci"—bear a close resemblance to those of Plotinus—"on ne cherche plus rien"—and the whole poem shows something of the mysticism of the Neoplatonists and of Marguerite. The words are from his *Œuvres chrestiennes* and were written during that period of his life when the king and his court were very much preoccupied with penitential reform and sacred oratory. However, the following lines spring directly from the Socratic thought, quoted elsewhere, that every soul of man seeks its Good:

> Tout ce que l'univers enserre
> Tend au *bien*, le cherche et le suit
> Le feu, l'air, les eaux et la terre,
> Et tout ce qui d'eux est produit.[73]

The Good, the One, and the All are the same with the Neoplatonists, as they become with Marguerite. Plotinus says: The Authentic *All* is contained in *nothing*, since nothing is prior to It; at once Primal and veritable, of necessity anything coming after It must, as a first condition of existence, be contained by this All, since it depends upon That and without It can have neither stability nor movement." As we have seen, Marguerite speaks of being "uny au Tout" while carrying forward Plotinus' idea of returning to "nothing" or "Rien." Pantheism is implicit in the words of both Plotinus and Marguerite. Plato speaks of God as having used *all* the substance of the elements in the act of creation, and Desportes, with no overtones of pantheism and in a Christian context, speaks of God coming to judge the "tout" when he says:

> Au jour que tu viendras en ta majesté sainte,
> Pour juger ce grand *tout*, qui fremira de crainte.[74]

Continuing our consideration of the creation as presented in *Timaeus*, we find that the Creator, after having brought order out of disorder and created the universe, created the inferior gods, giving them creative powers of their own.[75] A plurality of gods was not acceptable to the Christians. St. Augustine had spoken of the one God, and said: " . . . let Him be worshipped, and it is enough. Let the train of innumerable demons be repudiated, and let this God suffice every man whom his gift suffices."[76] Desportes, therefore, in order not to commit heresy, could only play with the idea of a plurality of lesser gods, or demons. Thus he speaks of a demon who may forewarn us in the following manner:

> Je connoy maintenant que nostre ame divine,
> Tenant tousjours du ciel lieu de son origine,
> Presage nos malheurs devant que d'advenir,
> Et nous en advertit, afin d'y parvenir;
> Ou que quelque *démon*, ou quelque autre puissance
> Nous fait devant le mal en avoir connoissance.[77]

He is using the word "démon" in a Platonic sense, for, although Socrates himself denied their existence,[78] we find frequent mention of these intermediary spirits in the dialogues, either as having existed in a bygone age[79] or as still existing and being messengers between God and man,[80] or guides of men through their different cycles of existence.[81]

Plato assigns to the inferior gods the task of forming the bodies of men and animals. He has the Creator address the inferior gods in this manner: "Betake yourselves to the formation of animals, imitating the power which was shown by me in creating you. The part of them worthy of the name immortal, which is called divine and is the guiding principle of those who are willing to follow justice and you—of that part [the Soul] I will myself sow the seed."[82] In perfect consistency with these words Desportes in one of his *Complaintes* attributes the creation of his lady to the "troupes immortelles". He says:

> Car, dès l'eternité, les troupes immortelles
> La firent au patron des Grâces les plus belles,
> Afin qu'elle embellist ce monde vicieux.[83]

Again, in an *Epitaphe de Claude de Bastarnay*, he attributes the release of the soul from the body of his friend to the "dieux benins", saying:

> Les *dieux benins* luy on le corps mortel osté
> Luy donnant dans le ciel une gloire immortelle.[84]

In his *Commentary on the Symposium,* Ficino had identified the Platonic demons or gods, calling them "Angels, ministers of God, which is still not different from what Plato called them."[85] Desportes may have considered them in the same light.

In the tenth book of the Platonic *Laws* we find that the inferior gods inhabit stars,[86] and in the *Timaeus* they are spoken of as those "who visibly appear in their revolutions."[87] It may have been by combining these two concepts that Desportes arrived at the conclusion that we have a star for a guide, or the idea may have come from the very popular astrology of the times. At any rate he expresses the idea in these words:

> On dit que nous avons une estoille pour guide,
> Qui, forte, nous arreste ou nous lasche la bride,
> Et qui tient de nos jours le terme limité;
> Mais ma deesse seule est mon astre prospere.[88] . . .

It is curious, if Desportes' source is not Platonic here, that he should tie up his thought with the idea expressed in the words "nous arreste ou nous lasche la bride," almost certainly an allusion to Plato's myth of the charioteer,[89] which will be more fully treated later.

There are two other aspects of the creation as presented by Plato—that having to do with the Soul, and that having to do with the patterns followed in the creation (Ideas)—which might be presented here but are of so great importance in themselves, both in Plato and in Desportes, that it has been considered better to devote a complete chapter to each of them. We shall see that they too are treated Platonically by our poet, and that he has therefore touched upon every important aspect of the creation as it is presented in the dialogues. First, it was a process of bringing the elements from a state of disorder into one of order. The universe resulted. Love played a great role, in that it was the force which brought about the order, set the universe in motion, and now holds it together. The universe was given a spherical shape and a circular motion, thus causing it to conform to one of the Platonic ideas of perfection. The spheres in their motion produce a heavenly music.

The Creator is responsible for the creation, which he brought about through love. The Good emanates from Him, even if He is not identified with it. He created the inferior gods, who in their turn created the animals, but he reserved to Himself the creation of the Soul. The gods, besides being creatures themselves, are beneficent.

For Desportes' ideas concerning the creation there are many possible sources. For the more Neoplatonic concepts he could have gone to Marguerite de Navarre, though her only interest in the creation was with the "souverain Bien." Héroët had been the purest Platonist of the first half of the sixteenth century, but his interests were limited to Platonic love and he drew primarily upon the *Symposium*. Desportes could have found his concepts among the Italian poets, from whom he made such copious borrowings in other matters. There is little evidence that he did, for only two of the poems which have been drawn upon in this chapter show evidence of having been borrowed. He could have gone directly to Plato, and particularly to the *Timaeus,* and this he seems to have done. As we have seen, that particular dialogue was known and revered at the School of Chartres as early as the twelfth century and had formed the basis of the beliefs of the masters there with respect to the creation. But Desportes' words on this subject do not call for a specific source. They are inserted without effort into almost any context, thus showing that they are a part of the Chartrain's general culture and beliefs.

Chapter III

THE SOUL

The Soul occupied a place of first importance in the speculations of Plato as it had in those of early Greek philosophers in general. The life of the soul is the life of reality. In the *Timaeus* one finds that after God had brought the universe into being "in the center he put the soul, which he diffused throughout the body."[1] This was the World-Soul. It was made by the best of intellectual and everlasting natures and was therefore the best of created things. God entrusted the creation of living creatures to the inferior gods, but to them he said: "The part of them worthy of the name immortal, which is called divine and is the guiding principle—of that divine part I will myself sow the seed, and having made a beginning, I will hand the work over to you. And do ye then interweave the mortal with the immortal, and make and beget living creatures, and give them food, and make them to grow, and receive them again in death."[2] The individual souls created by God did not immediately fall into bodies. First, they were created from what remained after God had created the soul of the universe: ". . .he divided the whole mixture into souls equal in number to the stars, and assigned each soul to a star; and having there placed them in a chariot, he showed them the nature of the universe, and declared to them the laws of destiny, according to which their first birth would be one and the same for all."[3]

Between the time of Plato and the era of the Renaissance the Christian religion had been born and had come to dominate western thought. Its adherents, like those of Platonism and Neoplatonism, placed much emphasis on the life of the soul. However, they went to the Old and New Testaments for their doctrine, and there they found that God, and not some inferior gods, created man in his own image. Each individual has an immortal soul, but nothing is said about the existence of that soul before it comes to inhabit the body. If there is a disagreement here between the Platonic and the Christian, there is none in the emphasis which both put on the necessity of freeing the soul from the prison house of the flesh, though the means whereby one is to accomplish this may differ.

Although a Christian, Ficino, in his *Commentary on the*

Symposium, speaks of the immortality of the soul but also gives to it an existence before it descends into the body.[4]

Desportes seems to have preferred the Platonic concepts concerning the life of the soul to the Christian ones. Perhaps it is because they are more poetic that he made use of them. In the following lines he does not specifically say that the soul existed before coming into the body, but he intimates as much when he speaks of heaven as the place of the soul's origin:

> Je connoy maintenant que nostre ame divine,
> Tenant tousjours du ciel, lieu de son origine,
> Presage nos malheurs devant que d'advenir.[5]

The Platonic origin of his thought in these lines is still further supported by his reference to the theory of anamnesis, of which more will be said later. As for the immortality of the soul and its relation to the element-composed body, he says:

> En la mort seulement se corrompt la matiere
> Qui tient des elemens; l'ame demeure entiere,
> Franche et libre du corps, et s'en revolle aux cieux.[6]

It will be noted that the poet does not say "volle aux cieux" but "revolle aux cieux," thus implying that the soul goes back to a place where it had already been and thus giving it a pre-existence before being implanted in body. In the lines which follow we have an almost complete interpenetration of Platonic and Biblical precepts:

> Ta main d'ame et de corps a mon tout façonné,
> De corps foible et mortel à la terre addonné,
> Qui retourne à la terre au soir de sa journée;
> D'ame immortelle et vive à jamais demeurant,
> Tousjours, comme à son bien, vers le ciel aspirant,
> Si le monde abuseur ne l'en rend destournée.
> . . . .
> Tu me gardes au ciel une eternelle vie.[7]

One will remark that our poet makes the life of the soul both "immortelle" and "eternelle," the latter quality being of Platonic but not of Biblical origin. And when he speaks of the soul "comme à son bien, vers le ciel aspirant, / Si le monde abuseur ne l'en rend destournée," he is expressing himself more in the manner of the Neoplatonic mystic than in that of a Christian, for the emphasis is on the longing of the soul to return to the source of its being. The last few lines seem to be a remembrance of the passage in the *Timaeus* in which it is maintained that if man conquers the evils of the flesh he will live righteously, and, if he is conquered by them, unrighteously. "He who lived well during his appointed time was to return and dwell in his native star, and there he would have a blessed and congenial existence."[8]

In Plato the mind, which is also referred to as the soul, is the seat of all knowledge. It is sometimes difficult to find a clear distinction between the two, but in the twelfth book of the *Laws*, the Athenian says: "The soul, besides other things, contains mind, and the head, besides other things, contains sight and hearing; and the mind, mingling with the noblest of the senses, and becoming one with them, may be truly called the salvation of all."[9] Other philosophers have been more specific. In the famous three hypostases of Plotinus we find the One, or the Good, at the top, and from that proceeds Intelligence, or Mind, from which, in its turn, proceeds the Soul.[10] St. Thomas, the voice of authority on Church dogma, says in his *Summa Theologica*: "The intellect is a power of the soul and not the very essence of the soul."[11]

Like Plato, Desportes fails to make a clear distinction between the mind and the soul. Above we saw him speaking of the "ame immortelle" which "revolle aux cieux." In the following lines it is the "esprit" rather than the "ame" which holds his attention:

    Car, bien que mon *esprit* ait celeste origine,
    Il se tient bien-heureux d'estre à vous asservy.[12]

Again the "celeste origine" seems to intimate a pre-existence. In the lines which follow he states that his mind originated in heaven:

    Mon *esprit*, nay du ciel, au ciel tousjours aspire.[13]

And elsewhere he combines the idea of the immortality of the mind with its longing to regain the knowledge of things which it had known before coming into body. This longing became for Plotinus the "feeling of uneasiness" with which one begins his return to first principles.[14] With Desportes it is the less formal and therefore more Platonic "cherchant tousjours d'apprendre":

    S'il est vray que l'esprit, d'origine immortelle,
    Cherchant tousjours d'apprendre, aime la nouveauté.[15]

Reason is a faculty of the soul which receives much consideration in Plato, where we find, in the sixteenth book of the *Republic*, these words: "There are four faculties in the soul—reason answering to the highest, understanding to the second, faith (or conviction) to the third, and perception of shadows to the last."[16] In the *Symposium* the lover and the philosopher are shown by Socrates to be one and the same, and dialectics is the gradual process by the aid of which we pass from the sensible to the

The Soul

ideal.[17] In the sixth book of the *Republic* we learn that the hypotheses of science are to be used not as final results, but as points from which the mind may rise into the higher heaven of Ideas and behold truth and being.[18] Desportes addresses Reason, as a faculty of the soul leading him to celestial heights, when he ennobles it as "Royne":

> Royne, qui tiens en nous la divine partie,
> Qui nous conduits au ciel. lieu dont tu est sortie.[19]

Reason is then not only a faculty of the soul, it is man's divine essence.

Timaeus, after explaining the original dwelling place of the individual souls and how they are implanted in bodies, goes on to say that the soul can overcome "by the help of reason the turbulent and irrational mob of later accretions, made up of fire and air and water and earth," and can return to its first and better state.[20] Our poet recognizes that it is through the aid of reason that he can extinguish the fires in his body. He says:

> Puis que par ton secours mon brasier est estaint,
> Et qu'avec la *raison* ma vólonté je donte.[21]

The idea of souls having had stars assigned to them as their permanent homes has intrigued men of all ages. Dr. Robert V. Merrill, in his work on Du Bellay, traced this idea from pagan theology through Christian literature and said that it entered poetry with Dante's words, "Dice che l'alma a la sua stella riede."[22] To carry the thought of Dante a step further one might mention the fact that in the *Paradiso* he finds the once ambitious souls not on separate stars but all inhabiting Mercury.[23]

Desportes could have found this poetic idea in any one of a number of contemporary poets, but he no doubt knew it through his familiarity with the *Timaeus*. In Plato the soul not only inhabits its star before falling into body, but returns to that star after being released from body. It is to this latter phase of the soul's peregrinations that our poet refers when eulogizing his friend, Claude de Bastarnay, for whom he wrote this *Epitaphe*:

> Pour le recompenser de sa fidelité
> Les dieux benins luy on le corps mortel osté
> Luy donnant dans le ciel une gloire immortelle,
> Car il luit maintenant en astre transformé,
> Il sera bien-heureux à bon droit estimé
> Qui naistra desormais sous planette si belle.[24]

He carries the concept to its very limits when, in a curious tribute to the water spaniel of that celebrated favorite and patroness of the poets, Mme de Villeroy, he attributes a soul to the animal and also assigns it a star:

> Or, si le ciel, qui tout embrasse,
> Comme jadis aux chiens fait place,
> Il ne faut douter nullement
> Que cette Barbiche si belle
> Bien tost d'une clarté nouvelle
> Ne flambe au haut du firmament.[25]

It is in the *Phaedrus* that the soul is more fully treated, and in that dialogue we learn that through "some double load of forgetfulness and vice" the wings of the soul "fall from her and she drops to the ground." In the same context the speaker refers to the era when the soul was "not yet enshrined in that living *tomb* which we carry about, now that we are imprisoned in the body, like an oyster in his shell."[26] We shall note that, although Plato speaks, on occasion, as if life on this earth were a punishment, a prison of the soul, in general the true significance of his soul lies not in its once celestial and now imprisoned state, but rather in the nobility of its nature as the seat of the intellect, through which man can arrive at that rapturous state where he is in the presence of the eternal beauties, represented by truth and goodness.

For Plotinus and the Neoplatonists, the individual soul is, quite naturally, a part of the All-Soul.[27] It is not in the body but the body is in it.[28] Plotinus says: "There is a great difference between the souls: one, never having fallen away from the All-Soul but dwelling within it, looks toward the Universal Mind and is capable of becoming one with It; others are capable of striving and almost attaining, while a third rank is much less apt."[29] However, he goes on to say: "With the individual souls the appetite for Divine Mind urges them to return to their Source, but they have, too, a power apt to administration in this lower sphere. . .In the Intellectual they remain with soul entire and are immune from care and trouble; but there comes a stage at which they descend from the universal to become partial and self-centered. This state, long maintained, the soul is a deserter from the All; it is a partial thing, isolated, weakened, full of care, intent upon the fragment; severed from the whole, it nestles in one form of being, caring only for the one, for a thing buffeted about by the world full of things. With this comes what is known as the casting of the wings,[30] the enchaining in body; the soul has lost that innocency of conducting the higher which it knew when it stood with the All-Soul, that earlier state to which all its interest would bid it hasten back. It has fallen, it operates through sense, it is a captive. This is the burial, the encavernment of the soul."[31] Plotinus' whole concept of reality lies in the life of the soul, and all of his emphasis is upon the reascension of the soul to its original source.

Christianity combines the two aspects of the soul found in Plato and in Plotinus. Man is corrupt, and his main purpose in this life is the salvation of his immortal soul by the subjugation of the flesh or corporeal side of his nature. Where his own powers are insufficient the redeeming power of Christ or divine grace may come to his aid. The emphasis is not on the intellectual attribute of the soul, as in Plato, but rather on the Neoplatonic intuitive yearning of the soul toward its good—*summum bonum* of Aristotle, and *souverain Bien* of Marguerite de Navarre.

Toward the end of her life Marguerite seems to have had an insatiable yearning for release from the flesh. This yearning is best expressed in her *Prisons*, in which she gains successive release from the bonds of earthly love, ambition, and learning, all of which serve, nonetheless, as rungs of the ladder by which she mounts to that realm where the loving soul may be united to the object of its love.[32]

Desportes echoes something of the weariness with life which we find in Marguerite in a *Complainte*, when he addresses his body thus:

> O pauvre corps! jusqu'a quelle journée
> Retiendras-tu mon *ame emprisonnée*
> En tant de fers, la gardant qu'elle volle
> Apres son bien, dont l'espoir me console?[33]

In one of the *Sonnets spirituels* our poet regrets that part of his life which he has wasted and hopes for release from the prison of the flesh. Platonically interpreted this release would have to come through the poet's own efforts through the love of beauty, or the seeking of truth. He appeals, however, directly to Christ, who is, for the Christian, Goodness, Truth and Beauty:

> Je regrette en pleurant les jours mal employez
> A suivre une beauté passagere et muable,
> Sans m'eslever au ciel et laisser memorable
> Maint haut et digne exemple aux esprits desvoyez.
> . . . .
> Que j'abhorre le monde et que, par ton secours,
> La prison soit brisée où mon ame est captive.[34]

The idea of the soul being in bondage to the body is a frequent one. In an elegy of a light nature the poet, speaking to his lady, says:

> Pour gage de ma foy, qui vous est dediée
> Tout le tans que ceste ame au corps sera liée.[35]

In the *Phaedrus* Socrates, while describing the soul, uses one of the most beautiful myths attributed to him by Plato in all of the dialogues. He speaks of the three parts of the soul and compares them to two horses and the charioteer who drives them. "And one of the horses was good and the other bad... The right-hand horse is upright and cleanly... The other is a crooked lumbering animal...Now when the charioteer beholds the vision of love, and has his whole soul warmed through sense, and is full of the prickings and ticklings of desire, the obedient steed, then as always under the government of shame, refrains from leaping on the beloved; but the other, heedless of the pricks and of the blows of the whip, plunges and runs away, giving all manner of trouble to his companion and the charioteer." However, the charioteer struggles with the unruly steed, "and when this has happened several times the villain has ceased from his wanton way, he is tamed and humbled, and follows the will of the charioteer, and when he sees the beautiful one he is ready to die of fear."[36] He goes on to say that the beloved is then led to receive the lover into communion and that when they are together both cease from their pain and enjoy the bliss of each other's presence.

This myth enjoyed great favor among the poets of the Renaissance. It was so well known by the time of Desportes that he makes obvious use of it without mentioning either the charioteer or the steeds, while not departing an inch from the original Platonic significance:

> Si la fureur d'amour, rendant l'ame agitée,
> La ravit dans le ciel de son corps l'elevant,
> Et si l'ame rebelle et qui s'en va privant,
> Tousjours foible et pesante en terre est arrestée;
>   Que n'aimez-vous, deesse, afin d'estre portée
> Par la fureur d'amour dans le ciel en vivant?
> Plein de ravissement je vous iroy suivant,
> Et mon ame à son gré seroit lors contentée.[37]

The idea behind the myth is, of course, that the soul is inspired to love by the desire for the possession of beauty, but that whereas the heavenly soul would soar to the realm of true Beauty, the sensual one wishes to enjoy earthly pleasures. The poet seems to be suggesting that the lady submit to the transports of love for him so that he may follow her to heavenly realms. This is an ingenious poetic interpretation of a basically Platonic concept.

Again in the *Phaedrus* we learn that: "The wing is the corporeal element which is most akin to the divine, and which by nature tends to soar aloft and carry that which gravitates downward into the upper region, which is the habitation of the gods. The divine is beauty, wisdom, goodness, and the like; and by these the wing of the soul is nourished and grows apace."[38]

This idea of being transported, of being carried away on wings, is not limited to Platonism. It is a poetic idea which has found favor perhaps from earliest times and is found in the words of the Psalmist when he speaks of taking the "wings of the morning."[39] Petrarch approaches the Platonic meaning of the wings of the soul when he says:

> Ancor (e questo é quel che tutto avanza)
> Da volar sopra'l ciel gli avea dat' ali
> Per le cose mortali
> Che son scala al Fattor, chi ben l'estima.
> Chè mirando ei ben fiso quante e quali
> Eran virtuti in quella sua speranza,
> D'una in altra sembianza
> Poeta levarsi all'alta cagion prima.[40]

Michelangelo, one of the most truly Platonic poets of the Italian Renaissance, uses the concept when speaking of the single mind which governs two loving hearts, "Ambos levando al ciel e con pari *ali*."[41]

Desportes speaks repeatedly of the wings that transport one to the "sejour des choses immortelles" without always coming to grips with the true Platonic significance of those wings which are grown by the soul. In his *Proces contre Amour*, it is the God Love who, defending himself before Reason because of the accusations of the poet against him, says:

> Je luy ay fait dresser et la veuë et les *ailes*
> Au bien-heureux sejour des choses immortelles.[42]

The reference to Platonic doctrine is obvious here but somewhat less so in the following lines where our poet speaks of his wing as being "trop basse," meaning, probably, not yet sufficiently developed, or still clinging too much to things of the flesh:

> Mais depuis sa beauté d'heure en heure augmenta
> La feit plus que deesse, et si haut l'emporta,
> Que, pour voler apres, trop basse fut mon *aile*.[43]

The inspiration which causes the soul to take wings varies.

The eyes of the beloved are of infinite importance in the psychology of love both in Plato and in poets from time immemorial. Desportes credits the beautiful eyes of his lady with the responsibility of carrying him aloft:

> Qui veut au ciel d'amour voir ses *ailes* haussées,
> Et de tous vieux ennuis la memoire bannir,
> Vienne au jour de vos yeux s'il les peut soustenir,
> Beaux yeux, les deux meurtriers de mes paines passées.[44]

It is strange to find the poet saying that he is transported, not on his own wings but on those of the beloved:

> Vostre esprit tout divin me rend plain de savoir,
> Je volle au plus haut ciel, emporté sur vos *ailes*.[45]

The contemplation of earthly beauty opens up new vistas and leads one upward to the final contemplation of absolute Beauty. It is the wings of one's own soul which grow as one contemplates beauty. Being borne heavenward on the wings of the soul of one's lady is an interesting subtlety not found in Plato, though the idea is certainly not far removed from his.

Sometimes the poet speaks of the wings of love rather than the wings of the soul, as in these lines where they are contrasted with the wings of the daring Icarus:

> Car les ailes d'Amour ne sont faites de cire,
> Le plus ardant soleil si tost ne les fondra.[46]

At other times he speaks of the wings of love which transport him to the realm of the "plus haut" where he comes to understand "la gloire et les merveilles," so that no matter whether he is speaking of the wings of the soul or the wings of love, the purpose which they serve is consistent with the Platonic concept:

> Quand j'ay l'heur de jouyr d'un bien tant souhaité,
> Sans partir de la terre aux cieux je suis porté,
> Et comprens du plus haut la gloire et les merveilles.[47]

When he speaks of the transient beauty of his lady as a shadow of eternal beauty and credits that beauty with being responsible for the growth of his wings he is expressing the full import of Plato's idea concerning the growing of wings:

> J'aimoy vostre beauté passagere et muable
> Comme un ombre de l'autre éternelle et durable,
> Qui sur l'aile d'amour dans les cieux m'élevoit.[48]

The Platonic concept of anamnesis, or recollection, as a power of the soul, seems not to have been used a great deal by the poets of the Renaissance, except in so far as it is implied in the poetic gift they liked to attribute to themselves. This doctrine is based on the belief in the pre-existence of the soul and is found throughout the dialogues. We have seen that after their creation the individual souls, before being assigned their stars, were placed in a chariot and shown all things.[49] In the *Meno* we read: "The soul, then, as being immortal, and having been born again many times, and having seen all things that exist, whether in this world or the world below, has knowledge of them all; and it is no wonder that she should be able to call to remembrance all that she ever knew about virtue, and about everything; for as all nature is akin, and the soul has learned all things, there is no difficulty in her eliciting or as men say learning, out of a single recollection all the rest, if a man is strenuous and does not faint; for inquiry and all learning is but recollection."[50] In the *Phaedrus* we find that when the lover "sees the beauty of earth, he is transported with the recollection of the true beauty."[51] Finally, the theory of recollection is connected with that of the Ideas, which we shall have occasion to treat much more fully in a later chapter of this study.

Boethius was acquainted with the theory of anamnesis, for we find him saying in his *Consolation of Philosophy*: "If any man search for truth with all his penetration, and would be led astray by no deceiving paths, let him turn upon himself the light of an inward gaze, let him bend by force the longdrawn wanderings of his thoughts into one circle; let him tell surely to his soul, that he has, thrust away within the treasures of his mind, all that he labours to acquire . . . For the body, though it brings material mass which breeds forgetfulness, has never driven forth all light from the mind. The seed of truth does surely cling within, and can be roused as a spark by the fanning of philosophy. . . And if the Muse of Plato sends through those depths the voice of truth, each man has not forgotten and is but reminding himself of what he learns."[52]

Michelangelo, a half century before the epoch of the popularity of Desportes, approached the concept of recollection in these lines:

> Non so se e' s' è l'immaginata luce
>   Del suo primo fattor, che l'alma sente,
>   O se dalla memoria O dalla mente
>   Alcuna altra beltà nel cuor traluce;
> O se nell' alma ancor resplende e luce
>   Del suo primiero stato il raggio ardente,
>   Di sè lasciando un non so che cocente,
>   Ch'è forse quel ch'a pianger me conduce.[53]

If this idea was not overworked during the period of the Renaissance it is perhaps because the Church did not teach the pre-existence of the soul. Although Ficino says in one place that the soul descends into a body,[54] thus implying its existence before that descent, elsewhere he says: "We learn that the soul possesses innate concepts of all its own qualities from its desires, its material of inquiry, its imagination, its judgment, and its comparison. Who will deny that the soul, from tender babyhood desires the true, good, honorable, and beneficial? But no one desires what he does not know. Therefore, there are some notions of those things in the soul even before it desires them; through these notions, like models and examples of the things themselves it judges them to be desirable."[55] Accordingly his words can be interpreted to mean that the notions are God-given but perhaps only at the moment when the soul comes into being with the body, rather than in a previous existence.

In dealing with the subject of recollection, Leone Ebreo, a disciple of Ficino with little concern over varying points of difference between the Christian and the Platonic, did not hesitate to substantiate his own beliefs by those of Plato and of Aristotle. He says: "Plato says that our reason and understanding is the recollection of things pre-existing in the soul in a state of oblivion, and this is the same potentiality of Aristotle, and the latency of which I have told you."[56]

Among the French, Marguerite de Navarre seems to play with the idea of anamnesis in these lines from her mystical *Prisons*:

> Voz jeunes yeulx ont vostre cueur tiré
> A la beaulté, puys il a desiré
> De ce bien la, *dont avoit congnoissance*,
> Par ung plaisir en avoir jouyssance.[57]

And her protégé, Héroët, had broached it in connection with the famous myth of the Androgyne, of which he gave the first complete poetic treatment in France:

> Apres aussi que les recouvrements
> Nous avons faicts par divers changements
> Et chascun vient à la *recongnoissance*
> Et sa moytié par longue experience,
> Soubdain toute aultre alliance s'oublie
> Et le vray neud deslié se relie.[58]

Desportes boldy uses the Platonic concept with all its implications—allied with other Platonic allusions—when he says in one of his sonnets to Diane:

> Si tost que je la vey si divine et si belle,

> Mon ame incontinant *recogneut* bien en elle
> Le parfait qu'autre fois elle avoit veu aux cieux;
> C'est pourquoy de depuis saintement je l'adore
> Pour la divinité qui la suit et l'honore,
> Et croy qu'en l'adorant je fay honneur aux Dieux.[59]

The idea is repeated in the *Procez contre Amour*, already mentioned in another connection above, where the little god Love carries on a discourse with Reason and makes this appeal:

> Pense, un petit, Raison, aux thresors desirables,
> Graces, beautez, douceurs et clartez admirables
> Que tu as veus là au cabinet des cieux.[60]

From the discussion above we find that the soul occupied an important place in the thought of Plato. It was to dominate the whole thought of the Neoplatonists for whom it became the real part of man. Following in the footsteps of Aristotle, the Christians were inclined to attribute reality to both body and soul, placing the greater emphasis on the soul, which was still recognized as the God-given part of man. Like Plato, Desportes makes of the soul the immortal part of man and sometimes seems to attribute to it a pre-existence. He is intrigued by the poetic aspect of the soul, along with the Athenian philosopher, that is to say, with the soul's dwelling place in its own star; with the wings of the soul; with the myth of the charioteer and the two steeds; and with the theory of anamnesis. Like a true Christian he also finds matter for poetic contemplation in such subjects as the soul's *summum bonum* and the prison of the soul, which can also be traced to Plato through the Neoplatonists.

Certain affectations of the earthly soul, having to do in particular with the virtues on the one hand and with fear on the other, with which Desportes was preoccupied at one time or another in his life, might have been included in this chapter. However, they are of so great importance and are so intimately tied up with his activities in the Académie du Palais of his protector, Henri III, that they will have entire chapters devoted to them.

CHAPTER IV

THE IDEAS

No concept in all of Plato has occasioned so much discussion as has the doctrine of Ideas, which has already been mentioned in connection with the subject of anamnesis. This doctrine is at the center of all of Plato's speculations upon metaphysical questions and comes up time and again in his dialogues. It is closely associated with his treatment of beauty, of truth, and of goodness. The Ideas themselves are treated as "patterns," as that which "can never change or be moved," as that "which always is," as "reality," as "forms," as "universals," and as "the one in many."

Although Plato spoke of them repeatedly, nowhere did he define the Ideas, for, concerning them, as concerning God, one can only guess at the truth. However, he knew that there is a truth which is beyond sense, and which is perceived by the mind alone when freed from the disturbing elements of the body.

If Plato did not try to define the Ideas he did attempt to explain them objectively. They can be reached by the aid of dialectic, which uses the senses as steps to mount to the realm of the absolute. No where is an estimate given as to their number, but in the *Cratylus* true beauty, which is never in a state of flux and remains always the same, is considered one of them.[1] And in the *Phaedrus* they are designated as universals and are contrasted with particulars. The reason has a recollection of them from that period when the soul was following God and "raised her head up toward true being."[2]

One may arrive in the realm of the Ideas through the love of beauty—a concept particularly intriguing to the love poet—as well as through the accumulation of knowledge leading to truth. The true lover, if led aright, will, through contemplating beautiful earthly forms, cultivate fair thoughts, and will soon perceive that the beauty of one form is akin to that of another and that beauty is therefore general; then that the beauty of mind is more to be desired that that of outward form. Thus he will progress from the material to the ideal, until he perceives that beauty which is separate, simple, and everlasting. The Ideas are inextricably bound up with love, by which we arrive at the vision of them. However, the love through which we arrive at final principles is of the intellectual nature and not of the senses, for we learn that "he attains to the purest knowledge of them [the Ideas] who goes to each with the mind alone."[3]

The soul of man was in the presence of these Ideas before falling into the body, as we learn from Socrates, who says: "These ideas must have existed before we were born as our souls existed before we were born; and if not the ideas, then not the soul."[4] The Ideas entered into the creation, since they were the patterns followed by the Creator. In the *Timaeus* one learns that "the work of the creator, whenever he looks to the unchangeable and fashions the form and nature of his work after an unchangeable pattern, must necessarily be made fair and perfect. .... It is manifest that he must have looked to that which is eternal ... for ... the world has been framed in the likeness of that which is apprehended by reason and mind and is unchangeable, and must therefore of necessity, if this is admitted, be a copy of something."[5]

So much for Plato's own treatment of the Ideas, summarized in the passages quoted above. One could go on quoting from him indefinitely, for the Ideas are, as we have said, the foundation on which all his metaphysics rests. These quotations, however, are sufficiently broad to cover his most significant thought on the matter. Let us look for a moment at the fate of the Ideas between the time of Plato and that of our poet.

Aristotle conceived of the Ideas as Forms. The Form of any thing represented its intelligible nature. The Form differs from the Platonic Idea in that it is immanent in the thing rather than existing apart from it.

For Plotinus and the Neoplatonists the Ideas were similar to those in the Platonic concept. They do not exist in things, since there is no reality in matter. They differ from the Platonic concept in that they are identical with Intelligence.

Plato believed that the Ideas are in the soul when it comes into the body. The Stoics conceived of them as coming from experience. St. Augustine and the early Christians, with their belief in revelation, held that man has natural knowledge of the world about him sufficient to the ordinary needs of living and that there is a higher knowledge which is revealed and comes through faith. This developed into the doctrine of the two-fold truth which was basic in St. Thomas Aquinas' thought.

During the eleventh century there arose in the School of Chartres a sect known as the Nominalists, headed by a doctor named Jean, who was in his turn the master of Roscelin.[6] There developed between its adherents and the Realists—those who held to the Platonic doctrine of Ideas—a conflict which lasted for many years and spread all over Europe. The Realists held that the Ideas are general concepts having an existence independent of things or experiences. The Nominalists insisted that ideas are the results of experience and can have no existence except as they are supported by experience.

Whatever interpretation may have been placed on the ideas, the basic Platonic conception remained alive in metaphysical speculation, and was especially so from the time of the quarrel of the Realists and the Nominalists until the period of the Renaissance.

Dante, in his *Convivio,* made mention of the Ideas but conceived of them in the Neoplatonic sense as Intelligences. He says: "Others were there such as Plato, a man of supreme excellence, who laid down not only as many Intelligences as there are movements of the heaven, but just as many as there are kinds of things; .... and Plato calls them Ideas, which is as much as to say Forms, and Universals."[7] Later Petrarch followed the Platonic concept when he spoke of his Laura as being fashioned after a heavenly pattern in the words which follow:

>   In qual parte del Ciel, in quale *idea*
>   Era l'esempio onde Natura tolse
>   Quel bel viso leggiadro, in ch'elle volse
>   Mostrar quaggiù quanto lassu potea?[8]

For Ficino and the members of the Florentine Academy, who were in possession of all the works of Plato, the theory of the Ideas took on new meaning. In his *Commentary on the Symposium* Ficino says: "For God, who is omnipotent, created in Angelic Mind, as it cleaved to Him, the forms of all things to be created.... These Prototypes or Forms of everything conceived by the dispensation of God in the Angelic Mind are, we cannot doubt, the Ideas."[9] Thus, like Dante, Ficino is interpreting the Ideas in a Neoplatonic fashion. The theory was taken up by all the idealists of the Italian Renaissance—Bembo, Leone Ebreo, Lorenzo de' Medici. Without mentioning the Ideas themselves Michelangelo makes allusion to them in this beautiful sonnet, which is a conversation between the poet and Love:

>   Poet: Dimmi di grazia, Amor, se gli occhi miei
>   Veggono'l ver beltà ch'io miro,
>   O s'io l'ho dentro il cor, ch'ovunque io giro,
>   Veggio più bello il volto di costei.
>   Tu'l dei saper, poichè tu vien con lei

>   A tormi ogni mia pace, ond'io m'adiro;
>   Benchè nè meno un sol breve sospiro,
>   Nè Meno ardente foco chiederei.
> Love: La beltà che tu vedi è ben da quella;
>   Ma cresce poi ch'a miglior loco sale,
>   Se per gli occhi mortali all'alma corre;
>   Quivi si fà divina, onesta, e bella,
>   Come a se simil vuol cosa immortale;
>   Questa, e non quella, agli occhi tuoi precorre.[10]

The theory of the Ideas was revived in sixteenth-century France and became an important part of the poet's storehouse of conceits. Maurice Scève's *Délie*, a long sequence of *dizains* celebrating the idealized love of the poet for his lady, was supposed until recently to have owed its name to an anagrammatical reworking of the word *Idée*.[11] In her *Heptaméron* Marguerite de Navarre makes allusion to the Ideas in a clearly Platonic manner. She speaks of the lover "cuidans trouver en une beaulté extérieure, en une grâce visible & aux vertuz morales, la souveraine beaulté, grâce & vertu."[12] Héroët in his *Parfaicte Amye* gives a complete treatment of the Idea of beauty, saying that the beauty we see on earth

> ... n'estoit qu'une estincelle
> De ceste qu'il nommoit immortelle
> . . . .
> Que l'aultre estoit entiere et immortelle.[13]

The poets of the Pléiade also made allusion to the theory, and it had not lost its attractiveness to any of the men of letters of Desportes' age. Guillaume de Salluste Sieur Du Bartas (1544-1590), a Protestant contemporary of our poet who was famous for his long epic poems—*La Semaine* (1578) and *la Seconde Semaine* (1784)—speaks of "revenant disciple studieux/ De l'Attique Platon...."[14] He is obviously referring to the Ideas as patterns for substantial things when he introduces the World-Soul into his long poem in this manner:

> Puis l'ame comme forme inspirant dans le corps
> Et ses membres sans nombre, et ses divins accords,
> Eust paré sa beauté d'une beauté suprême.[15]

Again he implies the flight through love to the realm of the Ideas when he says:

> O doux ravissement, saint vol, amour extrême
> Qui fais que nous baisons les lèvres d'amour mesme.[16]

It was inevitable that Desportes should avail himself of this concept. He does so when praising his lady, pointing out that she is a copy of a heavenly pattern:

> Sur la plus belle *Idée* au ciel vous fustes faite,

> Voulant nature un jour monstrer tout son pouvoir,
> Depuis vous luy servez de forme et de miroir,
> Et toute autre beauté sur la vostre est portraite.[17]

He makes the very poetic point that nature, not being satisfied with having created the lady after the pattern of perfect beauty, then uses her for a pattern. In another instance his lady, who is the "ombre de beauté," will some day be transformed into perfect beauty:

> Cette ombre de beauté, qui vous fait renommer,
> Quand vous seriez au ciel, se verroit transformer
> En la beauté parfaite et d'essence éternelle.[18]

No clearer statement of the Platonic concept could be found than that embodied in the following lines of our poet which have already been quoted in the chapter on the Soul:

> J'aimoy vostre beauté passagere et muable
> Comme un ombre de l'autre éternelle et durable,
> Qui sur l'aile d'amour dans les cieux m'élevoit.[19]

Finally, the lady herself is the "Idée" on which the poet's love is founded:

> Aussi, pour dire vray, mon amour j'ay fondée
> Sur la perfection d'une si belle *idée*.[20]

In Plato matter takes its form by having the Ideas impressed upon it, and "the mother and receptacle of all created and visible and in any way sensible things, is not to be termed earth, or air, or fire, or water or any of their compounds or any of the elements from which these are derived, but is an invisible and formless being which receives all things and in some mysterious way partakes of the intelligible, and is most incomprehensible."[21] The concept of the Ideas carries over into art. Plotinus speaks of a "creation in which the sculptor has concentrated every loveliness," and he says: "Now the stone thus wrought by the artist's hand to beauty of form is beautiful not as stone—for so the crude block would be as pleasant—but in virtue of the form imposed on it by art. This form is in the designer before ever it enters the stone; he holds it not by his equipment of eyes and hands but by his participation in his art. The beauty, therefore, exists in a far higher state in the art; that original beauty is not transferred; what comes over is a derivative and a minor, and even that appears in the statue only in so far as the stone yielded to the art. Art, then, must itself be beautiful in a far higher and purer degree, since it is the seat and source of that beauty; in the degree in which the beauty is diffused by entering into matter it is so much the weaker than that concentrated in unity."[22]

The concept of the Ideas found its way into both the sculpture and the poetry of the great Italian Michelangelo, who subscribed to the theory of intuitive genius and believed that God impressed the Ideas on matter, so that the hand of the sculptor could not find in the stone what was not already there. Thus, unlike Plotinus, he believed that the form was inherent in the uncut stone rather than in the designer, and that the sculptor only served to bring out the form. In his *Story of Art* E. H. Gombrich says of Michelangelo the sculptor: "He wanted to release the figures from the stones in which they were slumbering.... Michelangelo always tried to conceive his figures as lying hidden in the block of marble on which he was working; the task he set himself as a sculptor was merely to remove the stone which covered them."[23] In one of his most famous sonnets the poet himself says:

>Non ha l'ottimo artista alcun concetto
> Ch'un marmo solo in se non circoscriva
> Col suo soverchio, e solo a quello arriva
> La man che obbedisce all'intelletto.
>Il mal ch'io fuggo, e'l ben ch'io me prometto,
> In te, donna leggiadra, altera, e diva,
> Tal si nasconde, e, perch'io più non viva,
> Contraria ho l'arte al desiato effetto.
>Amor dunque non ha, nè tua beltate,
> O fortuna, o durezza, o gran disdegno,
> Del mio mal colpa, o mio destino, o sorte,
>Se dentro del tuo cor morte e pietate
> Porti in un tempo, e ch'l mio basso ingegno
> Non sappia ardendo trarne altro che morte.[24]

Desportes borrows Michelangelo's concept in the following lines:

>Le sculpteur excellent desseignant pour ouvrage
>Une plante, un lion, un homme, un element,
>Si la main obeit et suit l'entendement,
>Trouve en un marbre seul toute sorte d'image.[25]

He, like Michelangelo, conveys the thought that the desired form is contained in the stone and can be brought out by the hand of the artist who follows his intuitive genius, "intelletto" or "entendement."

As we have seen, the subject of the Ideas readily lends itself to poetic variations, for the Ideas can be interpreted in many different ways and can cover many aspects of metaphysical speculation. The concept is not abundantly used in Desportes because it is apropos only when one is dealing with things most sacred and divine. However, when our poet does use it, he does not depart from its exact sense, and he uses it in connection with subjects which are beyond all explaining. Being a love poet, for the most part, he limits the subject to the divine beauty of his lady. Of that we shall have more to say when we consider more particularly the lover and the beloved.

Perhaps it should be noted here that the theory of the Ideas entered into literary criticism—through a rationalization of Aristotle—as a part of the seventeenth-century classical doctrine. Presupposing an ideal form for all things to be found in nature, the poet—and the artist in general—was advised to seek perfection in his works by improving on nature.

CHAPTER V

LOVE

A short resumé of the evolution of the concept of idealized love from the period when it was first recorded by Plato to that of the Renaissance may help in the clarification of Desportes' interpretation of it in his verse, though this evolution may be familiar to most of those who will read these pages.

Even before Plato, certain Greek philosophers had come to look upon love as the great creative and motive force behind the universe as well as the medium through which one arrives at a knowledge of the essence of things and the link between the human and the divine. However, such considerations had scarcely gone beyond the philosopher and the metaphysician, and the poet of antiquity does not seem to have been influenced by them to any considerable degree. For the poet of antiquity love might at times represent a beautiful, sincere, and tender emotion, but more frequently it was something to be enjoyed through the physical associations of the lover and the beloved, who shared alike its delights of the moment and did not think of it as leading to the non-sensual, immaterial realm of the divine.

It was left for the medieval poet to rediscover the ancient Greek concepts of love and to embody them in his verse, to shift emphasis in matters having to do with love from the physical to the intellectual and moral. Under the influence of all that had transpired between the age of Plato and his own, his concepts became somewhat modified but developed, by the time of the Renaissance, into a pattern not far removed in essence from the basic concepts of the Greeks. To be sure the beloved was no longer a youth but a lady. However, she had become a thing apart. The relationship between lover and beloved was comparable to that existing between vassal and lord. The lover owed fealty, devotion, and service to the lady as the vassal owed them to the lord.

This new development in love psychology grew up among the troubadours of Provence. Its rationalization is best represented in the well-known twelfth-century Latin treatise *De arte honeste amandi*, prepared for Marie de Champagne by Andreas Capellanus, which formulates a code of courtly love. It is comparable to Ovid's *Ars amatoria*, if less pragmatic in its techniques, but introduces the element of decorum and deals with the question of inequality. The courtly love which Andreas portrays, or rather summarizes from the previous work of the troubadours, varies considerably from Ovidian love. Although he defines love as a "certain inborn suffering derived from the sight of and excessive meditation upon the beauty of the opposite sex," he goes on to say that "it can endow a man even of humblest birth with nobility of character" and that it "makes a man shine with so many virtues and teaches everyone . . . so many good traits of character." The author relates his own love ventures of a sensuous nature, but he says that love "adorns a man, so to speak, with the virtue of chastity," and that "an excess of passion is a bar to love." He goes on to say that "the man in love becomes accustomed to performing many services gracefully for everyone."[1]

Thus we see that love had become for the troubadours much more than the mere satisfaction of physical appetites and the most effective manner of accomplishing this end. From what source did they receive their new concepts of love? Professor Urban Tigner Holmes summarizes the numerous theories in his *History of Old French Literature.*[2] In the introduction to his translation of the work of Andreas Capellanus, John Jay Parry concludes that the most reasonable of the theories presented by Holmes is that which traces the influence to the culture of Moslem Spain.[3] He says that when the Califate of Cordova fell in 1031 the Moslem lands were divided among twenty petty kings. They encouraged literature as a sign of royal power and each had his own court poets, some of whom wandered from court to court. Among these poets there were two different attitudes toward love: that of the sensual tradition which owed something to Ovid; and that of the intellectual tradition, which went back to Plato and was based on a knowledge of him passed down by the Arabian scholars. Already in about 1022 the Andalusian poet Ibn Hazm had written his *The Dove's Neck-Ring*, in which one finds the Ovidian sighings, weepings, paleness, and thinness of the lover, as well as the idea that love should be secret and that jealousy is one of its pleasant aspects. Otherwise, the love he represents is essentially different from that of Ovid. The lover trembles in the presence of his beloved. Love is defined as the union of souls separated in creation. It is born at the sign of an outwardly beautiful form. The soul itself is beautiful and wishes to possess the beautiful. True love does not ignore physical effects, but the union of souls is of far greater worth. Love makes the lover better. It may be conceived for a great lady or for a slave girl and may even exist between men. The lover is ever submissive before the beloved. In these respects the love painted by Ibn Hazm was not unique among Arabian poets. For elsewhere these poets proposed that man shows his good character and breeding by practicing chaste love; that true love has an ennobling effect on the lover; and that submission to the will of the lady brings him honor.

The work of the Moslem poets became known to Guillaume d'Aquitaine,[4] the first of the troubadours of Provence, and to his friend and vassal Ebles II de Ventadorn, and these men and their colleagues embodied the new concepts they found in the works of the Moslem poets in their own verse.[5] Theirs was an aristocratic attitude toward love, and their works have become known as courtly poetry. This courtly poetry spread into Italy when many of the troubadours had to flee France in the wake of the Albigensian Crusade (1209). The Italian poets learned much from them, but they began a still further refinement of the psychology of love, which is first clearly visible in the verse of a thirteenth-century poet of Bologna named Guinicelli.

With Guinicelli the lady takes on a new meaning. She is a symbol of the divine. Through love of her the poet is wounded to death. The beauty of the lady represents a form of perfection, the reflection of a divine cause. The lover is inspired in his turn to perfect himself. True love is the monopoly of the well-born, noble, delicate heart. Finally there is no nobility apart from love. The poet no longer celebrates the beauties of the lady, which are perishable, but sings the effects which her beauty has on the one who contemplates her.[6] Guinicelli is the precursor of a school of poets who cultivated the *dolce stil nuovo*.[7] His concepts were introduced among the Florentine poets by Guido Cavalcanti, whose poem *Donna mi prega* is the first great expression of the new school. Guido introduces philosophy into the considerations of love. He suggests hidden symbolisms to be sought in his work and in the beauty of the lady. Love has now lost the aspect of joy and acquired that of contemplation.

These new developments were to enlist almost immediately the great poetic powers of Dante, who carried the ideals of the *dolce stil nuovo* to their most exalted level. His lady, Beatrice, not only became the earthly embodiment of the angelic but was herself an angel and the guide of the poet through the realms of the supernatural. She became the very link between the poet and God. While the poet's juvenile love for her may have caused him uneasiness and suffering, the true love which he ultimately conceived for her was his salvation. Dante finally clarified all the symbolism behind the new concepts in his *Convivio*,[8] which served as a handbook on philosophic love for future poets because of the keenness of its reasoning and the nobility of its sentiments.

Petrarch was the heir of this brilliant school of poets. However, his love for Laura was something more than, something different from, the love of Dante for Beatrice. Beatrice was scarcely a person of flesh and blood. She represented all that was beautiful and good and pure, and she served as an inspiration for Dante's verse. Petrarch obviously wanted to make his Laura a representation as divine as Beatrice, but he expresses considerably more than the yearnings of his immortal soul. Whereas in the *Vita nuova* Dante had suffered from being dumbfounded in the presence of Beatrice, Petrarch, in his *Rime*, suffers certain physical privations, comparable to those suffered by the troubadours. His sonnets and *canzoni* are frequently sad laments. Nevertheless, Laura is the source of all his inspiration and his guide to a virtuous life.[9]

The advances of the poets of the *dolce stil nuovo* and Petrarch in the idealization of love, the higher intellectualization of their concepts of love, may have been due to the fact that they were in possession of a greater accumulation of Platonic materials—the Latin translations of the work of the Neoplatonists and early Church Fathers; the works of such Romans as Cicero and Boethius; the few Platonic dialogues which had survived in the western world—than their predecessors. Thus Petrarch had arrived at a point where he could say of his lady:

> Gentil mia Donna, i'veggio
> Nel mover de' vostr' occhi un dolce lume
> Che me mostra la via ch'al Ciel conduce;
> Et per lungo costume,
> Dentro la dove sol con Amor seggio
> Quasi visibilmente il cor traluce.
> Quest'è la vista ch'a ben far m'induce,
> E che me scorge al glorioso fine.[10]

In the next breath, however, he might be very humanly lamenting in this manner:

> Fera stella (se'l Cielo ha forza in noi
> Quand' alcun crede) fu sotto chi'io nacqui,
> E fera cuna dove nato giacque,
> E fera terra ov'e pie mossi poi;
> E fera donna che con gli occhi suoi

> E con l'arco a cui sol per segno piacqui,
> Fe la piaga ond' Amor, teco non tacqui,
> Che con quell'arme risaldar la puoi.
>
> Ma tu prendi a diletto i dolor miei;
> Ella non già: perchè non son più duri,
> E'l colpo è di saetta e non di spiedo.
>
> Pur mi consola che languir per lei
> Megl'è gioir d'altra; e tu mel giuri
> Per l'orato tuo strale, e io tel credo.[11]

Petrarch has been called the singer of the divided heart.[12] His immediate successors simply reworked the rich poetic vein which he had helped to open and perfect, adding their own ingenious subtleties, retaining little or nothing of his sincerity, and lacking, for the most part, his true love experience which added verisimilitude to the love which he sang.

Petrarchism was well established among the poets of Italy when the Greek scholars—Chrysoloras, Plethon, Bessarion, and others—came to Italy in the fifteenth century and brought with them the storehouse of ancient Greek learning in general and the complete dialogues of Plato in particular. The men of Florence —for the new learning was adopted first and most enthusiastically in that city—already worshiped at the shrine of beauty, and were therefore carried away by the new beauties and truths revealed to them by those brilliant scholars. It was "Platonic Love" —first so called by Ficino[12]—which primarily captivated their attention. James A. Notopoulos says: "The foundation for the communion of the Florentine Platonists was Ficino's cult of love and friendship, which was based on *amor divinus*, the love of the soul for God, and was sharply opposed to the vulgar concept of love."[13] Not satisfied to stop with Plato, the men of this group studied the works of the Neoplatonists as well and thus absorbed ideas of questionable orthodoxy, so far as Platonic doctrine is concerned. Of prime importance, of course, were the translations and commentaries of Ficino. His commentaries, particularly the one on the *Symposium*, influenced greatly the men of letters of the age, such as Pico della Mirandola, Benivieni, Leone Ebreo, Bembo, and Castiglione.

Each poet or writer found inspiration in this new and vast storehouse to suit his own particular temperament and special preoccupations. In Benivieni, as in his master Ficino, a gentle mysticism is apparent. In Leone Ebreo an eclectic philosophical strain, tending toward a closer *rapprochement* among Greek, Hebraic, Arabic, and Christian thought was the result. And in

Bembo and Castiglione the teachings of the dialogues gave meaning to the love which every courtier should cultivate, and brought new significance to the role of the courtier in his relations with his prince. The *uomo di virtù* was the ideal of the Italian gentleman, but there had to be some ultimate reason for his cultivation of the perfections. To the continuing and growing school of Petrarchist poets—Sasso, Sannazaro, Tebaldeo, Costanzo, and a host of others,—all this meant a new flood of poetic conceits, to add to those they had inherited from Petrarch. At the same time their inspiration became more and more conventional, and their techniques increasingly ingenious. The new Platonic element did not serve to eliminate the courtly element nor the constant lamentations which had found their way into the verse of these poets.

We should consider for a moment those lamentations and sufferings which occupy so much space in the verse of the Petrarchists and are to be found all too frequently in the works of Desportes, for in the minds of some critics they serve to minimize the possibility of any serious Platonic intent on the part of these poets. Many men participated in the dialogues, and they expressed varying points of view on the various subjects which were introduced for consideration.[14] Later writers who went to the dialogues for inspiration used what they found, sometimes indiscriminately, to suit their own purposes and tastes.

When one reads then the inexhaustible stream of *Rime*[15] from the Italian Renaissance and becomes weary of the despair of the lover, of his hotness and coldness, his paleness and blushing, his tremblings, faintings, jealousies, and deprivations, one must remember that the same reactions are found in the dialogues. There we find that the lover waxes hot and cold in the presence of the beloved and that his "whole soul is in a state of ebullition and effervescence";[16] that "the entire soul is pierced and maddened and pained"; that in his "madness" the lover can neither sleep by night nor stay in one place by day; that he wishes to be as near as possible to his beloved, who is the object of his worship.[17] "He may pray and entreat, and supplicate, and swear, and lie on a mat at the door, and endure a slavery worse than that of any slave."[18]

Suffering from love was common in courtly poetry and is said to come from Ovid,[19] who conceived of love as an illness. The Petrarchists adopted the *dolce-amaro* concept of love, first found in Sappho,[20] which looks upon it as a suffering, but of the bitter-sweet kind, so that the poet does not wish under any circumstances to be rid of it. In his *Vita nuova* Dante laments the suffering he endures because of his love for Beatrice, but later finds the reason for his suffering in his inability to understand the true nature of love. This is similar to Plato's rationalization in the Myth of the Cave,[21] in which he tells of the distress man feels when first in the presence of the sun's light after having lived for so long in the midst of shadows. The pain he feels in his eyes makes him turn away, as does the lover in the presence of the beauty of his beloved.

Desportes, as we have pointed out, leaned quite heavily on the Italian Petrarchists for inspiration, and sometimes we find him lamenting thus:

> Quand premier Hippolyte eut sur moy la victoire,
> Et que j'ouvry mes yeux au jour de sa beauté,
> Je ne sçay qu'il m'advint, je fus si transporté,
> Que de moy-mesme, helas! je perdy la memoire,
> Mes sens estoient ravis en l'amoureuse gloire,
> Et mon œil esblouy de trop grand clarté,
> Craignant ses chauds regards, s'abaissoit arresté
> Sur son beau sein d'albatre et sa gorge d'yvoire.
> Je senty mal et bien, chaud et froid à l'instant:
> J'esperay sans espoir, j'eu peur, j'osay pourtant,
> Et parlay dans mon cœur mainte chose inconnuë,
> Je le fortifiay pour les maux à venir,
> Et pour mieux y penser, chassay le souvenir
> De toute autre beauté que devant j'avoy veuë.[22]

The very thing which causes pain and sadness, love itself, when full blown, is the balm which assuages them. Socrates says that "the beauty of the beloved meets her eye and she receives the sensible warm motion of particles which flow toward her, therefore called emotion, and is refreshed and warmed by them and then she ceases from her pain with joy."[23]

Our poet blesses the flame of love which is the cause of his sufferings:

> Amour brûle mon cœur d'une si belle flame
> Et suis sous son pouvoir si doucement traité,
> Que, languissant ainsi captif et tourmenté,
> Je beny la prison et le feu de mon ame.[24]

When the richness of the Italian Renaissance began to make itself felt in France, it offered to the poet an abundance of new and intriguing conceits, both Petrarchan[25] and Platonic. Imitation was the order of the day among the poets of the Pléiade, and they drank at any spring which appeared refreshing. They Petrarchized, Platonized briefly, foreswore Platonism, and then relied upon their own inspiration.[26]

When Desportes appeared at the court of France, the Platonic matter was available in its entirety, not only in Ficino's Latin translations but also in French translations, as far as most of the dialogues were concerned.[27] The young Chartrain had received a thorough classical education, both as to languages and to literature, and had then accompanied the Bishop of Puy to Italy where he remained for several years.[28] While he read and absorbed everything the Italian poets had written he must also have come under the influence of some of the various academies which were still thriving in Italy and where Plato was still revered. When he returned to the court at Paris he found it subjected to innumerable Italian influences, as one might expect with a son of Catherine de' Medici on the throne and with Catherine herself in the wings directing the court drama. Charles IX and the young courtiers grouped around him were more interested in the subtleties of the Petrarchists than in the idealism of the Platonists. Desportes, however, soon found, in the salon of the maréchale de Retz where he became a favorite, the atmosphere favorable to his poetic temperament, an atmosphere where love was idealized.

In discussing Platonic love in the work of Desportes, we should not expect that all of his loves measured up to the ideal to be found in the *Symposium*, the great dialogue on idealized love. In Castiglione's *Cortegiano* we find Bembo, in his very serious and beautiful discourse on true love, saying that such love is reserved for men of a ripe age: "Whereupon most commonly it happeneth, that young men be wrapped in this sensuall love, which is a very rebel against reason, and therefore they make themselves unworthie to enjoy the favors and benefits which love bestoweth upon his true subjects, neither in love feele they any other pleasures, than what beastes without reason doe, but much more grievous afflictions .... As I judge therefore, those young men that bridle their appetites, and love with reason, to be godly: so doe I hold excused such as yeelde to sensuall love, whereunto they be so enclined through the weakenesse and frailtie of man: so they show therein meekness, courtesie, and prowesse, and the other worthie conditions that these Lords have spoken of, and when these youthfull yeares bee gone and past, leave it off cleane, keeping aloofe from this sensuall coveting as from the lowest step of the stayres, by the which a man may ascend to true love."[29] Whatever Desportes' loves may have been, his verse is characterized by "la parfaite convenance, la chasteté."[30] If one can judge from the following lines the love to which he aspired was pure and high and noble:

> Pardonnez-moy, deesse, et perdant la memoire
> De ces longues erreurs, n'y pensez nullement;
> Et pour le tans suivant songeons tant seulement;
> A combler nostre amour d'heur, de joye et de gloire,
> Rendons--la si parfaite, et si claire et si belle,
> Qu'elle serve d'exemple aux siecles à venir;
> Et que l'effort des ans, au lieu de la finir,
> Fasse que sa memoire à jamais soit nouvelle.[31]

He expects no reward from his lady:

> Or ne m'estimez point estre si temeraire,
> D'attendre en vous servant quelque plus grand salaire,
> . . . .
> Je desire, sans plus, que vous soyez contente
> Que je prenne de vous ce bien qui me tourmente,
> Que je vive pour vous, que je meure par vous,
> Et que vos yeux cruels ne me soient jamais doux,
> Car de mon seul penser je reçoy tant de gloire,
> Et de ce que j'osay debattre la victoire
> En la guerre d'Amour, où je perdy le cœur.
> Qu'estant de vous vaincu, je m'estime vainqueur,
> Et sens mon amitié trop bien recompensée,
> Me souvenant sans plus du vol de ma pensée.[32]

Concerning Desportes' capacity for loving and his own loves, not a great deal is known. He was destined for the Church from youth and had been tonsured while still in Chartres, although he did not receive minor orders until some twenty years later (1582).[33] These steps did not prevent him, or any other man of his age, from loving, and the loves which he celebrated in his verse were not only for idealized ladies but also for the young male friends of his youth and his protegés of later years.[34]

With the foregoing prospectus of the varying aspects of love and their evolution down through the ages to guide us, and with the conflicting influences brought to bear on the Renaissance poet in mind, let us now turn to the place which specific Platonic concepts concerning love occupied in the works of Desportes.

First we should find a definition of love in Plato's own words if we are to be sure that our poet understood Platonic love, keeping in mind the fact that from time immemorial poets have treated love in at least two lights—as a sentiment or passion, and as a personality. Plato was no exception in having done so.

We shall look first at the intangible thing, the sentiment which we call love.

In the *Symposium* Socrates explains that love is a desire for the possession of eternal beauty, and concludes that in seeking the beautiful the lover also seeks the good, and in desiring these things he longs for something which is non-existent in himself.[35] This is only the beginning of the description of true love, which continues with a minute treatment of its every aspect. This definition was reflected in every work into which a consideration of love entered in the Renaissance period, and we shall take time to summarize its various expressions. The early Neoplatonists, who influenced so greatly the men of the Renaissance, were particularly interested in the nature and force of love, as they were in all metaphysical considerations, and Plotinus echoed Plato when he said: "Everyone recognizes that the emotional state for which we make love responsible rises in souls aspiring to be knit in the closest union with some beautiful object. . . . Pure love seeks the beauty alone."[36] More than a thousand years later the Italian Ficino, commenting on the concept of Plato and his disciples, said: "When we say Love, we mean by that term the desire for beauty, for this is the definition of Love among all philosophers."[37] Following in the footsteps of Ficino, Bembo, in the *Cortegiano*, says: "Love is nothing else but a certaine coveting to enjoy beautie."[38]

The definition of love was thus hallowed and enjoying an honored tradition when it was taken up by the French poets. Already, under the patronage of Marguerite, the poet Héroët was saying in his *Parfaicte Amye:*

> Ne voyez vous qu'en amytié divine
> L'ung ne crainct point que l'aultre le ruine?
> Qui ayme Dieu ne celle son desir,
> Et ne recoyt gueres plus de plaisir
> A estre aymé qu'a veoir aultre attiré
> De la beaulté que tant a desiré.[39]

Thus we could only expect that Desportes might have made full use of this definition in his verse. Whether he went back to the *Symposium* or merely repeated what his more recent predecessors had said, the following line is nearly word for word from Plato:

> Aussi l'amour n'est rien qu'un desir de beauté.[40]

The definition is somewhat drowned in the Petrarchism of the next lines, but it is there none the less:

> Amour, qui des yeux prend naissance,

> Court aussi tost vers *le desir*,
> Se conserve avec l'esperance,
> Et trouve repos au plaisir.
> Mon amour est d'une autre sorte:
> Le desespoir la rend plus forte,
> Elle renaist de son trespas;
> Perdant, elle acquiert la victoire.
> C'est une chose forte à croire
> Aussi, vous ne le croyez pas.[41]

In one of his *Chansons* Desportes reiterates the definition in all its Platonic purety when he addresses himself thus to a lady whom he considers unworthy of true love:

> Quand vous aurez un cœur plein d'amour et de foy,
> Pur, entier et constant, pour m'offrir en eschange
> De celuy si loyal que vous avez de moy,
> Ne vous desfiez point qu'autre part je me range
> . . . .
> Vostre bouche et vos yeux, riches de mille appas,
> Meritent bien qu'on meure en leur obeïssance,
> Mais vostre esprit leger ne le merite pas;
> A ce que l'un contraint, l'autre nous en dispanse.
> Amour est un desir de jouyr et d'avoir
> Pour soy tant seulement l'object qui beau nous semble.
> Jamais de compagnon il ne veut recevoir:
> Cupidon ne sauroit lier trois cœurs ensemble.[42]

Here we have the faintest allusion to the Platonic conception that true love is an intellectual thing, and he who seeks it cannot be satisfied with an "esprit leger." The theme under consideration becomes more ethereal and more poetic, but no less truly Platonic, when the poet, reflecting the words of Diotima in the *Symposium*[43] and suggesting the progressive nature of the advance toward true beauty through love, says to Love:

> Purge moy tout par tout, le cœur, l'esprit et l'ame,
> Et m'eschauffe si bien de ta divine flame,
> Que je puisse monstrer ce que je vay suivant,
> Et que l'amour, volant qui jusqu'au ciel m'emporte,
> Apres la beauté sainte, est bien d'une autre sorte
> Que l'aveugle appetit qui nous va decevant.[44]

Our poet indicates that the beauty which love causes him to desire is not corporeal in nature but rather intellectual. It is "beauté sainte," which has its seat among the Ideas. Of this beauty, which is the ultimate goal of all our strivings, we shall have more to say in a later chapter.

It is evident that in Plato's thought love and beauty are inseparably tied together. Beauty not only inspires love but provides the steps for mounting to celestial spheres. But before abandoning the idea of love as a desire for the possession of beauty, we should examine one last instance of its manifestation in our poet's work, where he goes to the length of finding in one of the king's *mignons*, Quélus, the idea of love, beauty, and desire of man for man, which reflects something of the relationship between Socrates and Alcibiades. The verses cited are taken from an *Epitaphe* entitled, *Sur la mort de Jacques de Lévy, sieur Quélus*:

> Quélus, que la nature avoit fait pour plaisir,
> Comme une œuvre accomplie, admirable et divine,
> Portoit Amour aux yeux et Mars en la poitrine;
> Bien d'égal, entre nous, ne se pouvoit choisir.
> Le voyant, on bruloit d'envie ou de desir.[45]

Socrates, in the *Phaedrus*, speaks of the "unusual heat and perspiration" generated in the lover when "he receives the effluence of beauty through the eyes."[46] Poets from time immemorial have spoken of the flame of love, and we might conclude that Desportes is simply following in their footsteps, except for his allusion to "amitié parfaite," when he speaks of "une vive ardeur":

> Si c'est la peur qui vous retient,
> Pensez que la crainte ne vient
> Qu'à faute d'amitié parfaite.
> Amour est une vive ardeur,
> Et la crainte est une froideur,
> Soudain par vraye amour desfaite.[47]

The general tone here is Platonic, but our poet probably owes something to Héroët's *Parfaicte Amye,* where the lady says:

> Mais mon amy tient de la deité
> Et contre peur me donne immunité.
> Ne voyez vous qu'en amytié divine
> L'ung ne crainct point que l'aultre le ruine?
> Qui ayme Dieu ne celle son desir.[48]

However, love is something more than a desire, or perhaps one might better say that desire itself takes on certain attributes beyond the control of the lover. At any rate, in the dialogues of Plato we find love becoming one of the divine furies, or a madness. In the *Phaedrus*, Socrates, discoursing on the four kinds of madness, says that "there is also a madness which is a divine gift, and the source of the chiefest blessings granted to men." He goes on to say that love is a madness of the noble sort, and that the "soul through all her being is immortal, for that which is ever in motion is immortal."[49] Ficino devoted considerable space to the treatment of the divine madness in his

Commentary on the Symposium. In one place he seems to identify himself with the Neoplatonists when he says: "But by divine madness, man is raised above the nature of man and passes over into God."[50] In a later chapter he continues: "Of all these, the most powerful and most noble is the amatory madness. 'Most powerful,' I say, because all the others necessarily depend upon it. For we achieve neither the poetic, the religious, nor the prophetic madness without a great zeal, flaming piety, and sedulous worship of the divine. But zeal, piety, and worship, what else do we call them but love?"[51]

In France Héroët spoke thus of the love fury:
> Bien vous diray ce que j'en imagine.
> Ceste union est *fureur tres divine*,
> Dont les esprits quelque foys agités
> Sentant l'odeur de tant de deités.[52]

In the following lines Desportes is concerned with the fury which lifts his soul from the body and carries it into celestial realms:
> Si la fureur d'amour, rendant l'ame agitée,
> La ravit dans le ciel de son corps l'elevant. . . . [53]

He misinterprets Plato, however, when he says that this madness is responsible for "rendant l'ame agitée," for Plato says that the soul is ever in motion, and that motion is an attribute of the immortal. Desportes may, however, be referring to the Platonic "state of ebullition" to which Socrates refers further along in the *Phaedrus* when he says: "But he whose initiation is recent, and who has been the spectator of many glories in the other world, is amazed when he sees any one having god-like face or form, which is the expression of divine beauty . . . Then the wings of the soul of the lover begin to grow and . . . the whole soul is all in a state of ebullition and effervescence.[54] Our poet seems to be in some such state when he speaks of the "fureur" which has seized him:
> J'estoy en mon accez, la *fureur* me tenoit,
> Et de vous seulement ce transport me venoit.[55]

He introduces a Petrarchan note into the following lines, and the fury of which he speaks, associated with jealousy and termed "maudite," is somewhat divorced from the Platonic love fury:
> Puisque ces vains pensers sont reçus en mon cœur,
> Et que la jalousie, avec toute sa glace,
> Parmy de si grands feux peut encor avoir place?
> O maudite *fureur*, sans les soucis mordans
> Amour tousjours enfant n'auroit griffes ny dans![56]

Addressing his lady, he queries:

> Seul but de mes desirs, ma celeste deesse,
> Helas! voyez-vous point la *fureur* qui me presse?[57]

His extreme fury transports him aloft:

> Mais je suis transporté de ma *fureur* extreme. . . . [58]

Here and there our poet questions the nature of his fury, and he is right in doing so, for though love may bring emotional disturbances in its wake, at the end both lover and beloved "cease from their pain," so that the fury which has been experienced by the lover is eventually therapeutic:

> Quoy! je ne puis dormir; O Dieu! quelle amitié,
> Qui, comme une *fureur*, me poursuit sans pitié,
> . . . .
> Non, ce n'est amitié; "L'amitié n'est jamais
> Du prince à son sujet, de l'esclave à son maistre."[59]

He is thus recognizing that friendship (love) cannot exist where the breach is too great, and thereby admits that the Petrarchan kind of love is insufficient.

In his *Chant d'Amour* our poet quite naturally ties up the love fury with poetic fury, when thus deifying Love:[60]

> O Dieu puissant et bon, seul sujet de ma lyre,
> Si jamais que de toy, je n'ai rien voulu dire,
> Et si ton feu divin m'a tousjours allumé,
> Donne-moy pour loyer qu'un jour je puisse faire
> Un œuvre à ta louange eloigné du vulgaire,
> Et qui ne suive point le trac accoustumé.[61]

The transports of love may be either corporeal or spiritual. Desportes disavows the former when addressing God in his *Sonnet spirituel*:

> Le feu de ton amour, dans mon ame eslancé,
> Soit la sainte *fureur* dont je seray poussé,
> Et non d'un Apollon l'ombrageuse folie.
> Cet amour par le foy mon esprit ravira,
> Et, s'il te plaist, Seigneur, au ciel l'elevera
> Tout vif, comme sainct Paul ou le prophete Elie.[62]

But he departs from the significance of the love fury as portrayed by Plato when he attributes malevolence to it:

> Cette *fureur* d'amour, de raison la maistresse,
> Aveugle, impatiente et qu'on ne peut cacher,
> Veiller, pleurer, jurer, s'appaiser, se fascher,
> Lettres, faveurs, regards, ce sont tours de jeunesse.
> . . . .
> Qu'amour à l'homme meur n'est que perte et mépris,
> Au lieu que sa folie au jeune est profitable.[63]

He may be referring to the unruly steed of the charioteer in the lines above, as well as in those which follow:

> Arriere, ô *fureur* insensée!

> Jadis si forte en ma pensée,
> Quand d'amour j'estois allumé;
> Rempli d'une flamme plus sainte,
> Je sens maintenant toute estrainte
> L'ardeur qui m'a tant consumé.[64]

The idea of the ennobling effects of love particularly intrigued the medieval poets, as it did also those of the Renaissance. The views of the participants in the discussion of the true nature of love in the *Symposium* vary, but nearly all agree that the lover is ennobled through his love. The poet, Agathon, personifies love, and says that it is "the fairest and best," and "the cause of what is fairest and best."[65] Others add their comments, but it is left for Socrates to establish the role of love as the means whereby one perfects himself and thereby becomes the ideal citizen of the ideal state. Love is a desire for the possession of beauty. It has its inception in the contemplation of innumerable beautiful faces and forms and mounts to the contemplation of innumerable beautiful things, seeking behind them not the copies but their patterns—eternal beauties—and learning that beauty is one with truth and goodness. One proceeds from fair forms to fair practices, from fair practices to fair notions, and from fair notions to the notion of absolute beauty. If one has true knowledge he cannot do evil; the good man is just. Man should cultivate wisdom so as to understand justice and be able to occupy his rightful position among the rulers of the state.[66] The emphasis here seems to be on the life of the intellect, but Plato could not justify existence on that basis alone and he gave wisdom an important practical end.

For the Neoplatonists universal love is contained in the All-Soul. As the single soul is embraced in the All-Soul, so the single love holds to the All-Love. "Good men have no other love than for the Absolute and Authentic Good and never follow random loves of a different kind."[67] In attaining likeness to God man acquires order, distribution, and harmony. These are qualities which ennoble us by setting bound and measure to our desires and sensibility, and by dispelling false opinion.[68]

The poets of the *dolce stil nuovo* looked upon love as a great ennobling force, both moral and intellectual. Ficino and his academic circle emphasized the mystical aspects of love. There is little evidence that Ficino himself was interested in the ideal state or the training of statesmen as Plato had been. However, this aspect of Platonism is emphasized in the works of Bembo and of Castiglione. In the third book of his *Asolani* Bembo exalts intellectual love in what amounts to a paraphrase of what Plato had said, omitting all of the Neoplatonic interpretations which Ficino had woven into his *Commentary*. And in the *Cortegiano* we find that Castiglione, before putting into the mouth of Bembo the intellectual interpretation of love which appears in the fourth book, outlines a course of education for the ideal courtier, or statesman, who will use his influence and talents in the service of his prince and therefore in the service of the state. Of course certain conditions of birth enter into the considerations of Castiglione, but these are inherent in Plato's thought as well.

The French Renaissance poet, Héroët, speaks thus of the effects of love:

> Si c'est au ciel que sont les lieux heureux,
> Et qu'aymer bien purge ung cueur amoureux,
> Tant qu'il le leve à celeste science,
> J'ayme si bien que j'ay seure fiance
> Et mon amour, que tost m'eslevera,
> Et les secrets du ciel m'enseignera.[69]

The poets of the Pléiade were very emphatic about the need for knowledge if one were to be a worthy poet. However, their concept of knowledge was not necessarily identical with the Socratic concept of wisdom, attained through love, and they were interested in knowledge not so much because it would serve the good of the state, as because it would bring them glory and would add to the glory of the literature of France when reflected in it. They frequently imitated the style of the ancients and what they had to say, without emulating in their lives the precepts they taught or sounding to their depths the true meanings of those precepts. Our poet, Desportes, seems to have taken those precepts more seriously. He was a worthy statesman; he gave his protection to promising youths; he served his prince faithfully and honorably. Into these aspects of his life entered his own concept of love as an ennobling force, which is reflected in his verse, and therein we see love passing through all the stages from the earthly to the divine, progressing from a thing of the senses to the realm of the intellect and to a state of wisdom. He tells us in the following lines that love is a guide to perfection:

> L'Amour est faible à sa naissance
> Mais le tans luy donne accroissance,
> Et le guide à perfection.[70]

It is also a pathway to knowledge:

> Vostre esprit divin me rend plain de sçavoir,
> Je volle au plus haut ciel, emporté sur vos ailes.[71]

The poet's love has nothing to do with the senses but "est de l'essence de mon ame":

> Ravi de vos perfections,
> Je ne peu voir les passions,
> Sortans des rais de vostre veuë;
>
> . . . .
> Car mon amoureuse chaleur
> Est de l'essence de mon ame.[72]

It cannot be said that the following lines refer to any specific passage in the dialogues, but the tone is Platonic and the theme is the beneficial effects of love:

> C'est pourtant un grand heur que d'aimer hautement,
> Car un esprit divin tend aux choses hautaines,
> Puis mille beaux pensers adoucissent les paines.[73]

When the poet speaks of "aimer hautement" he is obviously referring to the two kinds of love which we find treated by Pausanias in the *Symposium* when he says: "For we all know that Love is inseparable from Aphrodite, and if there were only one Aphrodite there would be only one Love; but there are two goddesses and there must be two Loves . . . . The elder one is the daughter of Uranus; the younger, who is the daughter of Zeus and Dione—her we call common; and the Love who is her fellow-worker is rightly named common, and the other Love is called heavenly."[74]

The poet wishes to know from his lady whether he has not purged himself of his old errors in his desire to love her as he should:

> Donc, ô belle Diane, helas! asseurez moy
> Si, pour vous adorer seule, ainsi que je doy,
> De toute vieille erreur j'ai purgé mon courage.[75]

Her beauty, which has given birth to his love, cleanses him of all evil desire:

> Quand au premier le flambeau de mon ame,
> Mon beau soleil à mes sens éclaira,
> Tout bas desir de moy se retira,
> Ravi de voir les beautez de ma dame.[76]

Love is an honorable thing, as we learn again from Pausanias in the *Symposium*: "Consider, too, how great is the encouragement which all the world gives to the lover; neither is he supposed to be doing anything dishonourable; but if he succeeds he is praised, and if he fails he is blamed."[77] Concerning the love between himself and his lady our poet asks the question:

> Qui nous peut honorer d'assez digne louange?[78]

Again in the *Symposium* Diotima recommends that one remember how "in the communion only, beholding beauty with the eye of the mind, he will be enabled to bring forth, not images of beauty, but realities ... and bringing forth and nourishing true virtues."[79] Desportes thanks heaven that his eyes have beheld such things as made him dissatisfied with anything but the perfect:

> Que je suis redevable aux cieux
> De ce qu'ils m'ont ouvert les yeux
> Et si bien purgé ma poitrine,
> Que rien plus ne me satisfait
> Qui ne soit divin et parfait
> Et qui n'ait celeste origine.
>   Tout ce qu'Amour sçauroit trouver
> D'attraits pour un cœur captiver,
> Tout ce que la beauté peut faire,
> Le destin et l'election,
> Tout s'assemble en l'affection
> Qui rend mon esprit tributaire.[80]

By an extension of the idea that love is an ennobling influence, we find that love becomes an essential of the noble heart. Héroët expresses the idea thus in his *Parfaicte Amye:*

> Mais sans amour, et sans sçavoir, mal née,
> Merite pis que d'estre abandonnée.[81]

Plato does not go so far as to say this, but he does imply everywhere that the life of great worth is that of the lover of beauty, truth, and goodness—who is the philosopher. Desportes goes to great lengths to make love necessary to the "cœur hautain et genereux":

> Ainsi dedans un cœur hautain et genereux
> Se retirent tousjours les desirs amoureux,
> Les douces passions, les delectables peines,
> Et les cheres langeurs dont les amours sont pleines,
> Qui ne doivent jamais un amant retenir,
> Veu qu'un grand bien ne peut sans travail s'obtenir
>   Un cœur noble et gentil sans amour ne peut estre,
> Car avecque l'Amour Nature l'a fait naistre,
> Les a liés ensemble et les joint tellement,
> Qu'ils demeurent tousjours inseparablement.
> . . . .
>   Bref, quiconque est bien né sent tousjours dedans l'ame
> L'inevitable effort de l'amoureuse flame.[82]

And, as we see, he adds that the well-born will naturally feel within their souls the urge of love. This can only imply intellectual love. There is an interesting analogy here between the words of our poet and those of Rabelais, in his *Gargantua et Pantagruel*. After giving the only rule to be in force in his ideal abbey of Thélème—"Fay ce que vouldras"—Rabelais justifies the rule thus: "... parce que gens liberes, *bien nez*, bien instruictz, conversans en compaignies honnestes, ont par nature un instinct et aguillon qui tousjours les pousse à faictz vertueux, et retire de vice: lequel ilz nommoient honneur."[83]

Desportes goes on to develop the theme of the nobility of love. He says that the heart which has not known love is enclosed in stone:

> Celuy qui n'aime point, ou qui n'a point aimé,
> A le cœur tout autour de rochers enfermé.[84]

For love is necessary to perfection:

> Il n'est rien de si cher qu'une amour ferme et sainte;
> Aucun bien n'est parfait sans cette douce estrainte.[85]

Since the soul seeks for its highest good, and since that highest good is beauty, then our poet reasons, as poets have done for ages without the aid of Plato, that we are born to love:

> Car nous naissons icy seulement pour aimer.[86]

Like Plato, Desportes, raises true love above sensual things and sensual perceptions to the realm of the intellectual. In the following lines it is thought rather than the emotions which governs the love of the poet:

> O mort! si c'est le ciel qui te face avancer,
> Pour ravir la beauté qu'adore mon penser
> Las! change à mon destin la fortune d'Alceste![87]

He wishes to be lifted above corporeal things:

> Chassons donc nostre angoisse, ô seul bien de mes yeux!
> Et, vivans deshormais comme l'on vit aux cieux,
> Sans plus penser aux corps faisons l'amour des ames.[88]

The sentiments expressed here approach those of Socrates, in the *Phaedo*, when he says that "he attains to the purest knowledge of them [the essence of things] who goes to each with the mind alone, not introducing or intruding in the act of thought, sight or any other sense together with reason, but with the very light of the mind in her own clearness searches into the very truth of each."[89]

True love is an affection of the soul, and as such is immortal, as is the soul. We learn in the *Symposium* that "love is of the immortal ... the mortal nature is seeking as far as possible to be everlasting and immortal; and this is only to be attained by generation, because generation always leaves behind a new existence in place of the old.... Those who are pregnant in the body only, betake themselves to women and beget children ... but souls which are pregnant ... conceive that which is proper for the soul to conceive or contain. And what are these conceptions? —wisdom and virtue in general."[90] This idea has not been overlooked by poets who have treated the love passion. Dante's love for Beatrice did not end with her death and ascension into heaven, nor did the love of Francesca and Paolo end, although they were condemned to spend eternity in hell. Petrarch's love for Laura survived her death. Our poet adds his voice to support the immortality of love:

> La vraye amour est tousjours vive
> Et ne meurt point par le trepas.[91]

Speaking of true love as "l'autre", he gives his opinion that love is not defeated by death:

> L'autre estoit de deux cœurs une union parfaite
> Que l'oublieuse mort n'eust sçeu rendre desfaite.[92]

It is a mere extension of time for our poet to make love not only immortal but eternal, which he does in these lines:

> Aussi bien mon amour pure, éternelle et sainte,
> Du salaire mortel payer ne se pouvoit.[93]

He repeats this idea, adding that love has its origin in a perfection which is divine:

> Car la parfaite amour dure éternellement;
> Mesme alors qu'il advient qu'elle a son origine
> D'une perfection dont la forme est divine.[94]

Love is the immortal flame which watches over the poet:

> N'ayant pour me garder que ma flamme immortelle.[95]

We have seen already that love is a creative force or life-giving fire flowing from God, as does the World-Soul. Individual souls seek to return to the source of their being. The brightness of the sun and of flame are constantly used as figures to represent generative heat or love. Our poet says that:

> Amour n'est rien que flamme, et la flamme ard plus fort
> Quand par une closture on la pense restraindre.[96]

The little god Love carries a flaming torch and burns hearts with "flammes éternelles":

> Un enfant, un aveugle, un tyran inhumain,
> Qui porte au lieu de sceptre un flambeau dans la main,
> Dont il brûle les cœurs de flammes éternelles,
> Et tourmente plus fort ceux qui sont plus fidelles.[97]

The eyes of his beloved, which the poet speaks of as "astres clairs," give off "celestes flammes":

> Quelle ame est assez belle afin de vous mouvoir,
> Astres clairs, qui versez tant de celestes flammes?[98]

It is the eyes which give off celestial flames, or the flames of love. No part of man has occupied so important a place in love's psychology as have the eyes. One cannot say that the emphasis on the power of the eyes originated with Plato. He did not, however, overlook their power, and his words must have had their influence on later generations of writers who knew his dialogues. Plato considered the eyes the most divine part of man. They were the suns of man—the microcosm—as the great ball of fire in the heavens was the sun of the universe—or macrocosm. We find in the *Timaeus,* where the creation of man is described, the following words: "And of the organs they [the gods] first contrived the eyes to give light, and the principle according to which they were inserted was as follows: So much of fire as would not burn, but gave a gentle light, they formed into a substance akin to the light of everyday life; and the pure fire which is within us and related thereto they made to flow through the eyes in a stream smooth and dense. . . . The sight in my opinion is the source of greatest benefit to us."[99] In the sixth book of the *Republic* we find the following conversation between Socrates and Glaucon: "Yet of all the organs of sense the eye is most like the sun?—By far the most like.—And the power which the eye possesses is a sort of effluence which is dispensed from the sun?—Exactly.—Then the sun is not sight, but the author of sight who is recognized by sight.—Exactly."[100]

Medieval man was particularly captivated by the idea of the microcosm and the macrocosm, according to which the eyes of the body represented and had the power of the sun, providing light from both the standpoint of the senses and of the intellect and serving as sources of that heat which was one with love and was therefore divine. In his *Vita nuova* Dante speaks thus of the eyes of his lady:

> Degli occhi suoi, come ch'ella gli muova,
> Escono spirti d'amore infiammati,
> Che fieron gli occhi a qual, che allor gli guati,
> E passan si che'l cor ciascun ritrova.[101]

The eyes figure prominently in Dante but are nothing like the force which they become in Petrarch. Time and again in the sonnets of the *Rime* Petrarch speaks of the "begli occhi" of Laura. The following is typical:

> Era'l giorno ch'al Sol si scoloraro
>   Per la pietà del suo Fattore i rai,
>   Quand'i' fui preso, e non me ne guardai,
>   Che i be' vostr' occhi, Donna, mi legaro.
> Tempo non me parea da far riparo
>   Contra colpi d'Amor; però n'andai
>   Secur, senza sospetto; onde i miei guai

> Nel comune dolor s'incominciaro.
> Trovommi Amor del tutto disarmato,
>   Et sperta la via per gli occhi al core,
>   Che di lagrime son fatti uscio e varco.
> Però, al mio parer, non gli fu onore
>   Ferir me di saetta in quello stato,
>   E a voi armata non mostrar pur l'arco.[102]

As with the whole body of poetic conceits which they owed to Petrarch, the Italian Petrarchists exaggerated the power of the eyes. Ficino got back to their Platonic significance when he said: "The appearance of a man, which because of an interior goodness graciously given him by God, is beautiful to see, frequently shoots a ray of his splendor, through the eyes of those looking at him, into their souls. Drawn by this spark like a fish on a hook, the souls hasten toward the one who is attracting them."[103] In an age when woman was generally looked upon as the beloved, it is interesting to note that Ficino, like Plato, speaks of a man as the beloved. He constantly conceived of true love as the deep friendship existing between man and man. We have seen that Desportes also had something of this concept of love. However, when treating the eyes and their effects he always refers to those of his lady. In view of the great debt he owed to the Petrarchists, it is little wonder that he exaggerated the importance of the eyes and went from one subtlety to another concerning their benevolent and malevolent effects. In the following lines it is the divine eye of the lady which brings on the fury of love:

> Car, si son œil divin m'oste toute puissance,
> Me ravit, me transporte, et me rend furieux. . . . [104]

Repeating the theme that love is a desire for beauty, the poet says that this love is born in the eyes:

> Amour, qui des yeux prend naissance,
> Court aussi tost vers le desir
> Se conserve avec l'esperance
> Et trouve repos au plaisir.[105]

Castiglione, in the *Cortegiano*, emphasizes the importance of the eyes when he speaks of beauty which inspires love and "draweth unto it mens *eyes* with pleasure, and pearcing through them imprinteth himselfe in the soule, and with an unwonted sweetness all to stirreth her and deliteth, and setting her on fire maketh her to covet him."[106]

It is not only the beauty of the beloved striking the eyes of the lover which inspires love. In the lines which follow it is the rays from the eyes of the lady which have put love into the heart of the poet:

> L'ardant amour qu'en mon cœur j'ay reçeu
> Naist de vos yeux, leur rayons l'ont conçeu.[107]

Not only do the eyes of the beloved give off the rays of love, but those of the lover are designed to receive those rays.

The ears also play an important part in the birth of love. We find in the third book of the *Republic* that "beauty, the effluence of fair works, shall flow into the eye and *ear*, like a health-giving breeze from a pure region, and insensibly draw the soul from earliest years into likeness and sympathy with the beauty of reason."[108] Plotinus, too, holds to this idea, saying: "Beauty addresses itself chiefly to sight; but there is a beauty for the hearing too, for melodies and cadences are beautiful; and the minds that lift themselves above the realm of sense to a higher order are aware of beauty in the conduct of life, in actions, in character, in the pursuits of the intellect; and there is the beauty of the virtues."[109] Our poet says he has turned his eyes away from his lady to avoid looking upon such "hautes merveilles" only to have love enter his heart through his ears:

> Si tost que m'apparut ce chef-d'œuvre des cieux,
> En crainte et tout devôt je refermay les yeux,
> N'osant les hazarder à si hautes merveilles,
> Mais je n'avançay rien, car ses divins propos
> Me voleront d'un coup l'esprit et le repos,
> Et l'amour en mon cœur entra par mes oreilles.[110]

When Desportes addresses his lady thus:

> Deesse, à qui je fus en naissant destiné,[111]

and thereby attributes predestination to love, the lover, and the beloved, he does so on the authority of one of the most intriguing of the Platonic myths—that of the Androgyne. In the *Symposium* Aristophanes explains that primeval man was not as he is today. He was round, and therefore more perfect, and in his terrible strength and might he attacked the gods themselves. Zeus in his anger cut the individuals of this race in two. Thereafter the halves went seeking each other and, when they found each other, embraced and were whole again. Aristophanes continues his story thus: "So ancient is the desire of one another which is implanted in us, reuniting our original nature, making one of two, and healing the state of man. Each of us when separated, having one side only, like a flat fish, is but the indenture of a man, and he is always looking for his other half."[112] The sexes of these round humans were not two but three: male and female, and a union of the two. The most excellent of those individuals who were divided and went seeking each other were the males. Their intense yearning for each other does not come from a desire for lover's intercourse but from a desire which springs from the soul, a desire for the possession of intellectual beauties. Dr. Merrill, in his excellent article on "The Pléiade and the Androgyne," says that Plotinus was the first to desert this tradition and the first "transmitter of the story to make love of man and woman its cultural theme."[113]

During the period of the Renaissance this myth enjoyed great popularity both in Italy and in France. It was treated by Ficino, Bembo, and Leone Ebreo in their works and thereby received common currency. When the story was taken up by the poets, the two halves naturally became the lover and the lady. Rabelais seems to have been among the first to introduce this myth into French literature, though he does so without mentioning the word Androgyne. In the first book of *Gargantua et Pantagruel*, speaking of the emblem in Gargantua's hat he says: "Pour son image avoit, et une platine d'or pesant soixante et huyt marcs, une figure d'esmail competent en laquelle estoit pourtraict un corps humain ayant deux testes, l'une virée vers l'autre, quatre bras, quatre piedz et deux culx, telz que dict Platon, in *Symposio*, avoir esté l'humaine nature à son commencement mystic. . . . "[114]

Marguerite de Navarre mentions these primitive creatures in both the *Prisons* [115] and the *Heptaméron*,[116] but it was her protégé, Héroët, who developed the myth into a long narrative poem, thereby giving it its most complete treatment in modern times.[117] All of the poets of the Pléiade made allusions to the myth which had by this time become so well known that the two parts of the creature were now generally treated under the simple term of "moitiés." It is thus that Desportes refers to them, as we see in the following lines:

> Et sous le doux effort de ses poignantes flames,
> Chacun, pour s'alleger, sa *moitié* choisissoit,
> Ne cessant leur amour quand ce desir cessoit.[118]

There is still further evidence of the influence of the myth of the Androgyne in these lines by our poet:

> Deux que le trait d'Amour touche bien vivement,
> N'ont rien qu'un seul penser, qu'un desir, qu'une flame:
> Ce n'est dedans deux corps qu'un esprit et qu'une ame,
> Et leur souverain bien gist en eux seulement.
> . . . .
> L'esprit qui se divise et qui se plaist au change

N'est point touché d'amour, mais d'un sale plaisir.[119]

It is doubtless on the basis of a rationalization of this myth that the lover and the beloved were considered destined for each other, and our poet expresses this idea time and again:

>Car le ciel me fist naistre afin de vous aimer.[120]

Heaven created him for his lady:

>En vous gist mon salut, ma foy, mon esperance,
>Le ciel me fit pour vous, pour vous je pris naissance
>Pour vous je doy mourir; aussi je meurs pour vous.[121]

He is enchanted to find that heaven has destined him to his lady:

>Plus j'ay de connoissance et plus je suis ravy
>De voir que c'est à vous que le ciel me destine.[122]

He should not be considered bold for daring to love his lady, since destiny is at work:

>Or ne m'accusez point que je sois temeraire,
>Presumant vous aimer: car je ne sçauroy faire
>Qu'ailleurs tourne mon cœur, qui vous est destiné.[123]

Love did him a great wrong to keep hidden from him for so long the happiness to which he was destined:

>Ah! qu'Amour m'a fait tort de m'avoir tant celé,
>L'heur ou le ciel m'avoit en naissant appelé![124]

He would prefer to die rather than forsake the love to which he was predestined, or accept another:

>Car mon cœur, que le ciel vous a presdestiné,
>Aime mieux consentir au decret ordonné,
>Et mourir par vos mains d'une playe honorable,
>Qu'esprouver l'appareil d'autre amour favorable.[125]

It is significant to note that in his discourse on *la Crainte*—one of his few prose works which have been preserved for us—Desportes speaks of the soul as being born for the purpose of loving in these words: " ... durant nostre vie nous aymons tousiours quelque chose, une ame ayent en soy une puissance amoureuse et née pour aymer, tout aussi qu'elle en a pour sentir, entendre et retenir."[126]

There was some question among the poets of the Renaissance as to whether true love should be hidden or open for all to see. Pausanias said in the *Symposium:* "In our own country a far better principle prevails. .... For, observe that open loves are held to be more honourable than secret ones, and that the love of the noblest and highest, even if their persons are less beautiful than others, is especially honourable."[127] Courtly love, which was usually directed toward an already married woman of a higher social level than her lover, was hidden. Castiglione advised discretion[128] about letting anyone know about one's love, and so did Marguerite de Navarre.[129] Héroët followed the lead of his protectress in the *Parfaicte Amye,* saying:

> Quand est à moy, je ne veulx publier
> Le nœud qui sçeut ma voulunté lyer,
> Et me plaist bien, couvert et incongneu.[130]

Desportes is inconsistent as to whether love should be kept secret. In one of his elegies he says that perfect love cannot be hidden:

> Car la parfaite amour ne se peut déguiser.[131]

Elsewhere he maintains:

> Qui veut donc receler une amoureuse flame,
> Il faut qu'en adorant sa deesse en son ame,
> Il feigne aimer ailleurs, et le feigne si bien,
> Que le peuple s'abuse et n'y connoisse rien.[132]

In the *Symposium,* speaking of the god Love, Agathon says: "As to courage, even the God of War is no match for him ... he must be himself the bravest." And he goes on to say that he is "regardful of good, regardless of evil."[133] There should be no fear, then, in perfect love, as Héroët points out so well:

> Mais mon amy tient de la deité,
> Et contre peur me donne immunité,
> Ne voyez vous qu'en amytié divine
> L'ung ne craint point que l'aultre le ruine?[134]

Desportes, voicing the same thought, says that fear cannot be a part of perfect love:

> Si c'est la peur qui vous retient,
> Pensez que la crainte ne vient
> Qu'a faute d'amitié parfaite.
> Amour est une vive ardeur.
> Et la crainte est une froideur,
> Soudain par vraye amour desfaite.[135]

Tied up with the theory of Ideas is the concept that true love can be conceived for one person only. The lover proceeds from the love of particulars to that of universals; from the love of diverse beauties to that of absolute beauty. Desportes seems to have such considerations in mind when he proposes:

> Ainsi d'un seul desir la vraye amour est faite,
> Qui s'affoiblist par nombre et demeure, imparfaite,
> Le desir divisé ne se peut dire amour.[136]

Again, true love is mutual, as we see in the *Phaedrus,* and "no feelings of envy or jealousy are entertained by them towards their beloved, but they do their utmost to create in him the greatest likeness of themselves, and of the god whom they honour. Thus fair and blissful to the beloved is the desire of the inspired lover."[137] The ladies sung by the Petrarchists, like those sung by the troubadours, as frequently as not scorned, disdained, and were cold and heartless to their imploring lovers. In Ficino, however, as in Plato, true love is a mutual thing[138] and is based upon the mutual love of the lover and the beloved for God. Héroët, in a truly Platonic manner, causes his *Parfaicte Amye* to conclude:

> . . . Dames, je vous promets
> Qu'il n'adviendra, et il n'advint jamais,
> Que vraye amour n'ayt esté reciprocqué.[139]

Desportes says that if love is to become eternal it must be mutual:

> Mais, pour nourrir sa flamme et la faire éternelle
> Il le faut asseurer d'une amour mutuelle,
> C'est ce qui le retient quand la beauté l'a pris.
> . . . .
> Car il faut bien aimer pour estre bien aimée,
> Et de deux cœurs unis naist la perfection.[140]

In several places in the dialogues[141] Plato speaks of the Golden Age and the golden race. "In those days God himself was their shepherd, and ruled over the lower animals. Under him there were no forms of government of separate possession of women and children; for all men rose again from the earth having no memory of the past. And although they had nothing of this sort, the earth gave them fruits in abundance, which grew on trees and shrubs unbidden, and were not planted by the hand of man. And they dwelt naked, and mostly in the open air, for the temperature of their seasons was mild; and they had no beds, but lay on soft couches of grass, which grew plentifully out of the earth. Such was the life of man in the days of Cronos."[142] Elsewhere we find that "God, in his love of mankind, placed over us the demons who are a superior race, and they with great ease and pleasure to themselves and no less to us, taking care of us and giving us peace and reverence and order and justice never failing, made the tribes of men happy and united . . . So we must do all that we can to imitate the life which is said to have existed in the days of Cronos.[143]

Now this certainly was an age of love, when all things lived at peace and under the protection of God or the gods. Dr. Robert V. Merrill, in his study of Du Bellay, speaks of the Age of Love,[144] but is referring to that period during the creation when order was brought out of Chaos through the force of love. The Age of Love or the Golden Age to which we refer here has nothing to do with the creation itself, but has to do rather with one of the cycles through which the human race has passed. It does not seem to have been a common source for poetic treatment in France during the Renaissance period. However, Desportes is certainly referring to this age in one of his elegies, while tying it up with the creation and the role of love in that phenomenon. We have a strange combination here which is not, however, contrary to the separate Platonic concepts.

> En la saison premiere, apres que toutes choses
> Furent de leur chaos ordonnément decloses
> Lors que tous blancs de foy les mortels icy bas,
> Nouvelle œuvre du ciel, seulement n'avoient pas
> Entr'eux le nom de vice, ains guidez d'innoçance
> Faisoient bien par nature, et non par connoissance;
> Amour, puissant démon, qui, le premier des dieux,
> Avait franchy le sein du chaos ocieux,
> Ayant mis fin par tout au trouble et à la guerre,
> Amoureux des humains vint demeurer sur terre
> Bien qu'il fust immortelle, il ne les dédaignoit,
> Mais de jour et de nuict il les accompagnoit,
> Il logeoit dans leurs cœurs, il échauffoit leurs ames,
> Et sous le doux effort de ses poignantes flames,
> Chacun, pour s'alleger, sa moitié choissoit,
> Ne cessant leur amour quand ce desir cessoit.
> . . . .
> Mais comme peu à peu le vice s'avança
> Et que cette *saison* en une autre passa,
> . . . .
> Amour tout estonné de voir si-tost changé
> Un people, qui n'aguere estoit si bien rangé,
> Detestant leur malice, ainsi se prit à dire. [145]

From this point the poet lapses into a Petrarchan treatment of the cruel lady, the lamenting and imploring lover. But he refers elsewhere more specifically to the Golden Age in these lines:

> Amour, quand fus-tu né? Ce fut lors que la terre
> S'émaille de couleurs et les bois de verdeur.[146]

And finally he mentions specifically the "saison dorée" thus:

> O foy! grand' deïté jadis reverée
> Des innocentes mœurs de la *saison dorée*,
> . . . .
> Fille de Jupiter et sa ministre sainte,
> Qui joints la terre au ciel d'une aimable contrainte,
> Et par qui ce grand tout en devoir est tenu,
> Favorise et conduis, ô deesse immortelle,
> Ceste troupe guerriere, amoureuse et fidelle.[147]

The poet is obviously speaking of love here and of its role in the creation, but he also speaks of the "innocentes mœurs" of the age, which he ties up with the age of Cronos.

In this chapter considerations have been limited to Platonic love, that phase of Platonism which has had the greatest influence on literature itself. An attempt has been made to point out briefly the varying concepts of love from antiquity to the period of the Renaissance in order better to understand the influences brought to bear upon French poets during the age under consideration. In this development mention has been made of the profane poets of antiquity and of the Middle Ages—the troubadours—and of their contributions to love psychology. The various interpretations of idealized love from the time of Plato have been passed in review, so that the reader might see how they reacted upon one another, modified one another, and were reconciled to one another.

So far as our own poet is concerned, he inevitably fell heir to certain attitudes and conceits not essentially Platonic. We have mentioned his debt to the Petrarchists and his departures, under their influence, from the true Platonic spirit. Those departures have to do primarily with the inequality sometimes existing between the lover and the beloved and with a series of lamentings due to love. However, even these lamentings and sufferings can easily be rationalized as symbolic of Platonic concepts having to do with the inception of love, as we have seen.

With Desportes, as with Plato, true love is a desire for the possession of beauty; it is a divine fury; it is intellectual rather than sensual; it is a creative force; it ennobles both lover and beloved; it is immortal and therefore divine and deserving of honor and praise; the lover and beloved are predestined to each other, and their love is mutual and should be open and fearless; the eyes of the lady are the suns of the body which receive and give off the rays of love. All of these aspects of love we have reviewed, and we have seen too that there was an age when love ruled the race of men.

Let us turn now from these considerations in which love has been an abstract passion or sentiment and consider it as personified in the god Love.

Chapter VI
THE GOD LOVE

It was inevitable that the Greeks should deify love as they had deified every great force of nature, and that this deification should have taken place long before the time of Plato. However, if Socrates was right when he said to Eryximachus, "What a strange thing it is, Eryximachus, that, whereas other gods have poems and hymns made in their honor, the great and glorious god, Love, has no encomiast among all the poets who are so many,"[1] then the poets must have begun their high praises of this god after the time of Plato, who recorded Socrates' words. If the poets had not yet begun to sing the greatness of the god Eros, however, they had at least placed the power of love in the hands of certain members of the family of gods. From the time of Homer, at least, Aphrodite, the goddess of love, was already credited with exerting her irresistible influence over gods and men, and throwing her weight into the balance of such affairs as the Trojan War. Sappho spoke of this goddess, addressing her thus: "Aphrodite, splendor throned, immortal, wile-weaving child of Zeus, to thee is my prayer...blessed Lady, with a smile on that immortal face...sweet accents and winning laughter which have made the heart in my breast beat so fast and high....I am tongue tied...delicate fire has overrun my flesh, my eyes grow dim and my ears sing, the sweat runs down me and a trembling takes me altogether, till I am as green and pale as the grass, and death itself seems not very far away"[2]

The real significance of Plato's Eros is that he brings harmony out of disorder and oneness from multiplicity. When he is made to take part in the world of the senses, the abstract world of the intelligible takes on the concrete form of life. As Raphael Demos says in his article on Eros: "Eros is the primordial attraction of the actual by the ideal....Eros is desire. Now desire is neither immortal nor mortal; neither divine nor human. Not divine for desire implies a lack. Not mortal because total absence of the Good would entail absence of desire. Desire is a mixture of being and non-being...a demon...an intermediary between two realms, actively engaged in interpreting the Gods to men, conveying the commands of the ones, and the prayers of the others"[3]

But the god Love is also interpreted in various allegorical

ways in Plato, and the poets who followed him chose at random the interpretations which suited their purposes best. According to Diotima he is the son of Porus—his father, who represents Plenty, and Penia—his mother, who represents Poverty. Thus he springs from being and non-being, and represents on the one hand rational love and on the other the primitive impulse.[4] Love is presented by Phaedrus as a "mighty god, and wondrous among gods and men...the eldest of the gods...of his parents there is no memorial."[5] He quotes these lines from Hesiod:

> First Chaos came, and then broad-bosomed Earth,
> The everlasting seat of all that is,
> And Love.[6]

According to Pausanias, in the passage from which we have already quoted in part, "there are more Loves than one . . . Love is inseparable from Aphrodite, and if there were only one Aphrodite there would be only one Love; but as there are two goddesses there must be two Loves. And am I not right in asserting that there are two goddesses? The elder one, having no mother, who is called the heavenly Aphrodite—she is the daughter of Uranus; the younger, who is the daughter of Zeus and Dione—her we call common...The Love who is the offspring of the common Aphrodite[7] is essentially common... and is of the body rather than of the soul—the most foolish beings are the objects of this love which desires only to gain an end, but never thinks of accomplishing the end nobly, and therefore does good and evil quite indiscriminately. . . But the offspring of the heavenly Aphrodite is derived from a mother in whose birth the female has no part,— she is from the male only; this is that love which is of youths, and the goddess being older, there is nothing of wantonness in her. Those who are inspired by this love turn to the male, and delight in him who is the more valiant and intelligent nature...For they love not boys, but intelligent beings whose reason is beginning to be developed, much about the time at which their beards begin to grow."[8]

Of all those who describe Love in the *Symposium*, Agathon is most lofty in the praises he heaps upon the little god. He says: "Of all the blessed gods he is the most blessed because he is the fairest and best .. the youngest of the gods... and also tender... in the hearts and souls of both gods and men ...he walks and dwells and makes his home. And a proof of his flexibility and symmetry of form is his grace...The fairness of his complexion is revealed by his habitation among the flowers...he can neither do nor suffer wrong to or from any god or any man. For all men in all things serve him of their own free will."[9] Agathon goes on to say that the love god is just and temperate, courageous, brave, wise; he is a poet and maker of poets, an artist and creator of order; he is a peacemaker and savior.[10]

Thus we have the stage set and the material supplied for almost any interpretation the poet wishes to put on the nature of the god Love. In antiquity, after the time of Plato, the Alexandrian or Anacreontic concept of Eros was that of a mischievous child, carefree and playful. He was winged and armed either with a bow and arrow or with a flaming torch. He had many brothers, plump and pink like himself. He was tricky, capricious, and incorrigible, but he was not mean. Thus he is represented in the *Greek Anthology* and the *Anacreontea*.[11]

Among the Latin writers we find that certain modifications took place. In Ovid's *Amores, Ars amatoria,* and *Remedia amoris,* Love is a malicious, vindictive tyrant, causing all sorts of sufferings and tribulations. According to Lisle Cecil John this Ovidian conception of the appearance, power, and nature of love in time dominated the literature of the Middle Ages, especially the romance of Chrestien de Troyes.[12] In the *Roman de la Rose*[13] Love had finally developed into a young, handsome, and tyrannical feudal lord. With the poets of the *dolce stil nuovo* he was again a child but had taken on chivalric aspects and had lost most of his sensuality. Dante still further elevated him in the first part of the *Vita nuova* but then abandoned him, adopting the theological view of such men as St. Augustine that God is Love and Love is God—not a god.[14]

Petrarch's god Love, who appears everywhere in his works as a child rather than a young man, embodies aspects of both the Alexandrian and the Ovidian god. He both ennobles and causes grievous suffering; he is irresistible, and it is at his command that the poet writes. Petrarch introduced many conceits into his sonnets and *canzoni* which were imitated by his successors for several centuries. The Italian Petrarchists did little more than repeat what he had said in his verse, while adding some ingenious turns of their own, and when the works of both made their appearance in France, the French poets accepted the god Love as Petrarch and the Petrarchists had represented him.

In an age which made copious use of the gods of mythology

and of other mythological and legendary figures, Desportes is
remarkably free of them, and whereas a mythological dictionary
is needed in reading some of the poets of the Pléiade, such is not
the case in the works of our poet. He did, however, make frequent
allusion to the god Amour, and like Petrarch, used him frequently as an interlocutor. In at least one of his most Platonic poems
the poet and Love appear before the seat of Reason,[15] there to
argue their cases against each other. While Desportes' use of the
god inevitably owes something to the Petrarchan amalgam, he
very frequently speaks of him in words which seem to be para-
phrased from the dialogues. The whole tone of the following
lines, in which he speaks of Love as "un puissant dieu," is Platonic, for he also speaks of the yearnings of his soul to soar to
celestial heights:

> Un *puissant dieu* m'arreste, et pour gloire plus grande
> Il me met sous le joug d'une qui luy commande:
> Sçachant ne pouvoir rendre autrement captivé
> Mon esprit, qui tousjours au ciel s'est elevé.
> . . . .
> Moy donc, qui dresse au ciel mon vol avantureux
> Doy-je pas me nommer l'aigle des amoureux?[16]

Ficino, in his *Commentary on the Symposium*, had attributed
to the Thracian Orpheus of Argonautica fame the saying that
"Love is the oldest and wisest of the gods, and perfect in himself."[17] Desportes seems to be echoing this idea when he describes
Love thus:

> C'est un grand Dieu qu'Amour, il n'a point de semblable,
> De luy-mesme parfait, à luy-mesme admirable,
> Sage, bon, cognoissant, et le premier des Dieux.
> Sa puissance invincible en tous lieux est connuë,
> Son feu pront et subtil, qui traverse la nuë,
> Brüle enfer, la marine, et la terre et les cieux.[18]

But here he seems to be identifying Love with God Himself,
for he gives Him the attributes of perfection, of being capable
of admiring Himself, of having wisdom, goodness, and knowledge. Socrates had identified the good with the beautiful,[19] to be
found in the realm of the Ideas. The Neoplatonists identified
Goodness, Beauty, and Truth with God, and they thought of God
as contemplating Himself, of knowing Himself, and as the only
thing worthy of His contemplation.

In the *Symposium* Phaedrus quotes Parmenides as saying,
"First in the train of gods, he fashioned Love."[20] Desportes also
places Love in first position among the celestial band:

> Bien que tu sois premier de la bande celeste
> En âge et en pouvoir, tu as pourtant le geste
> D'un enfant delicat, gracieux et seant.[21]

He repeats the idea in these words:

> Amour, puissant démon, qui le premier des dieux,
> Avoit franchy le sein du chaos ocieux.[22]

Although Diotima had said that Love is neither mortal nor immortal, Desportes follows Phaedrus instead when he begs his lady to reciprocate his love, saying that Love is a god of divine nature—"Amour, est un démon de divine nature"[23]—and reasoning that if she is resisting his love because of some law, the laws have no meaning where gods are concerned. The god Love alone is worthy of the poet's songs:

> O dieu puissant et bon, seul sujet de ma lyre....[24]

He is irresistible, as the great Roland—the Orlando of Ariosto's long poem—learned to his sorrow:

> Le grand dieu des amours, dieu de telle puissance
> Qu'encore il n'a trouvé qui luy fist resistance,
> Un jour blessa Roland....[25]

There is none like him in power:

> Luy qui fut un dèmon nonpareil en puissance.[26]

As one might very well expect, the dividing line between love, the desire, and Love, the god, is very vague, since the latter is simply an allegorization of the former. Therefore, we shall not be surprised to see the same powers attributed first to the one and then the other. In our treatment of love, the desire, we saw that the act of creation—the bringing of order out of Chaos—was attributed to it. In the following lines, previously quoted, it is the god Love who accomplishes this act:

> Amour, puissant démon, qui, le premier des dieux,
> Avoit franchy le sein du chaos ocieux,
> Ayant mis fin par tout au trouble et à la guerre...[27]

Desportes seems to be speaking of Aphrodite, rather than of her son Eros, when he attributes to love the power to unify:

> Fille de Jupiter et sa ministre sainte,
> Qui joints la terre au ciel d'une aimable contrainte,
> Et par qui ce grand tout en devoir est tenu....[28]

We do not find illustrated in the verse of Desportes all of the accounts of the birth and parentage of Love, and the intricacies concerning them, to be found in Plato. He attributes to Aphrodite, or her Latin counterpart, Venus, the status of the mother of Love, without ever identifying his father. Therefore, we judge that his Love is the son of the heavenly Aphrodite. In at least

one place he speaks of the "foamborn" Venus, so dear to the artist from time immemorial:
> Venus, mere d'Amour, est fille de la mer.[29]

Sometimes, in his less Platonic moments, our poet curses the son of Venus, and denies that she had anything to do with him:
> Que maudit soit Amour, ses traits et son carquois,
> . . . .
> Jamais Venus la douce aux flancs ne l'a porté.[30]

Elsewhere he doubts the goodness of Love and brands him a god of blood and flame:
> Si l'Amour est un dieu, c'est un dieu d'injustice,
> Reconnoissant le moins ceux qui luy font service.[31]

And again he identifies him with the creation but in no flattering fashion when he says:
> Amour, quiconque fut qui te mit de la race
> De ce debat confus, *lourde et pesante masse,*[32]
> Il parloit sagement et disoit verité,
> Car, las! qui veit jamais confusion si grande
> Qu'aux miserables lieux où ton sceptre commande,
> Tousjours rouge de sang, d'ire et de cruauté?[33]

In another passage Desportes agrees to the characteristics given to love by Agathon, who had spoken of the god as delicate, graceful, beautiful and agile.
> . . . un enfant delicat, gracieux et seant
> Tu es plaisant et beau, tu as le corps agile.[34]

Plato does not specifically say that Love is blind, but we find the following words in the *Laws*: ". . . for the lover is blinded about the beloved."[35] Since the personification of the love passion is an attempt to bring concreteness into an abstract idea, the transfer of the quality of blindness from the lover to the god is but a step, and one which has been made by poets through the ages. Thus we find Desportes saying:
> Amour est un enfant sans prudence et sans yeux.[36]

In Plato we find Phaedrus quoting Homer thus, when speaking of the god Love:
> "Mortals call him fluttering love,
> But the immortals call him *winged* one,
> Because the growing of wings is a necessity to him."[37]

Desportes does not specifically say that Love is winged, but he does attribute to him the ability to fly, calling him "démon volant":
> O grand démon *volant*, arreste ta meurtriere
> . . . .
> Et delivre ma vie, en ses yeux prisonniere.[38]

On another occasion he calls him

> . . . l'Amour, *volant*, qui jusqu'au ciel m'emporte.[39]

The benefits of love have been pointed out in the chapter on love. The god Love is also a benefactor. He defends himself against the complaints of the poet before the seat of Reason, telling her of all the benefits he has visited upon him:

> J'ay purgé son esprit par ma divine flame,
> L'enlevant jusqu'au ciel et remplissant son ame
> D'amour, de beaux desirs, de constance et de foy.
> . . . .
> J'ay fait luire en cent lieux sa vive renommée
> Et des meilleurs esprits je l'ay rendu prisé,
> Je l'ay fait ennemy du tumulte des villes
> J'ay repurgé son cœur d'affections serviles,
> . . . .
> J'ay chassé loin de luy l'ardante convoitise,
> L'orgueil, l'ambition, l'envie et la feintise.
> . . . .
> J"ay fait par ses escrits admirer sa jeunesse,
> J'ay reveillé ses sens engourdis de paresse,
> Hautain et genereux je l'ay fait devenir;
> Je l'ay separé loing des sentiers du vulgaire
> Et luy ay enseigné ce qu'il fallait faire
> Pour au mont de vertus seurement parvenir.
> Je luy ay fait dresser et la veuë et les ailes
> Au bien heureux sejour des choses immortelles;
> . . . .
> Car de si grand' beauté son amour j'ay fait naistre
> Que moy, qui suis des dieux et des hommes, le maistre,
> J'atteste mon pouvoir que j'en suis amoureux.[40]

Nothing could express more clearly the Platonic significance of the power of true love than these lines. In another place the poet himself takes up the praise of Love:

> Tu delectes les bons, tu contentes les sages,
> Tu bannis les frayeurs des plus lâches courages
> Rendant l'homme craintif, hautain et genereux.[41]

As we have seen, Agathon says that Love "is a poet. . .the source of poetry in others. . .at the touch of him everyone becomes a poet."[42] Desportes voices the same thought when he says:

> Et sans toy, ne peut rien la douce poësie,
> Car un parfait poëte est tousjours amoureux.[43]

The poet's verses go under the name of Love:

> Amour, trie et choisis les plus beaux de ces vers,
> . . . .
> C'est dessous ton beau nom qu'ils vont par l'univers.[44]

Love is a desire for beauty, but it is the god Love who prepares its way by opening the eyes of the poet to this beauty:

> Amour, l'aveugle enfant, m'avoit ouvert les yeux
> Pour me faire connoistre un chef-d'oeuvre des cieux.[45]

There is no evidence that Desportes derives his implication of a plurality of little Love gods from Plato when he asks:

> *Amours*, qui voletiez à l'entour de nos flames,
> Comme gay papillons, où sont deux autres ames
> Qui redoutent si peu les efforts envieux?[46]

nor when he says:

> O beaux cheveux chatains d'une qui ce nom porte,
> Ondez, crespes et longs, où les Jeux inconstans
> Et les petits *Amours*, comme oiseux voletans,
> S'emprisonnent l'un l'autre en mainte et mainte sorte.[47]

As we have seen, according to the Alexandrian conception of this god, which the poets of the Pléiade had discovered in the *Greek Anthology* and the *Anacreontea*, Eros was a plump, rosy darling, mischievous but not malicious, and he had innumerable brothers resembling himself. Desportes was doubtless familiar with this concept of the god, and he could not have missed noting the paintings and sculptured pieces of the times, which represented the little cherubic figures flying about the head of some beauty.[48]

Concerning the Anteros, which deifies the passion aroused in the beloved as well as that aroused in the lover, there is only one passage in the verse of Desportes which can be interpreted as owing something to this idea, that enjoyed considerable popularity in our poet's day. Plato makes what may be considered a vague allusion to the Anteros in the *Phaedrus,* where we find Socrates saying, as he speaks of the beloved: "When he is with the lover, both cease from their pain, but when he is away then he longs as he is longed for, and has love's image, love for love (Anteros) lodging in his breast, which he calls and believes to be not love but friendship only, and his desire is as the desire of the other, but weaker; he wants to see him, touch him, kiss him, and probably not long afterwards his desire is accomplished."[49] The idea of the Anteros was doubtless popularized in France by Héroët in his *Aultre invention extraicte de Platon* (1542) where, in speaking of Eros, he says:

> Et, bien qu'il soit de Venus filz aisné,
> Semble tousjours qu'il vienne d'estre né,
> Tant est petit. Mais pour le faire croistre,
> Nous ont voulu les Grecs faire cognoistre
> Qu'ung frere fault luy forger promptement.
>   C'est pour la femme ung advertissement,
> Qu'elle ne doibt jamais se tenir forte,

> N'estimer grande amytié qu'on luy porte,
> Qu'amour ne soit au paravant entré
> Dedans son cueur, et qu'elle l'ayt monstré,
>   Car le puisné le filz aisné provoque;
> Lequel voyant son frere reciproque
> En peu de temps se pouvoir avancer,
> De grandeur veult comme d'aage passer.
> Ainsi concluds que l'homme n'est blasmé,
> S'il ayme peu, quand il n'est point aymé;
> Le faire ainsi nature luy commande.[50]

In the following poem, which is the epitome of Platonic doctrine, our poet longs for a love involving both Eros and Anteros, although he does not mention them by name:

> Si la fureur d'amour, rendant l'ame agitée
> La ravit dans le ciel de son corps l'élevant,
> Et si l'ame rebelle et qui s'en va privant,
> Tousjours foible et pesante en terre est arrestée;
>   Que n'aimez-vous, deesse, afin d'estre portée
> Par la fureur d'amour dans le ciel en vivant?
> Plein de ravissement je vous iroy suivant,
> Et mon ame à son gré seroit lors contentée.
>   Cette ombre de beauté, qui vous fait renommer,
> Quand vous seriez au ciel, se verroit transformer
> En la veauté parfaite et d'essence éternelle;
>   Tout volage desir en moy seroit esteint,
> Regardant vostre cœur je m'y trouveroy peint,
> Et vous verriez au mien vostre image si belle.[51]

Thus we see that Desportes, following in the steps of Petrarch and the Italian poets who imitated him, made the god Love a constant companion of his verse. He represents him most frequently in a traditional manner as the son of Venus or Aphrodite, the goddess of love, who goes about inflicting love upon his victims by shooting arrows into them or by imprisoning them in his chains. Although our poet sometimes complains of Love's actions, he generally admits that Love is the beneficent Platonic god rather than the malicious Ovidian one. Most of the powers Desportes attributes to the god are those found attributed to him by the various speakers in the *Symposium*. He is represented as the first of the gods and as having entered into the creation as an ordering force. He is powerful and irresistible before gods and men. In spite of his power he is in the guise of a delicate, gracious, pleasant, and handsome child; he is "subtil, gaillard, volage." He purges the mind of evil, raises the soul to the contemplation of immortal things, makes one generous, brings fame, inspires the poet, and is responsible for his verse. These are the true points of significance of the Platonic allegorization of love.

CHAPTER VII

BEAUTY

Having considered the various aspects of Platonic love found in the works of Desportes, as well as the place occupied by the Ideas, one should next give consideration to beauty, which is inseparable from the Platonic concept of love in that love is by definition a desire to possess it, and inseparable too from the Ideas, since absolute Beauty exists in the realm of the Ideas.

In Plato absolute Beauty is to be found only in the realm of the Ideas. As the Ideas cannot be defined, neither can such beauty. However, one can say many things about it. In the *Lysis* Socrates says: "Beauty is certainly a soft, smooth, slippery thing, and therefore of a nature which easily slips in and permeates our souls. For I affirm that the good is the beautiful."[1] Beauty is also harmony, whether in the human face and form, in music, in one's manner of living, or in the operation of affairs of state. In the harmonious workings of the universe the Greeks saw a reflection of the beauty of God. The soul yearns for the beautiful, for when man sees earth's beauties he is transported by the reminiscence of true Beauty. He who loves beauty partakes of that highest form of madness which is the madness of love. If goodness is one with beauty, so is truth, and if absolute Goodness, Truth, and Beauty are of the Ideas, then they are devine, and it follows that earthly beauty, which is a copy of the divine, also participates in divinity.

Socrates rises to his greatest eloquence when, having explained the "lesser mysteries of love," he describes the progressive stages of growth through which the true lover passes. He says that "he who would proceed aright in this matter should begin in youth to visit beautiful forms...and soon he will of himself perceive that the beauty of one form is akin to the beauty of another...how foolish would he be not to recognize that the beauty in every form is one and the same! And when he perceives this he will abate his violent love of the one...and will become a lover of all beautiful forms; in the next stage he will consider that the beauty of the mind is more honorable than the beauty of outward form. So that if a virtuous soul have but a little comeliness, he will be content to love and tend him and will search out and bring to the birth thoughts which may improve the young, until he is compelled to contemplate and see the beauty of institutions and laws, and to understand that the beauty of them all is of one family, and that personal beauty is a trifle...but drawing towards and contemplating the vast sea of beauty, he will create many fair and noble thoughts and notions in boundless love of wisdom...and at last the vision is revealed to him of a single science, which is the science of beauty everywhere...when he comes toward the end [he] will suddenly perceive a nature of wondrous beauty...the beauty absolute, separate, simple and everlasting...He who from these ascending under the influence of true love, begins to perceive that beauty, is not far from the end. And the true order of going, or being led by another, to the things of love, is to begin from the beauties of earth and mount upwards for the sake of that other beauty, using these steps only, and from one going on to two and from two to all fair forms, and from fair forms to fair practices, and from fair practices to fair notions, until from fair notions he arrives at the notion of absolute beauty, and at last knows what the essence of beauty is. This...is that life above all others which man should live, in the contemplation of beauty absolute...Remember how in that communion only, beholding beauty with the eye of the mind, he will be enabled to bring forth, not images of beauty but realities... and bringing forth and nourishing true virtue to become the friend of God and be immortal, if mortal man may."[2]

Such rationalization and intellectualization of beauty was limited to philosophers. Nevertheless, from earliest times poets have vaguely associated the beauty of their ladies with the divine. In the Homeric *Hymn to Aphrodite,* Anchises the mortal, who has fallen in love with the goddess Aphrodite, calls her a goddess because of her beauty, although he does not know that she is such. He thus identifies the beautiful with the divine and says: "I render your beauty the sacrifice of all my thoughts and worship you with all my desires."[3] With the troubadours the lady became once and for all idealized. And with the poets of the *dolce stil nuovo* her beauty was a reflection of divine beauty, the goal of the philosopher.

Dante says of his Beatrice:

>Vede perfettamente ogni salute
>   Chi la mia donna tra le donne vide;
>   Quelle, che van con lei, sono tenute
>   De bella grazia a Dio render mercede,
>   E sua beltate e di tanta virtute,
>   Che nulla invidia all'altre ne procede,

> Anzi le face andar seco vestute
> De gentillezza, d'amore e di fede.[4]

Petrarch calls the beauty of Laura divine:
> Ma canto la divina sua beltate;
> Che quand'i' sia de questa carne scosso,
> Sappia'l mondo che dolce à la mia morto.[5]

When Ficino made the *Symposium* available to readers of the western world and added his *Commentary* to it, the poets had their conceptions of beauty immeasurably enhanced, and they began to see in earthly beauty not only a reflection of the divine, not only an inspiration to virtue, but also the equivalent of the scales of a ladder by which they could attain intellectual as well as moral virtues. Ficino's own interpretation of the words of Plato is more Neoplatonic than Platonic, but nevertheless he emphasizes the supreme role of beauty in the lives of men when he says: "This Divine Beauty creates in everything love, that is, desire for itself, because if God draws the world to Himself, and the world is drawn [from Him,] there is one continuous attraction, beginning with God going to the world and ending at last in God, an attraction which returns to the same place whence it began as though in a kind of circle."[6] The Neoplatonists liked to think of everything as emanating from God and returning to Him, and Ficino's interpretation had a great influence on the French Renaissance poets particularly when they had a penchant for the mystical as did Marguerite de Navarre. They frequently likened God, goodness, and beauty to a radiance, a light, brightness, the sun. Ficino also explains beauty as a radiance of the Divine Goodness, and speaks of the "beauty of the soul which consists of brightness, of truth and virtue."[7]

Castiglione summarized beauty thus for the courtier: ". . . comely and holy beautie is a wondrous setting out of everie thing. And it may bee saide, that Good and beautifull be after a sorte one selfe thing, especially in the bodies of men: of the beautie whereof the nighest cause (I suppose) is the beautie of the soule: the which as a partner of the right and heavenly beauty, maketh sightly and beautiful what ever she toucheth, and most of all, if the bodie, where she dwelleth, be not of so vile matter, that she can not imprint in it her propertie."[8]

As a result of the work of Ficino and of the prose writers, such as Castiglione, who helped to popularize the efficacies of intellectual beauties, there was grafted on the amatory poetic stock, already composed of Greek, Latin, troubadour, dolce-stilnuovist, Dantesque, and Petrarchan elements, a whole new world of poetic conceits. It is not unusual to find the various elements side by side, and they occasionally contradict each other. The Petrarchan lover is constantly lamenting, usually sorrowing, frequently suffering because his love is not reciprocated. The truly Platonic lover may wax hot and cold, and may do foolish things because of his love, but these things are not done because of jealousies or because of the cruelty of the beloved, and in the end the lover undergoes a catharsis since both he and the beloved find peace and joy in mutual love.

Perhaps no poet of the Italian Renaissance had so clear a vision of true beauty as did the great sixteenth-century sculptor, painter, poet, Michelangelo. Certainly no Italian poet of the age was so purely Platonic. The whole Platonic significance of beauty is expressed in this sonnet:

> Per ritornar là d'onde venne fuora
> L'immortal forma, al suo carcer terreno
> Come angel venne, e di pietà si pieno,
> Che sana ogni intelletto, e'l mondo onora.
> Questa sol m'arda, e questa m'innamora,
> Non pur di fuor, che'l tuo lume sereno
> Sveglia amor non di cosa che vien meno,
> Ma pon sua speme ove virtù dimora.
> E se talor tua gran beltà ne muove,
> E'l primo grado la salir al cielo,
> Onde poi grazia agli altri s'apparecchi.
> Nè Dio se stesso manifesta altrove
> Più che in alcun leggiadro mortal velo,
> Dov' occhio sano in sua virtù si specchio.[9]

Transcendental beauty, so far as the ancient Greeks were concerned, had its earthly form in the handsome youth. Such beauty scarcely existed for the poets of antiquity, and when the medieval poets began the development which led to the idealization of love in their verse, the earthly beauty which inspired that love was embodied in the lady rather than in a youth. Some suggestions will be offered later as to how this transition from youth to lady as the object of the desire of the lover came about. It suffices here to say that it was a *fait accompli* in the period of the troubadours and was perpetuated for all time, perhaps, by the poets of the *dolce stil nuovo*.

With the revival of interest in Platonism in fifteenth-century Italy the youth as the beloved was not completely lost sight of, however. Ficino, reverting to the spirit of Plato and the Greeks in his interpretation of the true nature of love, said in his *Commentary on the Symposium*: "A man enjoys the physical beauty of a *youth* with his eyes; the youth enjoys the man's beauty with his mind. The youth, who is beautiful in body only, by this practice becomes beautiful also in soul; the man, who is beautiful in soul only, feasts his eyes upon bodily beauty. Truly this is a wonderful exchange, equally honourable indeed, to both, for it is equally honourable to learn and to teach. The pleasure is greater in the older man since he is pleased both in sight and intelligence, but the benefit is greater in the younger, for as much as the soul is more excellent than the body, so much is the acquisition of the beauty of the soul more valuable than of that of the body."[10]

Few Renaissance poets followed Ficino in his emphasis on male beauty in the rationalization of love. Like the earlier Italian poets—Dante, Petrarch, and the Petrarchists—they limited their attentions to the beauty of their ladies. Two outstanding exceptions were Michelangelo[11] in Italy and Shakespeare[12] in England. As for our poet Desportes, his sonnet sequences are dedicated to ladies bearing the names of Diane, Cléonice, and Hippolyte. We have already had occasion to remark, however, his close attachment for the young noble, Claude de Laubespine, the grief which he suffered upon his death, and the laments over his death which found their way into his verse,[13] but here it was a question of friendship rather than beauty. It is the beauty of one of the king's favorites, Jacques de Lévy, sieur Quélus,[14] which is celebrated in the following lines:

> Quélus, que la nature avoit fait pour plaisir,
> Comme une œuvre accomplie, admirable et divine
> Portoit Amour aux yeux et Mars en la poitrine;
> Bien d'égal, entre nous, ne se pouvoit choisir.
> Le voyant, on brûloit d'envie ou de desir;
> Il fut de grand courage et d'antique origine,
> Ayant l'ame invincible, aux vertus toute encline,
> Que la soir d'amasser n'eust sçeu jamais saisir.[15]

This is a rare exception, however, and it is of the lady that Desportes speaks when he advises as to the necessity of pursuing beauty, the object of his ardent desire:

> Lors, pour servir de guide à mon ardant desir,
> La jeunesse me fit une beauté choisir,
> Qui s'offrit favorable à mes yeux la premiere,
> Et que je reconneu pour ma seule lumiere.
> Son ardeur doucement mon esprit embrasoit,
> Je ne voyoy plus rien qu'ainsi qu'il luy plaisoit;

> C'estoit mon seul objet, mon desir et ma flame,
> Et sa seule influence avoit force en mon ame.[16]

One can almost hear Diotima saying here: "For he who would proceed aright in this matter should begin in youth to visit beautiful forms. . .,"[17] so nearly do Desportes' sentiments coincide with these words.

We have seen that true love is the desire for beauty. In the lines of a sonnet to Diane the emphasis is placed on beauty itself rather than on love:

> Bien que vostre *beauté* mon desir ait fait naistre,
> . . . .
> Qui ma flamme a nourrie et l'a fait ainsi croistre.[18]

Since beauty is of the realm of the Ideas it follows that it is divine. However, we have a more substantial basis than mere deduction on which to base the divinity of beauty, for in the *Phaedrus* we find Socrates saying: "But of beauty I repeat again that we saw her there shining in company with the celestial forms; and coming to earth we find her here, too, shining in clearness through the clearest aperture of sense. For sight is the most piercing of our bodily senses. . .But this is the privilege of beauty, that being the loveliest she is also the most palpable to sight."[19]

Time and again Desportes attributes the origin of beauty to heaven, as when he says:

> Le ciel, comme l'on dit, l'a voulu retirer,
> Pour apprendre aux mortels, trop pronts à s'égarer,
> Que la beauté parfaite est ailleurs qu'en la terre.[20]

Or when he says that heaven ornamented the youth of Hippolyte with the most precious gifts:

> Le ciel, ornant vostre jeunesse
> De dons les plus precieux.[21]

As our poet spoke in one of his epitaphs of the beauty of Quélus as arousing envy and desire, so in another he speaks of his beauty as originating in heaven:

> Quélus avoit du ciel les beautez plus parfaites:
> Il n'estoit point humain, l'œil, le geste et le port
> L'accusoient pour un dieu.[22]

Since the beauties of his lady are heaven born, and since such beauties can be seen with the mind only, the poet wonders why his lady looks at herself in a mirror:

> Pourquoy si folement croyez-vous à un verre,
> Voulant voir les beautez que vous avez des cieux?[23]

Not only are the beauties of the lady celestial, but all her graces are supernatural, and Love without her eyes would have no torch:

> Et vos douces beautez monstrant bien, l'origine,
> Que vous avez du ciel tout parfait et tout beau;
> Vous n'avez rien d'humain, vostre grace est celeste,
> Vos discours, vostre teint, vostre ris, vostre geste,
> Et l'Amour sans vos yeux n'auroit point de flambeau.[24]

The earthly beauty of his lady, which is a mere copy, will be transformed into perfect beauty, the pattern or idea of beauty, when she is in heaven:

> Cette ombre de beauté, qui vous fait renommer,
> Quand vous seriez au ciel, se verroit transformer
> En beauté parfaite et d'essence éternelle.[25]

Moreover beauty, besides being of divine origin, is, like love, of great good to the beholder. In the contemplation of beauty one rises from "l'ombre à la vérité":

> D'estre idolatrement de vos yeux amoureux,
> Souhaitant pour tout bien l'heure tant attenduë
> Par qui vostre beauté devoit m'estre renduë,
> Et que, sans plus me voir de penser enchanté,
> J'echangeasse à la fin l'ombre à la verité.
> . . . .
> Et bref, vous contemplant, bien-heureux, j'imagine
> L'entier contentement de la troupe divine.
> Je jouys icy bas de la gloire des cieux,
> Et d'un homme mortel je suis égal aux dieux.[26]

The poet regrets having followed passing beauty, for a time, rather than the changeless:

> Je regrette en pleurant les jours mal employez
> A suivre une beauté passagere et muable,
> Sans m'eslever au ciel et laisser memorable
> Maint haut et digne exemple aux esprits desvoyez.[27]

In the following *Sonnet spirituel* of Desportes we find another instance of the fusion of Platonic and Christian doctrine. The quatrains are of Biblical inspiration, and in reading them we are reminded of the following passages: "For a thousand years in thy sight are but as yesterday when it is past, and as a watch in the night,"[28] and, "Vanity of vanities, said Ecclesiastes, vanity of vanities; all is vanity."[29] Our poet speaks of life which is "moins qu'une journée" and of favors, treasures, and grandeurs which "ne sont que vanité." However, the tercets owe even more to Platonism or Neoplatonism, for there the poet speaks of the "heur souverain" or *summum bonum*, to which consideration was given in the chapter on the soul, and of the "beauté parfaicte" as the final goal of love:

> Si la course annuelle en serpent retournée

> Devance un trait volant par le ciel emporté,
> Si la plus longue vie est moins qu'une journée,
> Une heure, une minute, envers l'éternité;
> Que songes-tu, mon ame, en la terre enchaisnée?
> Quel appast tient ici ton desir arresté?
> Faveur, thresors, grandeurs, ne sont que vanité,
> Trompans des fols mortels la race infortunée.
> Puis que l'heur souverain ailleurs se doit chercher,
> Il faut de ces gluaux ton plumage arracher
> Et voller dans le ciel d'une legere traicte.
> Là se trouve le bien affranchi de souci,
> La foy, l'amour sans feinte et la beauté parfaicte
> Qu'à clos yeux, sans profit, tu vas cherchant ici.[30]

The sight of beauty has other virtues besides the transporting of the beholder to celestial realms. It aids in the enlightenment of the mind of the beholder as well as his eyes:

> Le ciel, ornant vostre jeunesse
> De ses dons les plus precieux,
> Pour mieux me monstrer sa richesse,
> M'éclaira l'esprit et les yeux.[31]

The beauty of the poet's lady is such that it drives away evil or corporeal desires:

> Ceste belle ennemie et d'amour et de moy,
> Qui presqu'en se joüant range tout en servage,
> A pour soldats choisi et pour riche équipage
> L'honneur, la chasteté, la constance et la foy.
> Un seul mauvais penser n'a place aupres de soy,
> La vertu toute vive est peinte en son visage;
> Si bien que qui la voit leve au ciel son courage,
> Et des desirs communs n'esprouve point la loy.[32]

It cleanses the mind of evil thoughts and introduces beautiful ones:

> Qui veut fermer l'entré, aux chastes pensées,
> Et par feu, comme Hercule, immortel devenir;
> Qui veut de beaux desirs son ame entretenir,
> Fuyant les vanitez du vulgaire embrassées;
> Qui veut au ciel d'amour voir ses ailes haussées,
> Et de tous vieux ennuis la mémoire bannir,
> Vienne au jour de vos yeux s'il les peut soustenir,
> Beaux yeux, les doux meutriers de mes paines passées.[33]

And finally the beauty of the lady assuages the pain of the poet:

> Vos beautez tout de mesme, entrans dedans mon cœur,
> Destrempant doucement son amere langueur,
> Et parmy mes ennuis la liesse est meslée.[34]

Desportes clearly shows in the passages quoted above that he looked upon earthly beauty as a gift from heaven and therefore as participating in divinity. He is primarily interested in the beauty of face and form which leads to the contemplation of higher things, and to a desire for greater perfection. The beauty which he contemplates is, for the most part, that of the lady rather than that of the youth. The contemplation of beauty is a great benefit to the beholder, who is, of course, the lover. It carries him to ecstatic heights; it enlightens his mind; it takes away evil desires. All of these aspects of beauty are to be found in the dialogues. They appear not once but repeatedly in the works of Desportes, and their appearance is frequently associated with other Platonic concepts, thus serving to identify them with Platonic doctrine in general.

CHAPTER VIII

THE LOVER AND THE BELOVED

Enough has been said concerning love and beauty to convey the idea that the goal of the Platonic lover is the realm of universals—the vision of absolute Beauty, Truth, and Goodness—to which he begins his ascent through the love and contemplation of earthly beauty. Through his knowledge of universals he enjoys a philosophic serenity, even in the midst of adversity. However, the lover does not arrive in one stride at such a state. As we have seen, he undergoes a period of perturbation after first having beheld the beauty of the beloved.

French Renaissance poets, following in the steps of the Petrarchists, all too frequently failed to recover from the disturbing elements of the very love which they idealized. Their laments were endless, and they rarely expressed the note of joy which should spring from a heart aflame. However, even when wounded to death by their love, they recognized that it brought them great benefits. Even in his earliest verse Desportes was aware of these benefits, which were intellectual rather than physical. We find him frequently "emporté sur les ailes d'amour" when contemplating the beauties and charms of his lady. However, having immersed himself in the works of the Petrarchists, he could not rid himself of all of their influences, and he wrote a number of *Plaintes* and *Complaintes*. Even so his lamentings do not usually carry bitterness with them, and he admits that he would not change the sufferings which he experiences. His lady, though sometimes cruel and indifferent, is always beautiful and chaste, and this he would not have otherwise.

In the *Phaedrus* Socrates says: "I have been speaking of the fourth and last kind of madness, which is imputed to him who, when he sees the beauty of earth, is transported with the recollection of the true beauty; he would like to fly away, but he cannot; he is like a bird fluttering and looking upward and careless of the world below; and he is therefore thought to be mad. And I have shown this of all inspirations to be the noblest and highest and the offspring of the highest to him who has or shares in it, and that he who loves the beautiful is called a lover because he partakes of it."[1] The lover, as represented in Desportes' verse, is not essentially different from the one whose madness is described by Socrates. Elsewhere we have remarked the benefits of love itself as depicted by him. Let us now seek to give a clearer picture of our poet's concept of the Platonic *lover*, of him who, "Ayant d'un coeur hautain jusqu'au ciel aspiré."[2]

This aspiration is expressed symbolically and without the introduction of specifically Platonic concepts in one of Desportes' most beautiful and most famous sonnets, having to do with the ambitions of the legendary Icarus. He says:

> Icare est cheut icy, le jeune audacieux,
> Qui pour voler au ciel eut assez de courage;
> Icy tomba son corps degarny de plumage,
> Laissant tous braves cœurs de sa cheute envieux.
> O bien-heureux travail d'un esprit glorieux!
> Qui tire un si grand gain d'un si petit dommage!
> O bien-heureux malheur plein de tant d'avantage,
> Qu'il rende le vaincu des ans victorieux!
> Un chemin si nouveau n'estonna sa jeunesse,
> Un pouvoir lui faillit, mais non la hardiesse:
> Il eut pour le brûler des astres le plus beau;
> Il mourut poursuivant une haut advanture;
> Le ciel fut son desir, la mer sa sepulture;
> Est-il plus beau dessein ou plus riche tombeau?[3]

From the words "le ciel fut son desir" one is justified in reading Platonic significance into this sonnet. According to the Greek legend Daedalus and his son Icarus were confined on an island, from which they escaped on wings of wax and feathers, fashioned by the father. Desportes does not mention the role of the father but centers his attention on the youth who takes the steps necessary to escape from the prisonhouse of the flesh in order to soar to the realms of the spirit. The loss of the flesh was a great gain to him, for it resulted in the liberation of the intellect. His enlightenment is particularly significant because "Il eut pour le brûler des astres le plus beau"—that is to say, the sun, a symbol among both Platonists and Neoplatonists for the Good, for wisdom.

Plato made of true love a mutual thing, equally enjoyed by both lover and beloved and equally benefitting them. In the *Lysis* we find these words: "Then the lover, who is true and no counterfeit, must of necessity be loved by his love."[4] The lover who has looked upon earthly beauty wishes to see its heavenly pattern. For the Neoplatonist, he who seeks the possession of beauty, truth, and goodness and is a lover of them is really only seeking to be reabsorbed into the Oneness of God from which he sprang. There developed among Italian Renaissance poets the idea that the lover, contemplating the beloved, loses himself but then lives in the person of the beloved, if his passion is reciprocated.[5] Michelangelo expresses this idea in one of his finest sonnets:

>   Veggio co' bei vostri occhi un dolce lume,
>   Che co' miei ciechi già veder non posso;
>   Porto co'vostri passi un pondo addosso,
>   Che de' miei stanchi non fu mai costume.
>   Volo con le vostr' ali senza piume,
>   Col vostro ingegno al ciel sempre son mosso,
>   Dal vostro arbitrio son pallido e rosso,
>   Freddo al sol, caldo alle più fredde brume.
>   Nel voler vostro sta la voglia mia,
>   I miei pensier nel cuor vostro si fanno,
>   Nel vostro spirto son le mie parole,
>   Come luna per se sembra ch'io sia,
>   Che gli occhi nostri in ciel veder non sanno
>   Se non quel tanto che n'accende il sole.[6]

Following this Italian rationalization of the processes of love, Desportes repeatedly places some part of himself within the being of his beloved, as when he says:

>   . . . Car dedans vostre cœur
>   Est ma vie et ma mort, mon repos et ma paine.[7]

Here it is his life which is in the heart of his lady. In the lines which follow it is his soul:

>   Je pars, non point de vous, mais de moy seulement,
>   Car je laisse mon ame afin qu'elle vous suive.[8]

Sometimes it is his entire being which takes up its dwelling in the lady:

>   Souvent par mes pensers aux cieux je m'enlevoy,
>   Et, ravy de moy-mesme, en elle je vivoy.[9]

Or he leaves both heart and soul with the lady:

>   Je ne vous laisse point, je me laisse moy-mesme:
>   Laissant l'ame et le cœur, n'est-ce pas me laisser?[10]

And he begs his lady that she

>   Fay que mon ame à la tienne s'assemble,
>   Range nos cœurs et nos esprits ensemble
>   Sous une mesme loy;
>   Qu'à mon desir ton desir se rapporte;
>   Vy dedans moy, comme en la mesme sorte
>   Je vivray dedans toy.
>   . . . .
>   Car tu n'as rien qui tien se puisse dire,
>   Ni moy pareillement;
>   . . . .
>   Mon cœur est tien, le tien à moy doit estre;

> Amour l'estend ainsi;
> Tu es mon feu, je dois estre ta flamme,
> Et dois encor, puisque je suis ton ame,
> Estre la mienne aussi...[11]

The Platonic significance here is that the poet abandons his corporeal self so that his soul may pursue the object of its love. Nesca Robb says in her *Neoplatonism of the Italian Renaissance* that the longing of the lover to transform himself into the beloved is the fundamental longing of man to become a god. He sighs because he leaves and destroys himself; he rejoices because he becomes worthier by transferring himself into a nobler being. He grows cold because he loses his natural heat; warm because heated by divine rays. In these alternate states he is either timid or bold.[12]

The ultimate goal of the beloved is the same as that of the lover—the vision of celestial beauties. Therefore, by pursuing the same goal they become one, so far as their divine natures are concerned. A definite precedent for this idea can be found in Plato's dialogues, for Diotima says in the *Symposium:* "Above all when he [the lover] finds a fair and noble and well-nurtured soul, he embraces the two in one person."[13] Concerning this concept our poet is most explicit:

> Ah! que j'ay de regret, quand je mets en memoire
> Combien j'ay reçeu d'heur, de plaisir et de gloire,
> Depuis l'heure qu'Amour devers vous m'adressa,
> Et que son feu divin par vos yeux me blessa;
> Car, presqu'au mesme instant, vous eustes connoissance
> Combien pour vous aimer j'enduroy de souffrance;
> Dont vous fustes touchée, et, chassant mon soucy,
> Vous me fistes sçavoir que vous m'aimiez aussi.
> Alors trop fortuné de vous je prenoy vie,
> Alors ma flamme estoit de la vostre suivie,
> Alors un mesme esprit nos deux corps animoit,
> Ainsi qu'un mesme trait nos deux cœurs entamoit.[14]

So joined the lover and the beloved are never absent from each other in spirit:

> Toutefois quand les corps n'ont moyen de se voir,
> L'ame pourtant n'est serve et peut, à son vouloir,
> Voleter invisible où la guident ses flames.[15]

It is Diotima again who gives authority to such sentiments. She had said: "...and at the touch of the beautiful which is ever present in his [the lover's] memory, even when absent, he brings forth that which he had conceived long before."[16]

Our poet tells us that the love through which the lover and the beloved become one is rare, just as the Neoplatonists maintained that the love which carried one to the celestial vision while still in the flesh is rare:

> Deux que le trait d'Amour touche bien vivement,
> N'ont rien qu'un seul penser, qu'un desir, qu'une flame;
> Ce n'est dedans deux corps qu'un esprit et qu'une ame,
> Et leur souverain bien gist en eux seulement.
> Ils ont en mesme tans mesme contentement,
> . . . .
> Cet Amour qui, si rare, en la terre se treuve
> Ne fait qu'un de nos cœurs; les effets en font preuve;
> Nous n'avons qu'un vouloir, qu'une ardeur, qu'un desir.[17]

He reiterates the same idea in the following lines:

> Deux corps par sa vertu d'un vouloir sont compris,
> Ils ont mesme desir, mesme espoir, mesme crainte,
> Tousjours d'un mesme trait leur poitrine est attainte,
> Et rien que veuille l'un de l'autre n'est repris.[18]

The beloved is another self for the lover, and when she dies the lover will die with her:

> La seule mort a causé ma tristesse,
> La seule mort y pourra mettre cesse,
> Ne m'empeschant plus longuement de suivre
> Cet autre moy, pour qui j'aimois à vivre.[19]

The lover, along with the other tribulations which he suffers and which we have discussed earlier, spends sleepless nights. Socrates says in the *Phaedrus*: ". . .and in her [the soul's] madness [she] can neither sleep by night nor abide in her place by day."[20] Many a poet who never heard of Plato has known the sleeplessness of the lover. Desportes may not have been conscious of anything other than the state of his own mind when he wrote the following sentiments. However, they express an aspect of the condition of the lover which can be traced to the dialogues:

> O lict! s'il est ainsi qu tu sois inventé
> Pour prendre un doux repos, quand la nuict est venue,
> D'où vient que dedans toy ma douleur continue,
> Et que je sens par toy mon tourment augmenté?
> Je ne fay que tourner d'un et d'autre costé,
> . . . .
> J'assemble bien souvent mes paupieres lassées,
> J'invoque le sommeil pour guarir mes pensées,
> Mais il fuit de mes yeux et n'y veut demeurer.[21]

The lover, whether intellectual or sensuous, naturally shows deference to his beloved, because he wishes to possess the beauty of the latter. He may carry this deference to the point of adoration. Such is not uncommon with the Platonic lover, for we find again in the *Phaedrus* that " . . . looking upon the face of his beloved as a god he [the lover] reverences him, and if he were not afraid of being thought a downright madman, he would sacrifice to his beloved as to the image of a god."[22] Our poet says that he wishes to build a temple to his goddess and to worship her:

>Solitaire et pensif, dans un bois ecarté,
>Bien loin du populaire et de la tourbe espesse,
>Je veux bastir un temple à ma fiere deesse,
>Pour apprendre mes vœux à sa divinité.
>
>Là, de jour et de nuit, par moy sera chanté
>Le pouvoir de ses yeux, sa gloire et sa hautesse;
>Et, devot, son beau nom j'invoqueray sans cesse,
>Quand je seray pressé de quelque adversité.
>
>Mon œil sera la lampe ardant continuelle,
>Devant l'image saint d'une dame si belle;
>Mon corps sera l'autel, et mes soupirs les vœux.
>
>Par mille et mille vers je chanteray l'office,
>Puis, espanchant mes pleurs et coupant mes cheveux,
>J'y feray tous les jours de mon cœur sacrifice.[23]

One would probably not be far from wrong in reading a great deal of symbolism, closely related to Platonic doctrine, into the poem just quoted, which, superficially read, seems nothing more than the height of *préciosité*. In solitude one contemplates the eternal beauties until one comes to see no reality in anything but those beauties. One therefore comes to worship them as divine things, and becomes himself the lamp which lights up the beautiful image for others, the body being only the bearer of the lamp. The heart is sacrificed to this end. The verse of the poet is devoted to singing the praises of beauty.

We have seen that the lover, after ascending the degrees to absolute Beauty, which he beholds with the eyes of the mind, arrives ". . . to become the friend of God and be immortal, if mortal man may."[24] And we have seen that, according to the Neoplatonists, the goal of man is to be God. The lover then, through his all-consuming desire for beauty, which participates in the divine, himself becomes divine. Desportes holds to the divinity of the lover in these lines:

>Si jamais un secret fut par toy retenu
>Bien serré sous la clef, c'est or' qu'il le faut faire,
>Cachant mesme aux pensers le celeste mystere
>Par qui d'homme mortel *dieu* je suis venu.[25]

His divinity is of a greater degree than that of the beloved:

>Et puis j'ayme trop mieux vous aimer sans espoir

> Que, ne vous aimant point, à mon gré vous avoir,
> Car l'amant est tousjours plus divin que l'aimée.[26]

In Plato we find that the lover is a poet. Agathon tells us that "...at the touch of him [Love] everyone becomes a poet, even though he had no music in him before; that also is proof that Love is a good poet and accomplished in all the fine arts; for no one can give to another that which he has not himself, or teach that of which he has no knowledge."[27] Desportes distorts this idea somewhat, but expresses it in a roundabout fashion:

> Car un parfait poëte est tousjours amoureaux.[28]

Heavenly love is in possession of his heart, for he is captivated by divine beauty:

> Puis que je suis épris d'une beauté divine,
> Puis qu'un amour celeste est roy de ma poitrine,
> Puis que rien de mortel je ne veux plus sonner,
> Il faut à ma princesse eriger ce trophée.[29]

It is frequently obvious in the verse of our poet that he, as the lover, is preoccupied with transcendental beauty, although at other times this meaning must be read into the verse which he addresses more directly to his lady. In life he was a lover in an even truer sense of the word, or at least in a sense to which the men of the Renaissance gave great consideration. The words of Ficino in his *Commentary*, which were inspired by Plato, were never far from the minds of the learned men of that day: "This love stimulates the soul which has reached maturity with a powerful desire for teaching and writing, so that in knowledge, generated either in writing or in the minds of students, the wisdom of the teacher (and truth) may remain eternal among men."[30] Desportes' own preoccupations with such considerations are evidenced by his activities in the Académie du Palais, of which the purpose was the pursuit of philosophic truth; by the open house which he kept for his wide circle of friends, which can well be likened to that of the Florentine Careggi; by the prodigious periods of study in which he engaged; by the protection, encouragement, and instruction which he gave to promising youths; and by the fact that the king, Henri IV, had chosen the poet, shortly before the latter's death, to be the tutor of the Dauphin.

But now let us look at the other "moytié" of the androgynous pair (for we should not forget the myth of the Androgyne in considering the lover and the beloved). One should bear in mind that it is the tangible beauty of the beloved, vaguely reminding the lover of absolute Beauty, which first attracts his eye, and that since his ultimate goal is that immaterial Beauty which has its seat in the realm of the Ideas, it is without sex. However, in the dialogues, and particularly in the *Symposium*, the beloved is a youth.

The process by which the youth, who exemplified beauty and was thus the beloved in ancient Greece, became the idealized lady of medieval courtly poets and their successors, has never been conclusively and systematically developed and set forth, though brief suggestions of the evolutionary process may be found here and there. The development seems to have been a slow, natural one, and not impossible of simple explanation.

In the Greek world of Plato womankind occupied a place of no great importance, although in the ancient religious beliefs—which were in Plato's day in the process of disintegration—numerous goddesses occupied important places in the divine hierarchy. As for woman's place in matters of love, it was the goddess Aphrodite who ruled over them. Among earthbound creatures it was the beauty and infidelity of Helen which had been directly responsible for the Trojan Wars, and the passions of such women as Clytemnestra and Phaedra had served to discredit their sex. Perhaps it was the actions of like women which had made them seem unworthy of true love to the philosophers. At any rate they receive little consideration in the dialogues, even though it is the priestess Diotima who is credited by Socrates with having spoken so knowingly and so eloquently on the subject of the nature of true love.

Later, among the Latin poets, it was the sensuous love of woman that was most frequently celebrated. Aeneas had his celebrated affair with Dido, and Ovid's loves were famous not only in his own age but down through the Middle Ages and into the Renaissance. Still, there was no idealization of women by the Latins.

With the advent of Christianity womankind took on more dignity and worth when Mary became the mother of God, in the person of Christ, and when such women as Mary Magdalene and the sisters of Lazarus, Mary and Martha, figured so prominently in His life. In early Church history women played an important role. Some of them were among the early saints, and one will recall Monica, the mother of Augustine, who was responsible for his conversion to Christianity. These women exemplified the spirit of true love.

Although Dr. Robert V. Merrill says that Plotinus was the first to designate woman as the copy of ideal beauty,[31] the Neoplatonists in general seem to have placed little emphasis on material beauty and were, for the most part, seeking ecstatic reintegration with God. Furthermore, they were ascetics and frequently withdrew from the world of material things.

In Boethius' *Consolation of Philosophy* woman, as a symbol, took a new turn in that she came to represent philosophy itself, and in that role she became the hope of the author of this work in his last days of supreme trial. His works were to be found in every library of any importance after his time.

Numerous other circumstances served to bring about the idealization of the fair sex during the Middle Ages. Under the feudal system the wife of the feudal lord was honored by the vassal not only because of the exalted position she occupied but also to please the lord. The crusaders, far from their women in distant lands, remembered them with longing, for it is doubtful that they succeeded in finding complete consolation in the women of another race with whom they came into contact, so accustomed are we to idealizing and finding most desirable those things which have entered intimately into the experiences of our childhood and youth. It was with the troubadours, some of whom had taken part in the crusades, that womankind began to be exalted in the poetry of medieval France.

The Virgin Mary had always occupied a place of honor in Church teachings, but it was only after the Albigensian crusades that the cult of the Virgin began[32] and that the great cathedrals were dedicated to her. Then all Christendom became united in her.[33] If that phenomenon had little influence on the medieval courtly poets, it nonetheless influenced those of the *dolce stil nuovo* who, like Boethius in his prose work many centuries before, made of woman the symbol of philosophy. Dante and Petrarch carried this idealization to its highest point, and with them the lady became for all time the beloved.

It seems evident in the light of the developments sketched above that no one thing brought about the change in the object of love from the youth to the fair lady. It was more probably a combination of many factors and took place over a period of many centuries. Certainly Desportes did not need the immediate influence of the Petrarchists or of such disciples of Ficino as Leone Ebreo—whose beloved Sophia in his *Dialoghi d'amore* is the symbol of truth—to cause him to center his love in woman.

The most significant quality of the beloved is beauty. In Plato the beloved is blessed in that he reflects divine beauty, of which he is a copy. Diotima says: "For the beloved is truly beautiful, and delicate, and perfect, and blessed."[34] When discussing love, we saw that it has its concrete side, represented by the god Love, who is used allegorically to represent its abstract side, that is to say, the desire for the possession of beauty. There is something of the same parallel to be drawn in the consideration of beauty. There is the beauty of face and form—that of the beloved—which we long to have as our own, and there is abstract Beauty, perfect and absolute, one with Goodness and Truth, which is the ultimate goal of our strivings and yearnings. Man longs after the inexplicable beauty only after having contemplated the ascending scale of earthly beauties and after having come to realize that, in spite of their imperfections, individual beauties have certain qualities in common, such as harmony and proportion. Such qualities are unchangeable. The unchangeable can only be God or a reflection of Him. Thus the unchanging qualities of earthly beauty share in the divine.

So far as earthly beauty was concerned Plato was primarily interested in those things which are harmonious. The universe, a creation of God, works harmoniously. Man should emulate the universe and direct all of his attention toward understanding it and toward bringing harmony into his own existence through the wisdom which comes from knowing himself, the microcosm, or little world, and through knowing the macrocosm, or great world, of which he is a miniature harmonious reproduction.

Interest in earthly beauty—which had been relegated to the unimportant realm of corrupt, material things by the early Christians and Neoplationists in their preoccupation with the afterlife—was revived by the humanists of the Renaissance and became manifest in the works of painters, sculptors, architects, landscape gardeners, musicians, and writers. Already Dante and Petrarch had extolled the various beautiful features of their ladies: the "begli occhi," the mouth, the neck, the breasts, the hands. And they agreed with Plato that there was a reflection of the divine in the beauty of their loved ones. There is then no wonder that later poets should have placed such emphasis on the divinity of beauty, or of the lady who embodied that beauty. In speaking of his beloved Petrarch says:

> Ma canto la divina sua beltate.[35]

He extolls

> . . .i celesti e rari doni
> C'ha in sè Madonna.[36]

Nearly two centuries later Michelangelo, having the advantage of the newly introduced Platonic thought in its entirety, intimates that the beauty of his beloved is heaven-given, and he speak of its virtues:

> Ben posson gli occhi presso e lontano
> Veder come risplende il tuo bel volto,
> Ma, mentre i passi a te seguir rivolto
> Spesso le tue bell'orme io cerco invano.
> L'anima, l'intelletto intero e sano
> Per gli occhi ascende più libero e sciolto
> All'alta tua beltà, ma l'ardor molto
> Non dà tal privilegio al corpo umano
> Grave e mortal, sicchè mal segue poi
> Senza ale aver d'un' angeletta il volo,
> E della vista sol si gloria e loda.
> Deh, se tu puoi nel ciel quanto fra noi,
> Fa di mie membra tutte un occhio solo,
> Nè fia parte in me poi che non ti goda.[37]

The simple description of the beloved as a goddess and of her beauty as divine is no indication that the poet is Platonizing, for a love poet might sing thus of his lady in any age. One must examine the sincerity of his sentiments, their setting and tone, before drawing any conclusions. As for Desportes, it is significant that he addresses his first songs to a beloved to whom he gives the name Diane, and that traditionally Diane was a chaste goddess. But his Cléonice is also pure, or so he tells us:

> Chere et chaste deesse, honneur de ces bas lieux,
> Orient de mon ame, astre de ma pensée.[38]

Whether he is singing the praises of Diane, Hippolyte, Cléonice, or some other, unknown lady, the contemplation of her divine beauty renders him happy:

> Je seroy bien-heureux, voyant incessament
> La divine beauté qui me tient en servage.[39]

The following lines would seem to belie this happiness, except when we remember that the cold and heat of the lover in the presence of the beloved have special significance. He grows cold because he loses his natural heat, since in a sense he dies; he becomes warmed by the divine rays of beauty.

> Si par vostre beauté, digne d'une immortelle,
> Je sens geler mon ame et mon cœur enflamer,
> J'en accuse le ciel plustot que vous blasmer;
> La faute en est à luy, qui vous forma si belle.[40]

The poet's love is conceived at the sight of the beauty of his beloved:

> On lisoit en ses yeux une paix éternelle,
> Lors qu'en sortant du ciel sa beauté m'apparut;
> Et mon jeune desir follement y courut,
> Comme un gay papillon au feu de la chandelle.[41]

After describing the beauty of the hair, the eyes, and the lily breasts of his lady, the poet says:

> Si tost que m'apparut ce chef-d'œuvre des cieux,
> En crainte et tout devôt je refermay les yeux,
> N'osant les hazarder à si hautes merveilles.[42]

The poet recognizes in the beauty of his beloved the beauties which his soul had known before falling into the body, and thus attests to his knowledge of the true significance of the relationship of the lover and the beloved:

> Si tost que je la vey si divine et si belle,
> Mon ame incontinent recogneut bien en elle
> Le parfait qu'autre-fois elle avait veu aux cieux;
> Pour la divinité qui la suit et l'honore.[43]

The love inspired by the divine beauty of the beloved is a divine love:

> Pius que je suis épris d'une beauté divine,
> Puis qu'un amour celeste est roy de ma poitrine. . . .[44]

It is the virtues of the beauty of the beloved—doubtless their ability to inspire the lover—which give her divinity:

> Aussi tant de vertus vous font toute divine.[45]

Her beauty, the divine element in her, causes the poet to identify her with the Neoplatonic "Tout":

> Belle race du ciel, ame claire et divine,
> Seule tout mon tout, ma creance et ma loy. . . .[46]

There is an intimation of the alliance of beauty of form and intellectual beauty when the poet speaks of the "esprit divin" of his lady:

> Si vostre esprit divin, tout au ciel adonné,
> Un jour tant seulement s'abaissoit en la terre.[47]

She has "mille vertus amassées":

> Les traits d'une jeune guerriere,
> Un port celeste, une lumiere,
> Un esprit de gloire animé,

> Hauts discours, divines pensées,
> Et mille vertus amassées
> Sont les sorciers qui m'ont charmé.[48]

The beauties of the beloved are mirrored in the mind of the lover, and thus they serve to make him emulate her perfection:

> Vous n'avez rien de rare et de caché,
> De beau, de saint, du ciel et de nature,
> Qu'Amour subtil n'ait partout recherché
> Pour faire en moy vostre vive peinture.
> Bref, mon esprit, ardant d'affections,
> Est miroir de vos perfections,
> Où vous pouvez vous voir toute depeinte.[49]

The beauty of the beloved is the prison which has fortunately incarcerated the reason of the lover:

> ... Or quelle autre prison
> Pouvoit plus dignement captiver ma raison
> Qu'une jeune deesse en beautés infinie?[50]

Although the Renaissance poets made extensive catalogues of the beautiful traits of their ladies, it was the eyes which invariably attracted most attention and to which most frequent references were made, for they represented a "puissance sainte" of a special order. Thus Desportes says:

> Car je jure vos yeux et leur puissance sainte
> Que je garde en cecy le respect et la crainte,
> Dont il faut reverer une divinité.[51]

Ficino in his *Commentary* had reasoned, concerning the eyes and their powers, "that mortals are best charmed when, in frequent gazes directing eye to eye, they join lights with lights and wretchedly drink in a long love. Really the whole cause and origin of this kind of illness...is the eye. Therefore, if a man is pleasing in the shining of his eyes, although he may be less well built in his other parts, for the reason we have mentioned, he nevertheless forces to fall in love those who look at him."[52]

As we have said, the beloved receives little attention in Plato, whereas the beauty of the beloved is of first importance. It is therefore very difficult to make a clear distinction between abstract Beauty, which is intelligible by nature and has its ultimate seat among the Ideas, and concrete beauties, appealing to the senses and usually reflected in the face and form of the beloved. The latter are copies of the former and share in its divinity, and the real significance of the beloved is that she is an emanation of the divine.

CHAPTER IX

THE POET AND POETRY

Plato, who was at heart a poet himself, both loved and feared other poets. He heaped high praises on them upon occasion and attributed to them prophetic powers, although his reason dictated that they should be exiled from the ideal Republic.[1] They should, however, be treated as sweet, holy, and wonderful beings before being sent on their way, and a few exceptional ones should be allowed to remain.

Poetry occupied a place of great dignity among the Greeks in general, and, like the related arts of music and the dance, it exerted a tremendous influence on the life of the people. The child's first lesson consisted primarily of learning to recite verse by heart.[2] The theaters were practically free, and all the great poets could be heard by everyone. At private gatherings their works were common subjects of discussion.[3] However, there was a standing quarrel between the poets and the philosophers on popular mythology. Therefore, in the *Republic*, Book II and III, Plato calls for a strict censorship of poetry. This leads in Book X to the banishment of the poet. In the *Laws*, written somewhat later, poetry is still suspect and must be censored although the poet is given a role to play in the state provided he is a man of years and is of good repute. He may remain a citizen under condition that he sing of noble thoughts and deeds.[4]

Let us look at what Plato had to say about the poet before he came to suspect him and his work. In the *Lysis* Socrates says of poets that "they are to us in a manner the fathers and authors of wisdom, and they speak of friends in no light or trivial manner, but God himself, as they say, makes them and draws them to one another."[5] In the *Phaedrus*, in discussing the four kinds of madness—prophetic, inspiration which purges wrath, poetic, and love—he says: "The third kind is the madness of those who are possessed by the Muses; which taking hold of a delicate and virgin soul, and there inspiring frenzy, awakens lyrical and all other numbers; with these adorning the myriad actions of ancient heroes for the instruction of posterity. But he who, having no touch of the Muses' madness in his soul, comes to the door and thinks that he will get into the temple by the help of art—he, I say, and his poetry are not admitted; the sane man disappears and is nowhere when he enters into rivalry with the madman."[6] In the *Ion* he continues: "...the Muse first of all inspires men herself; and from these inspired persons a chain of other persons is suspended, who take the inspiration. For all good poets, epic as well as lyric, compose their beautiful poems not by art, but because they are inspired and possessed...the lyric poets are not in their right mind when they are composing their beautiful strains . . . they bring songs from honeyed fountains, culling them out of the gardens and dells of the Muses; they, like the bees, winging their way from flower to flower....For the poet is a light and winged and holy thing, and there is no invention in him until he has been inspired and is out of his senses... they are simply inspired to utter that to which the Muse impels them... for not by art does the poet sing, but by power divine... God takes away the minds of poets and uses them as his ministers, as he also uses diviners and holy prophets... God is the speaker... the poets are only the interpreters of the Gods by whom they are severally possessed.'"[7] It is still Socrates speaking in the *Apology* when these words are uttered: "... not by wisdom do poets write poetry, but by a sort of genius and inspiration... say many many fine things, but do not understand the meaning of them."[8] From these quotations we can see that Plato looked with great esteem upon the poets, even as he suspected them and that he considered them divinely inspired, possessed of a poetic madness.

Aristotle does not mention the fact that Plato had proposed the expulsion of the poet from the state. For Aristotle poetry is an imitation of nature, and imitation is natural with mankind. We learn at first by imitation, and learning is the greatest of pleasures, not only for the philosopher but for all human beings.[9] Aristotle says that ". . . poetry demands a man with a special gift for it, or else one with a touch of madness in him."[10] He goes on to establish the rules for the poetic art which have exerted so great an influence on literature from his own day until ours, and which have been so variously interpreted, so freely and so dogmatically by turns. Many another scholar of antiquity had something to say about poetry and the inspiration of the poet. Among the most influential was Horace, who says in his *Ars poetica*: "Whether a good poem be the work of nature or of art is a moot point."[11]

It was inevitable that the idea of poetic inspiration as a divine gift should intrigue the poets of the Renaissance who had both Plato and Aristotle as authorities for such a concept. The French poets were not long in making the idea of *divinus furor* their own. Thomas Sebillet embodied it in his *Art Poétique Françoys* (1548).[12] Pontus de Tyard spoke of the four ways by which man may be seized by divine enthusiasm in his *Solitaire premier* (1552), saying that the first of these is poetic enthusiasm, proceeding from the gift of the Muses.[13]

The Pléiade attributed the poetic gift to every divine source they could find in Greek literature. Poets were favored, according to them, by the Muses, the Fates, Apollo; they were possessed of demons; they soared aloft on Pegasus; or they had drunk from the waters on Parnassus. These and a hundred other sources could be responsible for their poetic gifts. However, all of this contradicted another ever present experience of the poets of Ronsard's group, namely, that poetry was hard work.[14] It also contradicted the advice given in the *Deffense et Illustration de la langue françoise* of Du Bellay, "d'imiter les bons auteurs Grecs et Romains, voire bien Italiens, Espagnols et autres," and the further command that one "Lis donc, et relis premierement, ô poëte futur, feuillette de main nocturne et journelle les exemplaires grecs et latins, puis me laisse toutes ces vieilles poësies françoises..."[15] These poets were anxious to get away from the "Rondeaux, Ballades, Vyrelaiz, Chanz Royaulx, Chansons et autres telles épiceries" and to cultivate the nobler genres which they found in the literatures of antiquity. In their verse they maintained that the poet was a person apart, having divine gifts, while in practice they insisted upon hard work and study, if one were to succeed in the poetic art. Du Bellay is not consistent in his thought concerning poetic fury. In the *Deffense et Illustration* (1549) he says: "... le naturel n'est suffisant à celuy qui en poésie veult faire œuvre digne de l'immortalité."[16] In his *Regrets*, however, one finds the following lines:

> De quelque autre subiect, que i'escriue, Iodelle,
> Ie cens mon cœur transi d'une morne froideur,
> Et ne cens plus en moy ceste diuine ardeur,
> Qui t'enflamme l'esprit de sa viue estincelle.[17]

Desportes the scholar, as well as Desportes the poet, is very clear on this subject. In one of his discourses before the Académie du Palais he says, addressing himself to the king: "Les poëtes sont ignorans et ne laissent pour cela, inspirez et souflez de quelque esprit divin, de composer en leur fureur choses qui tirent en grande admiration les escoutans. Aussy n'est-ce pas tant de merveille de veoir sortir quelques beaux et doctes discours de raison de la bouche de ceux qui sont exercitez en la philosophie et en font profession, ainsi que font beaucoup de ceux qui sont en cette assemblée, comme quand un qui n'estudie point et qui semble ignorant jette en fureur des enfantemens de son esprit si beaux, si rares et si peu de luy attendus qu'ils font esbaïr les doctes et sçavans qui les oient."[18]

One should not be deceived by Desportes' use of the word "ignorans" when he speaks of poets. He had been on one occasion described by Du Perron—himself one of the great minds of the day—as the most learned man in Christendom.[19] Desportes was making no show of modesty in this case either, since by "ignorans" he had in mind those poets who compose under the compulsion of a frenzy.

As for the belief of Desportes the poet concerning the poetic fury, we find that one of his earliest works to draw the attention of the court—his *Mort de Rodomont*—opens with these lines:

>Je sens d'un feu nouveau ma poitrine allumée,
>Qui ne m'echauffe point d'ardeur accoustumée:
>Un subit mouvement que je ne puis donter
>Me ravit hors de moy, pour me faire chanter
>Je ne sçay quoy d'estrange et difficile à croire,
>Quittant de Cupidon le triomphe et la gloire,
>Les larmes des amans, leurs soupirs et leurs cris,
>Sentier trop rebattu des poëtiques esprits.[20]

It is interesting to see that our poet attributes the narration which he is about to make to a special inspiration which has seized him, and to find him doing so at such an early moment in his career. Perhaps this was a warning to prospective patrons as to what might be expected from him.

The Pléiade made little distinction between the inspiration of love and that of poetry. As we have seen, the two were treated side by side in Plato. In the following verse our poet looks to the god Love to supply him with the necessary inspiration to sing his praises worthily:

>O Dieu puissant et bon, seul sujet de ma lyre,
>Si jamais que de toy je n'ay rien voulu dire,
>Et si ton feu divin, m'a tousjours allumé,
>Donne-moy pour loyer qu'un jour je puisse faire
>Un œuvre à to loüange éloigné du vulgaire,
>Et qui ne suive point le trac accoustumé.[21]

In so doing he fuses love madness with poetic madness, but recognizes that they are both gifts.

In extolling Love in the *Symposium*, Agathon had said that "... he is a poet, and he is also the source of poetry in others, which he could not be if he were not himself a poet."[22] Desportes recognized this fact in the verses quoted above, and he gives credit to Love for guiding his pen in the following lines:

> Amour guide ma plume et me donne l'adresse,
> Pour vivement pourtraire une jeune deesse.[23]

Again he seems to be saying that he is possessed of both the love fury and poetic fury:

> O vers que j'ai chantez en l'ardeur qui m'enflame,
> Je deviens à bon doit de vostre aise envieux!
> . . . .
> Je sçay qu'il eust fallu, pour monstrer son pouvoir,
> Un esprit plus divin, plus d'art, plus de sçavoir;
> Mais, estant plein d'amour, je fuy tout artifice.[24]

And in the quatrain below he gives credit to Love for having drawn from the mind of the lady Callianthe her verse:

> Qui veut sçavoir de quels traits Amour blesse,
> Sans voir vos yeux trop pronts à martyrer,
> Lise ces vers qu'habile il sçeut tirer
> De vostre esprit, digne d'une deesse.[25]

The poets of the Pléiade were as inconsistent in their beliefs concerning the immortality of the poet and the cult of glory as they were concerning the special natural gifts he enjoyed. Diotima had shown that lovers and poets desire immortality.[26] Horace maintained: "The man of true worth is forbidden to die/ By the Muses, they find him his place in the sky."[27] And he had boasted: "I've reared a frame outlasting brass."[28] Brunetto Latini said to Dante, when the latter encountered him in the *Inferno*:

> Se tu sequi tua stella,
> Non puoi fallire a glorioso porto.[29]

In his *Trionfi* Petrarch wrote of the triumph of fame. The poets of the Pléiade were well aware of the considerations which had been given to the glory of their fellows, not only by the writers of antiquity but by their own Italian predecessors. Du Bellay, in speaking of the verse of another, could say:

> Ton œuvre sera plus durable
> Qu'un Théatre ou un Colisée,
> Ou qu'un Mausolée admirable.[30]

And Ronsard said that the better part of him, his verse, would not go to the tomb with him:

> Sous le tombeau tout Ronsard n'ira pas,
> Restant de luy la part qui est meilleure.[31]

But Ronsard questioned the immortality of the poet in the advice which he addressed to the young Desportes:

> Nous mourons les premiers, le long reply des ages
> En mourant engloutist nos œuvres à la fin:
> Ainsi le veut Nature et le puissant Destin.
> Dieu seul est éternel. . . .
> Chacun de son labeur doit en ce Monde attendre
> L'usufruit seulement, que present il doit prendre
> Sans se paistre d'attents et d'une éternité,
> Qui n'est rien que fumée et pure vanité.
> . . . .
> Des-Portes, qu'Aristote amuse tout le jour,
> Qui honores ta Dure, et les champs qu'à l'entour
> Chartres voit de son mont, et panché les regarde,
> Je te donne ces vers, à fin de prendre garde
> De ne tuer ton corps, desireux d'acquerir
> Un renom journalier qui doit bien tost mourir:
> Mais happe le present d'un cœur plein d'allegresse,
> Cependant que le Prince, Amour, et la jeunesse,
> T'en donnent le loisir, sans croire au lendemain,
> Le futur est douteux, le present est certain.[32]

The *carpe diem* theme was ever present in Ronsard, but here it is tied up with the transistory nature of the glory of the poet. Perhaps Ronsard already realized that the young poet might replace him in the favor of the court, and hoped by such advice to have him turn to some other pursuit; at any rate it was not long before he found himself being forgotten. His poetry was neglected for that of his young rival, so that he felt obliged to come out with a new collection of verse, the *Sonnets à Hélène*, in the manner which Desportes had brought to favor at court.

If the glory of Desportes suffered an eclipse after his death, it was not because he had not enjoyed great favor during his lifetime, nor was it because he had failed to trust in his continued fame. During his day he was acclaimed as one of the great poets of the age. Scévole de Sainte-Marthe had promised him immortality in these terms:

> Des-Portes, quand le temps, qui toute chose emmeine,
> L'usage du Françoys aura tout aboly,
> Par le meme destin, qui rend ensevely
> Et l'usage du Grec, et la langue romaine,
>
> Ton ouvrage sera une vive fontaine
> Où puiseront ceux-là, qui pour vaincre l'oubly

> Apprendront en lisant ce language accomply
> Dont aujourd'huy la voix est l'escolle certaine.
>
> Ils trouveront chez toy celle *naïveté*
> Qui joint une douceur à une gravité
> Et diront, en voyant tes rymes si faciles:
>
> Il paroist bien qu'alors que ce poëte escrivoit,
> Un prince tel qu'Auguste en la France vivoit
> Puis-qu'il fit de son temps renaistre des Virgiles.[33]

When Sainte-Marthe speaks of the "naïveté" that one finds in Desportes he uses the word in the sense of inborn. Robert J. Clements says: "The natural genius of a literature or language, its ethos, is sometimes called its 'naïveté' by the Pléiade."[34] It would appear from the following lines that Desportes did not minimize his own worth:

> Moy donc qu'un plus grand Dieu touche si vivement,
> Et qui veux que mon nom vive éternellement,
> Pour avoir mon amour sur tout autre elevée:
> Moy qui ay tant de fois ma vaillance esprouvée,
> Craindray-je maintenant à ce dernier assault?[35]

At times, however he disavows any desire for immortality through his verse:

> Je vous offre ces vers qu'Amour m'a fait escrire,
> De vos yeux, ses Flambeaux, ardemment agité,
> Non pour sacrer ma peine à l'immortalité.
> Car à si haut loyer ma jeunesse n'aspire.
> . . . .
> Et puis je n'escry pas pour gloire en acquérir.[36]

In the *Republic* there is a description of the three Fates, Lachesis (singing of the past), Clotho (singing of the present), and Atropos (singing of the future), and of the spindle which they keep going.[37] We find our poet attributing his misfortune to Clotho, who, however, has destined

> Qu'il ait l'ame hautaine, et qu'une belle audace
> L'affranchisse du peuple et le retire à soy,
> Que par ses longs travaux, son merite et sa foy
> Il s'eleve un renom que le tans ne defface.[38]

The Fates, of course, do not originate with Plato, but Desportes, in writing these lines, seems to have been under the influence of the above-cited passage. He continues with a recital of the ills that Clotho has visited upon him:

> Que son heur des jaloux soit tousjours empesché,
> Que le flux de ses pleurs ne puisse estre estanché,
> Qu'il trouve à ses desseins la fortune opposée![39]

In ancient Greece there was no distinction made between music and verse, for the Greek poets wrote their verse to be sung, and the rhythmic step of the dance could accompany the song. As Plato proposed to allow certain poets and certain kinds of poetry to exist in his ideal Republic while others would be forbidden, so there were certain musical modes which were reputed to produce good effects, and others evil. We find authority given this idea in the *Timaeus*: "Moreover, so much of music as is adapted to the sound of the voice and to the sense of hearing is granted to us for the sake of harmony; and harmony, which has motions akin to the revolutions of our souls, is not regarded by the intelligent votary of the Muses as given by them with a view to irrational pleasure . . . but as meant to correct any discord which may have arisen in the courses of the soul and to be our ally in bringing her into harmony and agreement with herself."[40] In the *Republic* Plato speaks of music which fosters temperance in the soul,[41] and in the *Laws* he says that licence in music leads to anarchy in the state.[42] Again in the *Laws* music is said to give a wholesome discipline in a pleasant form.[43] Children in the Greek schools were taught to play the lyre before they went to the gymnasium. The point of all this emphasis on music was to make the lives of the people more harmonious and gracious, and to implant in their souls true conceptions of good and evil. Music was a gift of the gods and was not intended for idle pleasure.

This emphasis which the Greeks had placed on the ethical values of music was not lost on the scholars of the Renaissance. Ficino, in his *Commentary*, spoke of the effects of music in this manner: "But there are said to be two types of melody in music: one serious and steady, the other soft and sensuous. The former is beneficial to those who hear it; the latter, Plato says (in the *Republic* and *Laws*) is harmful. In the *Symposium* he assigns to the former the name Urania, and to the latter, Polyhymnia. Some prefer the first type and others the second. The love of the former people ought to be indulged, and the sounds which they long for should be invited; but the desire of the latter should be resisted, for the passion of the former is heavenly love, and that of the latter, earthly love."[44] So music is tied up not only with *ethos* but with love as well. Kristeller says that Ficino had a deeper interest in music than in the other arts and in his *De amore* places the beauty of sound on a level with that of visible forms and thoughts. He speaks of the "effects" on the soul of music, which will dispel the troubles of soul and body, and goes on to say that in this work he treats of poetry in close connection with music but considers poetry as superior, for words speak not only to the ear but also to the mind.[45]

This tendency to identify music, poetry, and the dance as one was consistent with the Neoplatonic oneness of all things which made for a harmonious universe, and the use of musical terms in promoting harmony is well illustrated in the words of Guy Du Faur de Pibrac, spoken before the Parlement of Paris in 1572. He said: "The ancients assembled at these games [Olympic] not only to content their corporeal eyesight but also their minds and understandings and to exercise themselves in virtue. . . . There were sung hymns to Apollo, but before beginning a Herald came forward who cried so that all could hear, 'Sing, but in tune'. . . . Their words have often ravished me with admiration . . . and they can be accomodated to our exercise of Justice, for so we ought all to sing, justly and in legitimate measure, both those who plead and those who defend."[46]

Mention has already been made of the fact that "la musique est souveraine" at the Collège de Coqueret where Jean Dorat was preparing the members of the Brigade to play their prime role in French letters. The great interest that one of Dorat's charges, Antoine de Baïf, took in measured music, measured verse and the measured dance, and in the ethical "effects" attributed to them, has been pointed out. The Academie de poésie et de musique, which was originated with the idea of promoting such desired "effects," and which led in its turn to the great court festivals of which the *Ballet comique de la Reine* (1581) was the most brilliant, resulted from Baïf's preoccupations. The whole purpose of the *Ballet comique* was to present a lesson in morality. It was organized as a musical drama—thus consisting of both music and words—combined with dancing. The ballet was presented as a part of the festivities surrounding the wedding of the duc de Joyeuse, one of the king's favorites. Yates says that Ronsard and Desportes contributed a tournament "for and against Love" which was accompanied by music.[47] There were numerous celebrations in connection with the duke's wedding, and for one of the masquerades Desportes composed the following moralizing poetic dialogue:

   Pour la Masquarade des chevaliers fidelles
   Stances recitées par un des Flamines:
    O foy! grand' deïté jadis tant reverée
   Des innocentes mœurs de la saison dorée,

> Mais dont rien que le nom en ce tans n'est connu,
> Fille de Jupiter et sa ministre sainte,
> Qui joints la terre au ciel d'une aimable contrainte,
> Et par qui ce grand tout en devoir est tenu,
> Favorise et conduis, ô deesse immortelle
> Ceste troupe guerriere, amoureuse et fidelle.
>   Ce sont neuf chevaliers devots à ton service,
> Qu'un despit genereux de l'humaine malice
> D'un des coings de la terre a conduis en ces lieux.
> Amour est le sujet de leur juste querelle:
> Ils ne sçauroient souffrir que l'audace mortelle
> Le conduise en triomphe à la honte des dieux.
> Aide un si beau dessein, fortune leur prouësse
> Et delivre un grand dieu, toy, plus grande deesse.
>   **La Foy:**
>   Allez, mes chevaliers, marchez à la bonne heure.
> Je vous suivray partout; ma plus chere demeure
> Sera dedans vos cœurs pleins de ma deïté.
> Pour avoir constamment gardé la foy promise,
> Je vous ay reservez à si haute entreprise,
> Ornant de ce laurier vostre fidelité.
>   **La chœur de tous les Flamines:**
>   Dames, qui par vos yeux rompez tous les ombrages,
> Changeant la nuict en jour, esclairez leurs courages,
> Et de vos deux regards animez leur valeur.
> Rien ne leur donne crainte, ayant ceste assistance;
> Sinon peu leur vaudra leur fidelle constance.
> Si vous n'en faites cas, la foy n'est que malheur.[48]

Thus was the poet using his poetic gift in the composition of verse, to be allied with measured music in one of the numerous attempts to bring harmony into a society torn by civil war. He makes allusion to a former age of gold; to love which joins heaven and earth and holds the "grand tout" in its power.

Baïf"'s measured verse never met with great success, but the encouragement which he gave to "this new-old kind of poetry-music-dancing"[49] gave a new impetus to the development of music in France, and to the importance which words were to have in relation to music in this development. One of the significant characteristics of French opera from his day has been the subordination of musical effect to a clear understanding of the words being sung.

When Desportes was translating the Psalms of David into French verse he withdrew for at least part of the time to the home of Baïf because the latter had accumulated a great deal of source material in his own unsuccessful attempt to translate them. This material was placed at Desportes' disposal, and Baïf took particular interest in the progress of his work, which was being undertaken as a counter-revolutionary measure. A number of Desportes' *Psalms* were put to music by such well-known musicians as Denis Caignet and Didier Poncet,[50] and if they did not succeed in composing the difficulties of the poet's own age, they were esteemed highly in the following century.

We have seen how the idea that the poet gains immortality through his verse goes back to antiquity, and how this idea was expressed in Plato. It was no more than a step to the parallel concept that the person sung by the poet also gains glory. We find Ronsard warning Hélène that she should reciprocate his love during the days of her youth and beauty, for some day she will regret having spurned the love of the one who has immortalized her in his verse and will say: "Ronsard m'a célébrée, au temps que j'étais belle."[51] Desportes puts no such pressure on his lady, and speaks in a clearly Platonic manner when he says:

> Deesse, à qui je fus en naissant destiné,
> Ou plus que le malheur vous me serez cruelle,
> Ou vous me laisserez la partie immortelle,
> L'ame, à qui mes escrits tant de gloire ont donné.[52]

He calls his verses couriers of the glory of his lady:

> Angelique beauté, je sacre à la memoire
> Ces vers, avantureux courriers de vostre gloire,
> Qui n'atteindront pourtant au ciel de vostre honneur.[53]

In the following sonnet our poet praises Petrarch, saying:

> Le labeur glorieux d'un esprit admirable
> Triomphe heureusement de la posterité,
> Comme ce Florentin qui a si bien chanté
> Que les siecles d'apres n'ont trouvé son semblable.
>
> La beauté n'est ainsi, car elle est perissable;
> Mais Laure avec ses vers un trophée a planté,
> Qui fait que l'on revere à jamais sa beauté,
> Et qui rend son laurier verdissant et durable.
>
> Celle qui dans ses yeux tient mon contentement,
> En ce qu'un moindre esprit la veut rendre immortelle.
> La passant en beauté, luy cede seulement
> En ce qu'un moindre esprit la veut rendre immortelle.
>
> Mais j'ay plus d'amitié, s'il fut mieux écrivant,
> Car sa Laure mourut et il resta vivant;
> Si ma dame mouroit, je mourrois avec elle.[54]

He becomes very pragmatic about the whole matter of his ability to make his lady immortal in his verse in these lines:

> Si vous voulez immortelle durer,
> Nul mieux que moy ne vous peut honorer,

>   Et vos vertus à jamais faire bruire.
>   Je l'entrepren; mais, pour plus m'animer,
>   Permettez-moy que j'ose vous aimer:
>   L'affection me fera mieux escrire.[55]

Concerning the tendency of the Renaissance poets to seek immortality and to immortalize others, Clements says: "The facets of this immortalizing were as many and varied as they had been in classical literature. One immortalized oneself, one's work, one's friends, one's mistress, one's monarch, one's province, one's river. As a scholar one could immortalize one's language. As a bard one could pay homage to virtue and to gods Christian or pagan. One's glory would set one apart. . ."[56]

A last word remains to be said about Desportes and the Platonic poet. When he is not imitating one of the Petrarchists his verse is remarkably free of minor clichés, mythological allusions, and the innumerable motifs popular among poets of his day. When he is borrowing he uses what he finds, generally simplifying obscure passages by amplifying them and omitting vague allusions. The Petrarchists had made a practice of comparing themselves to all sorts of objects and animals, such as the bee which distills sweet honey and the salamander which can live in the flame. Desportes uses few such conceits, although they are by no means absent from his work. Many of them owe nothing to Plato, but at least one which our poet used, did.

From earliest times the swan and its sweet song have been symbolic of the poet.[57] The idea does not originate in Plato, for the swan was the bird of Apollo and of Orpheus. But, Plato speaks in the dialogues of the sacredness of this bird and of its beautiful voice. In the *Phaedo* Socrates says: "Will you not allow that I have as much of the spirit of prophecy in me as the swans? For they, when they perceive that they must die, having sung their life long, do then sing more lustily than ever, rejoicing in the thought that they are about to go away to the god whose ministers they are. But men, because they are themselves afraid of death, slanderously affirm of the swans that they sing a lament at the last, not considering that no bird sings when cold or hungry, or in pain, not even the nightingale, nor the swallow, nor yet the hoopoe. . . . But because they are sacred to Apollo, they have the gift of prophecy, and anticipate the good things of another world; therefore they sing and rejoice in that day more than ever they did before. And I too, believing myself to be the consecrated servant of the same God, and the fellow servant of the swans, and thinking that I have received from my master gifts of prophecy which are not inferior to theirs, would not go out of life less merrily than the swans."[58] After Plato the swan motif can be found in the works of numerous poets of antiquity. The Romans linked the swan with the goddess of love, Venus, and her son, Eros, and thus gave to the bird a double meaning for future poets.

During the Renaissance, French poets were attracted toward the swan motif as they were attracted toward the whole of their heritage from antiquity and from their Italian predecessors.[59] In Rabelais' great work, which is a melting pot for every conceivable idea that intrigued the age, we find: "Les cycnes, qui sont oyseaulx sacrez à Apollo, ne chantent jamais, si non quand ilz approchent de leur mort. . . chant de cycne est praesiage certain de sa mort prochaine, et ne meurt que praealablement n'ayt chanté. Semblablement les poëtes qui sont en protection de Apollo, approchans de leur mort ordinairement deviennent prophetes et chantent par Apolline inspiration vaticinans des choses futures."[60] Du Bellay mentions the swans as the sacred covey of Phoebus and calls himself:

> Nouueau Cigne, ce me semble,
> Je remply l'air de mes criz.[61]

Even in the sermons of the day profane imagery enjoyed a great favor and, we are told that at the funeral of the sponsor of the Académie du Palais, Guy Du Faur de Pibrac, Père Pain et Vin, who delivered the oration, compared the death of a just man to that of swans, who are filled with prophecy at death and express the goodness which death holds in their melodious songs.[62] Desportes makes use of the swan motif in this manner:

> Je me suis veu muer, pour le commencement,
> En cerf qui porte au flanc une fleche sanglante;
> Apres je devins cygne, et, d'une voix dolante,
> Je presage ma mort me plaignant doucement.[63]

Like Plato, then, Desportes conceived of poets in general, and of himself in particular, as being possessed of a divine fury—"ardeur," "fureur", "divin feu"—as being "inspirez et souflez de quelque esprit divin de composer en leur fureur choses qui tirent en grande admiration les escoutans," and as one who, even at the moment of death, sings sweet songs, prophesying the good things of another world. He held with Plato that the lover is a poet and that his songs bring immortality to himself and to those whose praises he sings.

Plato and the Greeks had tended to unify and interrelate all knowledge and the arts, with poetry and music occupying most important places. The men of Desportes' age followed the same tendency, as did he himself. After Plato decided it was best to exile the poets from his Republic and to censor poetry, he still proposed to give a place to the poets of mature age who glorified the national heroes and to those who sang the praises of the gods. Even in Desportes' profane poetry we find some elegies and epitaphs in celebration of men and women whom he considered worthy subjects of the king. In his more mature years, after he became an *abbé*, he gave up profane verse entirely and devoted his poetic talents to his *Œuvres chrestiennes* and to the translation of the Psalms. He, like Plato, and like his contemporary Baïf, hoped that the cultivation of the harmony of music and of verse might restore concord among the people of France.

CHAPTER X

THE VIRTUES

Desportes gained early favor and made a place for himself in the world through the cultivation of poetry devoted primarly to love. As he grew older and became more involved in the affairs of Church and State, and particularly after he received the abbeys of the Trinité de Tiron and Notre Dame de Josaphat in the diocese of Chartres in 1582, and thus took on the duties and responsibilities of an abbé, he abandoned such occupations and cultivated more serious ones. Among these were his contributions to the activities of Henri III's Académie du Palais, one phase of which—the consideration of moral and contemplative virtues—we shall discuss in this chapter.

Without referring specifically to the virtues we have seen that the lover perfects himself—and therefore acquires them—through the contemplation of beauty, goodness and truth. With reference to virtue Plato says: "Remember how in that communion only, beholding beauty with the eye of the mind, he (the Lover) will be enabled to bring forth, not images of beauty, but realities (for he has hold not of an image but of a reality), and bringing forth and nourishing *true virtue* to become the friend of God and be immortal, if mortal man may."[1]

There is probably no subject which so repeatedly occupies the attention of the men who take part in the Platonic dialogues as the matter of the virtues. Concerning them there are two questions of particular importance: "Can virtue be taught?" and "Is virtue one or many?"[2] There are varying answers given to both of these questions. In the case of the first the conclusion seems to be that virtue is knowledge and can therefore be taught, if one can find teachers. As to whether the virtues are one or many, it is generally agreed in the *Republic* that they are four: wisdom, courage, temperance, and justice. Socrates argues that if virtue is knowledge and can be taught, it is good, and the good man, having acquired virtue, will impart it to his fellow citizens.

In the *Phaedo* and the *Phaedrus* the virtues are idealized. The philosopher alone has true virtue and is desirous of keeping his soul pure from the contaminations of the body and ready, when the time comes, to fly back to its celestial place of origin. The earthly virtues are feeble copies of those absolute qualities which the soul saw when it accompanied God. The philosopher, who has a better memory than most men, is filled with rapture when he contemplates the earthly copies of the virtues to be glimpsed in a noble soul.

Aristotle's *Ethics* is largely devoted to a consideration of the virtues. There one finds that every art, inquiry, and action is directed to some good. The good is identified with happiness, and happiness is defined in terms of activity of the soul in accordance with perfect virtue. Two types of virtues are identified: the moral ones, proper to the appetitive soul which shares in the rational principle, and the intellectual ones, proper to the intellective soul. The moral virtues have to do with the rule of right or of practical reason, which is dependent on philosophic wisdom. Thus, wisdom may be considered the formal cause of happiness. The greatest happiness is found in the contemplative life.

The Neoplatonists were more interested in the destiny of the soul—the means of restoring it to its primitive Oneness—and in the philosophic problems having to do with structure and the rational explanation of reality than they were in matters having to do solely with earthly creatures. For them the true mission of the soul of man was to release itself from the prison of the flesh and to unite itself with God through purgative practices and illuminative contemplation. Thus were outlined the three important steps of the mystics: purgation, illumination, and union. One comes to know oneself through the intellect, not through the senses, and thereby arrives at knowing God. The kind of wisdom Plato would have man seek—wisdom based on the knowledge of all things and acquired through the dialectic method—was not emphasized by the Neoplatonists. Plotinus speaks, rather, of closing the eyes and awakening within oneself "that other power of vision,"[3] thus emphasizing intuitive wisdom. And yet Plotinus has much to say about the goodness in man which comes from the cultivation of the virtues, and he speaks of the beauty of the virtues and of the arts and sciences, all of which must be brought under one principle.[4] The virtuous man is happy even in adversity.[5] The emphasis of the Neoplatonists is thus on the contemplative side of man's nature.

The Christians placed considerably more stress on the virtues than did the Neoplatonists. Particularly was this true of the moral virtues. For even though man's ultimate goal is heaven, he arrives there only through virtuous living on earth. St. Augustine says that felicity is the reward of virtue.[6] To the four Platonic virtues the Christians added three: hope, faith, and charity. In the *Summa Theologica,* St. Thomas speaks of "virtues and vices and other like habits."[7] He has a great deal to say about the virtues, supporting Peter Lombard's definition that: "Virtue is a good quality [which St. Thomas would have changed to habit] of the mind, by which we live righteously, of which no one can make bad use, which God works in us without us."[8] Then St. Thomas divides the virtues into intellectual, moral, and theological ones, adding the theological ones to those already proposed by Aristotle. The intellectual virtues, he says, are three in number: wisdom, science, and understanding. Socrates had maintained that a man in possession of knowledge could not sin, but St. Thomas holds that, since men's appetitive nature opposes reason, sometimes "the intellect marks the way, while desire lags, or follows not at all."[9] This he quotes from St. Augustine. Moral habits can be considered human virtues only when in conformity with reason.[10]

In the fourth treatise of his *Convivio*[11] Dante treats at great length the question of nobility in man, which he defines as "perfection in each thing of its proper nature."[12] He speaks of the moral and the intellectual virtues, saying that the moral virtues are the road to the contemplative and that "the felicity of the contemplative life is more excellent than that of the active, and the one and the other may be and is the fruit and end of nobility . . . there is nobleness wherever there is virtue, but not virtue wherever there is nobleness."[13]

Although Ficino had no system of ethics he dwelt upon the virtues in his *Theologia Platonica,* dividing them into moral and speculative virtues. The end of the former is to purify the soul and separate it from the divisible body; and of the latter, to grasp the incorporeal and universal concepts of things, whose locus is far from divisible bodies. According to Porphyry he said that virtue is equivalent to the spiritual ascent of the soul and exists in four degrees; passing through the civic virtues, the purifying virtues, the virtues of the purified soul, and the exemplary virtues. Through these degrees the soul achieves union with God.[14] True happiness can exist only through the speculative or contemplative virtues which bring a knowledge of God, for the contemplative life has a part in eternity.

The traditional concepts concerning the virtues became somewhat distorted by the beauty-loving men of the Italian Renaissance, whose interpretations of them are reflected in Castiglione's

Cortegiano. This work served to fix, perpetuate and pass on to other countries the Italian ideas. Beauty, elegance, manners, the arts, music, dancing, and such skills as dueling all became attributes of the *uomo di virtù*.[15] Castiglione, in the fourth book of his work, treats of the virtues *per se*. The moral virtues are not in us by nature but must be learned and cultivated. However, we are born apt to receive them. First, we practice virtue or vice; then, we are either virtuous or vicious. He defines virtue as a wisdom and an understanding to choose the good. If the good and ill were well known and perceived, every man would always choose the good. The contemplative virtues are discussed in connection with idealized love.

This continuing preoccupation with the virtues by men of learning from antiquity to the period of the Renaissance naturally carried over into Henri's Académie, where the emphasis was on philosophical matters, and the aim was the cultivation of harmony within the individual and the state. By the time of its opening, which was probably about 1576, our poet was already well established as "messire Philippe des Portes . . . le bien-aymé et favori poëte du roy Henri III de France."[16] He became one of its leading spirits, and it was to him that was entrusted the *Livre d'institution de l'Académie*, in which were inscribed all the names of the members, a record of the proceedings, and perhaps many other interesting things. Unfortunately this book has been lost, and under strange circumstances.[17] There are preserved, however, a number of the discourses made before this learned body,[18] and among these are three delivered by our poet.

Let us look at the contents of two of the discourses by Desportes which have been preserved on the subject: *Quelles sont les plus excellentes, les vertus intellectuelles ou les morales*.[19] If we are to believe D'Aubigné this subject so preoccupied the Académie that even two of the learned women of the day—Mme de Retz, of whom we have already had occasion to speak, and Mme de Lignerolles—"se firent admirer" by their fine words.[20] Desportes' own discourses followed two others, on the same subject, by Ronsard. The latter championed the moral virtues and seems to have drawn heavily on Aristotle, Boethius, and the Christian teachings. He says that if a man could have both moral and intellectual virtues together he would indeed have "le souverain bien," and he concludes that "ce n'est pas grande vertu de comtempler et s'amuser à un subject qui ne peult faillir ny tromper," adding, "Car que sert la contemplation sans l'action?"[21] It is no more than we might have expected that Ronsard should have supported the pragmatic side of this argument, for he is simply repeating his familiar "Cueillez dès aujourdhui les roses de la vie"—or cultivate those things which have to do with immediate living.

Not so Desportes! He chose, or was given, the championing of the contemplative or intellectual virtues. We have seen how he opened his rebuttal of Ronsard's contentions by a Platonic consideration of "divine fury" or poetic inspiration. Although he seems to have been well acquainted with all that had been said before his time on the subject of the virtues, the basic sources for his arguments in favor of the contemplative ones are Platonic. He says that man is composed of soul and body; that the body is the tool of the soul; and that the workman is always superior to his tool. Furthermore, the intellectual virtues, having to do with the soul and being therefore divine, are superior to the moral ones, having to do with the body, which is only the servant of the intellect. The moral virtues have their seat in the appetite; the intellectual ones, in the reason. The latter proceed from the most excellent power of the soul, and are thus most perfect. They are concerned with a completely perfect subject, divine, pure, eternal, unchangeable, and constant; whereas the moral ones have to do with human, variable, and uncertain affections and actions. But let us draw parallels by quoting some words of Desportes followed by comparable ones from Plato.

Desportes: "Pareillement fault considérer que c'est que l'homme, lequel est, en ceste mortelle vie, composé de l'âme et du corps, non pas comme le corps et ses parties mais comme l'âme ayant et tenant le mesme rang envers le corps que l'ouvrier tient envers son outil. Or n'y a-il point de comparaison de l'outil à l'ouvrier ni aussi du corps à l'âme, laquelle est l'homme mesme ... l'homme est homme par l'honneur de son âme et non pas à cause de son corps."[22]

"... plus nous avançons en la contemplation des choses divines et plus nostre desir s'enflame et se faict poignant (ardent, irrésistible) sans s'estaindre ou se reboucher par le travail que nous ne sentons point, par ainsi nous cessons moins d'espérer et sommes plus excellans et plus parfaict par les speculations."[23]

"... la contemplation est sa fin mesme et n'est aymée et désirée que pour l'amour de soy. Il est certain que le bien désiré pour l'amour de soy surpasse de beaucoup celluy qui est cherché, aymé et poursuivy pour l'amour d'une autre; car les dernières fins sont tousjours les plus excellantes."²⁴

Socrates: "And were we not saying long ago that the soul when using the body as an instrument of perception, that is to say, when using the sense of sight or hearing or some other sense ... is dragged by the body into the region of the changeable, and wanders and is confused ... But when returning into herself she reflects, then she passes into the other world, the region of purity, and eternity, and immortality, and unchangeableness, which are her kindred, and with them she ever lives, when she is by herself and is not let or hindered; then she ceases from her erring ways, and being in communion with the unchanging is unchanging. And this state of the soul is called wisdom ... When the soul and the body are united, then nature orders the soul to rule and govern, and the body to obey and serve. Now which of these two functions is akin to the divine? and which to the mortal? Does not the divine appear to you to be that which naturally orders and rules, and the mortal to be that which is subject and servant? ... The soul is the very likeness of the divine, and immortal, and intellectual, and uniform, and indissoluble, and unchangeable; and the body is in the very likeness of the human, and mortal, and unintellectual, and multiform, and dissoluble, and changeable."²⁵ Plato is here speaking of the soul, but we must understand that according to him the soul is divided into reason, spirit, and appetite.²⁶

Desportes: " ... le contemplatif ne se propose autre fin que la cognoissance de la vérité qui est la contemplation mesme, au lieu que toutes les autres vertus morales regardent à d'autres fins."²⁷ The moral virtues are full of activity and uneasiness; the intellectual ones of rest and felicity: "Or toutes les opérations des vertus morales sont plaines de travaux et d'inquiétudes ... séparez et reculez entièrement du repos et de la félicité dont ils pourroient jouir en contemplant ... ceste opération et ceste félicité, qui est plus semblable à celle qu'on attribue à Dieu, est plus excellente et plus parfaicte que les autres, qui ne luy peuvent estre appropriées. On ne peult attribuer les vertus morales à Dieu, comme il se cognoist par leur diffinition et par le siège où elles ont place, qui est la puissance de l'appétit et des passions, qui ne tombent point en Dieu."²⁸

Socrates: "Then mind and science when employed about such changing things do not attain the highest truth? ... Let us say that the stable and pure and true and unalloyed has to do with the things which are eternal and unchangeable and unmixed, or if not, at any rate what is most akin to them has; and that all other things are to be placed in a second or inferior class . . . And are not mind and wisdom the names which are to be honored most? . . . And these names may be said to have their truest and most exact application when the mind is engaged in the contemplation of true being?"[29]

Desportes explains that all living things operate, and that there are three operations: active (born from moral virtue and prudence—making perfect him who possesses them); factive (born from art by which we make something—making perfect the work of the worker); and speculative or contemplative. He goes on to say: "Mais l'opération contemplative qui procède maintenant de l'habitude des principes et s'appelle *intelligence*, maintenant de l'habitude des conclusions et s'appelle *science*, et maintenant de la *sapience*, qui est une très-parfaicte habitude de toutes les deux, rendant parfaict non seulement celluy qui a telle habitude, mais aussi la puissance de l'âme, en quoy elle se retrouve et ne se proposant autre but que soy-mesme. La contemplative dy-je, paroist, par ces conférances, plus parfaicte que les deux autres, et, par conséquant plus digne d'estre attribuée à Dieu, père et autheur de toute perfection, dont la contemplation est unicque et perpétuelle, qui s'entend soy-mesme et conséquemment toutes choses."[30] He concludes that some men are disposed in one direction, some in another; and the dispositions of men change with changing age. Middle-aged men are disposed to affairs and action; older men, to rest and contemplation: "Platon nous en a monstré l'example, qui tant de fois, en jeunesse alla en Sicile pour aider Dion et pour rendre meilleur Dionisius et ses subgects, s'il eust peu, puis vint achever ses jours au doux repos de l'Académie."[31]

Socrates: "And thought is best when the mind is gathered into herself and none of these things trouble her—neither sounds nor sight nor pain nor pleasure—when she takes leave of the body, and has as little as possible to do with it, when she has no bodily sense or desire, but is aspiring after true being?[32]

". . . the true lover of knowledge is always striving after being—that is his nature; he will not rest in the multiplicity of individuals which is an appearance only, but will go on—the keen edge will not be blunted, nor the force of his desire abate until he have attained the knowledge of the true nature of every essence by a sympathetic and kindred power of the soul, and by that power drawing near and mingling and becoming incorporate with very being, having begotten mind and truth, he will have knowledge and will live and grow truly, and then, and not until then will he cease from his travail."[33]

In the parallels which have been drawn above, the words of Desportes are not by any means paraphrases of those of Plato, and it is doubtful that our poet had the dialogues at hand when he prepared his *discours* for the Académie. It is more probable that the strong Platonic accent which we find here was due to a thorough process of "innutrition" of Platonic doctrine received through the studies of Desportes' youth and in the intervening years of intensive reading and study.[34]

Plato speaks most lovingly of the contemplative life, but from the practical viewpoint he knew that man must serve his fellowmen, and he went about doing so. Nevertheless, his words concerning the contemplative life, the turning of the mind upon itself, the reascension of the soul to the realm of the Ideas, all gave ample foundation to the Neoplatonists for their mystical tendencies. Desportes, like Plato, devoted his life to the service of his king and his fellow men, but he was an important link in the great chain which connected the revival of Platonism during the period of the Renaissance with the wave of mysticism which swept through France at the beginning of the seventeenth century.[35]

Platonism was by no means the only philosophy originating in antiquity which was rediscovered and studied by the Renaissance scholars. In their considerations of the virtues the men of Henri's Académie doubtless owed much to Epicureanism,[36] which was perfectly exemplified in the works of Lucretius and to a lesser extent in those of Horace,[37] and to Stoicism, which had greatly influenced the whole Christian attitude toward life and which was exemplified in the works of Seneca.[38] Neither of these philosophies seems to have interested Desportes in the least. He neither adopted an attitude of indifference toward life—which was by no means cruel to him—and its problems, nor did he accept the idea that pleasure is the supreme good, even though that pleasure be intellectual.

CHAPTER XI

FEAR: A PASSION OF THE SOUL

We have spoken briefly, in the immediately preceding chapter, of the interest of the Académie du Palais in the moral and intellectual virtues, and of Desportes' support of the excellency of the intellectual ones. A much greater preoccupation was shown for the passions of the soul, as one might expect of an academic group whose chief concern was with harmonizing the deep passions of an age characterized by violence, bloodshed, and civil war. One has only to look at the titles of the discourses which have been preserved to be struck by this preoccupation. They are: *Des passions humaines de la joye et de la tristesse et quelle est la plus véhémente; Des passions de l'âme et de la joye; De l'ire et comme il la faut modérer; Discours de l'honneur et de l'ambition; De l'envie et des mœurs contraires à icelle; Discours de la crainte; Discours de la cognoissance; Discours de l'âme; De l'envie; De la Vérité et du mensonge.* Most of these discourses are included in Edouard Frémy's *Académie des derniers Valois.* Several of them, however, are still in manuscript, among them one on *la Crainte* which was delivered by Desportes and which has been transcribed from the manuscript in the Bibliothèque Nationale for inclusion in this study. This transcription may be found in the appendix.

It is not within the scope of this work to go into a full discussion of the discourses on the passions of the soul as treated in the Académie du Palais. Such treatment could not be justified on the basis of the Platonic doctrine embodied in them, for the speakers owed less to Plato, in their arguments, than they did to Aristotle, Cicero, Plutarch, Seneca, and many others of the ancients, not to mention the Churchmen and the Scriptures. Even if the Platonic doctrine were more abundant, Desportes' own contribution to the discussion of the passions is limited to one discourse, so far as we know.

Our poet had devoted his greatest literary talents to the cultivation of lyric poetry founded on Platonic love. Such love is a desire for beauty and is intellectual in nature. It has to do with the immortal soul and therefore with eternal and universal values, rather than with the passions which are temporal, terrestial and corporeal, and concerned with the mortal soul. Poetry of this kind adapted itself easily to other Platonic considerations, such as those having to do with the Creator and his creation, the soul, the Ideas, beauty, the lover and the beloved, poetry, and the poet. The good *abbé's* life as well as his verse seems to have been singularly free of the strong passions and perturbations of the soul, for he led the most composed existence imaginable in the midst of court intrigues and bitter struggles going on all around him. In his only other preserved discussions before the Académie he had chosen to champion the excellency of the contemplative virtues, rather than the moral ones, thus demonstrating his preoccupation with the unchangeable and everlasting things of the intellect rather than with the changeable ones of this world. He is then stepping out of his accustomed role as advocate of the celestial when he discourses on the passion *fear*. It is only because he seems even here to be borrowing the framework of his thought from Plato that mention is made at all of this discourse, for otherwise he refers to Demosthenes, St. Augustine, Solon, Aristotle, Virgil, Cicero, Epictetus, Seneca, Plutarch, Plautus, Isocrates, Tertullian, the Stoics, Epaminondas, Fabricius, Sextus, Julius Caesar, Diogenes, Socrates, Atilius Regulus, Cato, Brutus, Cassius, Lucretia, and Horace, to support his arguments.

But let us see what Desportes owes to Plato in this discourse. He says: "toutes nos affections ce font en la puissance appetitive de nostre ame et qu'elles regardent, vissent, et s'adressent à deux obietz, au bien, & au mal." In the *Republic* we find that there are three elements of the soul: reason, spirit, and appetite. Virtue is the harmony or accord of these elements, when the dictates of reason are enforced by passion against the appetites, and vice is the anarchy or discord of the soul when passion and appetite join in rebellion against reason.[1] And again in the *Laws* we find that there are two souls, the immortal and the mortal, "at any rate, we must not suppose there are less than two—one the author of good, and the other of evil."[2] Now, as we have seen, passion—which is identified with spirit[3]—is not in itself evil. It becomes evil only when it joins with appetite in rebellion against reason. Desportes does not say that the "affections" lie in the appetitive soul, but that they "ce font" there. He goes on to say: "Car naturellement nous suivons les choses qui nous semblent bones & profitables, et fuions les mauvaises come cellez qui peuuent nuire." This is Socrates' constant contention. He asks the question: "Do not all men, my dear sir, desire good?" and he gives the answer, "Yes."[4]

After having placed fear among our "affections" Desportes proceeds to define it: "Par ainsy donc naturellement ce qui nous semblera horrible, mauvais, & nuisible, nous causera crainte, si nous avons opinion qui nous nuyse, et nous soit prochain, mesme si nous auons pensé ce qui ne se puisse eviter: mais poʳ venir à la diffinition de la crainte, Je diré que la crainte n'est autre chose qu'une perturbation du cœur, d'une tristesse née de l'imagination d'un prochain qui soit poʳ nous apporter facherye ou destruction." In these words the *abbé* is practically quoting Plato, who put into the mouth of Socrates these words: "I should particularly like to know whether you would agree with me in defining this fear or terror as expectation of evil."[5]

In setting confidence against fear Desportes says: "Viola donc deux affections differentes, la crainte et la confience, l'une nous yrite & nous pousse, l'autre qui nous retire & nous espouvante." Socrates, in the *Protagoras*, speaking of cowardice rather than fear in connection with confidence, says, when asked if he means confident men when speaking of brave ones: "Yes ... I mean the impetuous, ready to go at that which others are afraid to approach."[6] And when asked if cowards go where there is safety and the courageous where there is danger, he says that they do. Continuing on the subject of fear and confidence, Desportes says: " ... mais de toutes les deux la force les guide & les modere, remede & rassure la crainte et rabaisse & reprime la trop grande confience." He seems to be referring to the will when he speaks of "force" here. In the *Laws* we find something of the same idea, when the Athenian says: "But the formation of qualities [of the soul] he left to the wills of individuals. For everyone of us is made pretty much what he is by the bent of his desires and the nature of his soul."[7] And he goes on to say that the soul receives " ... more of good or evil from her own energy and the strong influence of others."

Desportes continues: "J'ay dit au commencement que la force estoit la moderation de cez deux passions la crainte et la confience. ... Je parleray seulement de cez craintes alentour desquelles la force n'opere point: cõme est la crainte de l'infamie de la pauvreté, des injures, des tourmans et autres semblables ... la crainte d'infamie et de deshoneur procedant d'aucun malfaict par raison est tousiours à craindre." We find in the *Laws* that there are "two kinds of fear ... fear of expected evil ... fear of evil reputation."[8] Desportes says: "Aussy *Platon* dit en premier livre des loyx qu'il y a deux choses qui font naistre la victoire l'audace envers ses ennemis et la crainte d'infamie envers ses amis." Of all the men referred to in this discourse by our poet, Plato is the only one who is quoted exactly and with reference to the dialogue from which the quotation is taken.[9]

Finally Desportes says: " . . . s'il craignent le venin, qu'ils suivent l'example de Socrates, qui le prist sans s'estoner. . . Puisque la crainte n'est autre chose qu'une opinion, et une attente du mal, celuy qui s'assure qu'aucun mal ne luy peut arriver sera franc de toute crainte." In this connection Socrates explains to Glaucon in the *Republic;* "I mean that courage is a kind of salvation." Glaucon asks: "Salvation of what?" And Socrates replies: "Of the opinion respecting things to be feared, what they are and of what nature, which the law implants through education."[10]

Thus we see that in the discourse on fear Desportes not only goes to Plato for support but quotes him specifically, proving his direct debt to him. He proves furthermore that he has a knowledge of the Platonic dialogues beyond those which were the common sources of poetic conceits for all the poets of the age.

A study of the influence of the sixteenth-century academic considerations of the passions, reason, and the will on seventeenth-century drama and on such works as Descartes' *Traité des passions de l'âme* would be of the greatest interest. However, even though such a study were to involve Platonism, it would be beyond the limits of this work.

CHAPTER XII

CONCLUDING REMARKS

Let us review briefly the points which this study of the Platonism of the epoch, life, and works of Philippe Desportes—court poet of the last of the Valois—has sought to bring out, with a view of drawing certain final conclusions.

The new learning which was introduced into France in the first years of the sixteenth century by a relatively small number of humanists, and which was cultivated so assiduously by the Pléiade, had, by the time of Desportes, spread greatly and represented a unified culture. This unified culture can best be epitomized by the one word "music." As D. P. Walker says in his review of Frances Yates's book on the French Academies: "The center of this encyclopaedic culture was music. For the Platonic sense of this word includes all the liberal arts and sciences, and this usage is backed up by the Platonic-Pythagorean metaphysic which interprets both the whole universe and the microcosm of man's soul in terms of number and harmony. Thus music, both in its more restricted, modern sense, and as the symbol of an all-embracing philosophical and educative system, naturally takes a very important place in the history of these academies."[1]

This emphasis on the musical, or harmonious, aspect of everything takes concrete form in numerous ways: in the serious role of oracle and prophet assumed by the poet; in the attempt to make of the ruler a philosopher-king; in the organization of academies and of court festivals in which the purpose was to promote harmony in the individual and in the state; in the attention given to the cultivation of friendships; and, finally, in the numerous religious *confréries* sponsored by the king which represented the final mystical outgrowth of the academic spirit.

Of all the courtiers of this age who were preoccupied with Platonism, Desportes is one of the few who seems not only to have grounded his works in Platonic doctrine but to have tried to regulate his life according to that doctrine. He was a loyal and worthy courtier but succeeded in living above the intrigues and rivalries of the opposing factions at the court of France. He was almost universally revered by his contemporaries and enjoyed the favor of the three kings under whom he lived.[2] He was born, brought up, and educated in the city of Chartres, in whose schools the teachings of Plato had been honored for many centuries. Those years were complemented by a sojourn in Italy at a time when the Renaissance movement had reached its zenith, the academic spirit was in evidence everywhere, and the *uomo di virtù* was the ideal of the courtier. He gained his first substantial fame in the refined milieu of the salon of Mme de Retz and soon became the favorite of the young duc d'Anjou, who had himself been a pupil of the great humanist and Greek scholar, Jacques Amyot. A trip to Poland with his prince sobered him, as it did the prince, and upon their return from that country the poet entered enthusiastically into the attempts of the prince to bring harmony into his realm through the encouragement of philosophical pursuits. Having taken on the responsibilities of an *abbé*, the Chartrain gave up profane verse and devoted himself to his abbeys, to the activities of the Académie, to his studies, to the accumulation of a great library, to the translation of the Psalms, and to the encouragement of young men of promise. His home at Vanvres became a veritable Careggi, where all the learned men of the age, including the king himself, gathered. His library was famous throughout France, and his fame as a man of erudition grew until he was known as the most learned man of his age.

Desportes' bibliographers, and literary historians in general, have stressed the debt he owed to the Italians. That debt was indeed great, although entirely normal for a poet of his period. When the casual reader picks up the collected works of Desportes and begins to read them with no particular object in view, he is soon fatigued by the sameness he finds in the sonnets and by the poet's preoccupation with an idealized lady who can scarcely be understood unless one thoroughly projects oneself into the particular age when these sonnets were being composed. But this is true of the sonnets of any sonnet sequence of the time, if one takes them in too large doses. To be enjoyed, the Renaissance sonneteers should be read at one's leisure. Thus and only thus can one appreciate the ingeniousness, the care, and the beauty which were compounded by the poets in their miniatures. After criticizing Desportes for his "poésies de commande," Darmesteter and Hatzfeld, in their *Seizième siècle en France*, say: "... quand il décrit ses propres émotions, il a de la délicatesse et de la grâce: ses sonnets, ses chansons, ses odes expriment avec charme la passion, la volupté, le plaisir. Son vers est harmonieux et sa langue pure et correcte, si bien que Henri Estienne le cite, à bon droit, comme un modèle de bon langage ... son plus grand mérite est l'exactitude."[3] The purity and correctness of his language cannot be overemphasized, and when one reads the verses of the Pléiade poets, and then those of Desportes, one feels the progress which the language has made under his pen.[4] In spite of his criticism of the poetry of Desportes,[5] Malherbe owed to him a considerable debt, as an important precursor in the crusade to bring clarity, simplicity, and exactitude into French verse.

As for the philosophical preoccupations reflected in the works of our poet, one is safe in saying that they are basically Platonic, if exception is made of his Petrarchism. The latter, although copious in amount, affects essentially only one aspect of the psychology of love, that is to say, a certain inequality between lover and beloved which causes sufferings and results in exaggerated lamentings. As we have seen, however, this aspect finds some justification in Plato himself, and can be rationalized, as Dante rationalized it, to fit into the Platonic picture. Desportes' whole thought concerning the creation, the soul, the Ideas, love and its personification, beauty, the lover and the beloved, the poet and poetry, and emphasis on the intellectual virtues is based on the dialogues. These subjects cover, for the most part, the possible spheres of speculation open to the love poet, and take in a large number of those which have intrigued the philosopher and the metaphysician as well. One finds the same clarity, the same exactness, in Desportes' Platonizing that one finds in his poetic expression in general. It is not limited to vague allusions to Platonic concepts and to poetic meanderings on the fringe of the Platonic. Generally speaking it stands out more sharply and more exactly than that of any other poet of the age. And yet it fits naturally into the general scheme of things and does not seem to be forced. Others may have dealt more completely with specific phases of Platonism, but none covered so many different phases.

Desportes frequently quotes Plato almost word for word, as he does when he speaks of the act of creation as being a process of bringing order out of Chaos, or when he defines love as a desire for the beautiful. On other occasions he paraphrases him in long passages, as in the case of his *Chant d'Amour*. Occasionally his Platonic concepts are hidden away in a non-Platonic setting, and only with difficulty can one recognize them for what they are. Then there are certain passages which can be classified as Platonic not because they are common only to that doctrine but because of the context in which they are found. It has been the purpose of this study to isolate not just a few illustrative examples of the Platonic concepts to be found in the works of our author, but to isolate every one of them and to classify them according to subject matter.

There is the final question as to the sources of Desportes' Platonism. We have pointed out the fact that his sources in general have been the subject of extensive studies, and that we can be reasonably sure that those works which are borrowed from some specific poet have been isolated. Except for the Petrarchan note in his poetry, these studies concerning Desportes' sources have dealt with words rather than with ideas, and until this time no one has sought any specific expression of Platonic doctrine in his works.

In the treatment of Desportes' specific use of such doctrine, we have indicated those lines involving Platonism which were borrowed from some other poet. They are comparatively few. Desportes was doubtless well acquainted with all the poets, both Italian and French, of his age, but when he Platonized he usually did so in his own words and from his own storehouse of Platonic doctrine. From where then did he get it? It is doubtful that he went to any one source. All of the great Platonic dialogues were available to the poets of his age in Greek, Latin, Italian or French, and any distinguished scholar had read them. Besides the dialogues there had already been built up a considerable Platonic literature, which included the *Commentaries* of Ficino on the various dialogues he had translated, the works of his fellow Italians, Pico della Mirandola, Leone Ebreo, Lorenzo de' Medici, Bembo, Castiglione, and Michelangelo, and in France much that had already been done in both philosophical and poetic Platonism by such persons as Symphorien Champier, Marguerite de Navarre, Maurice Scève, Héroët, and Pontus de Tyard. Our poet was almost certainly well acquainted with this accumulated literature. It seems safe to conclude, then, that he owed his knowledge of Platonic doctrine to his early studies, to his stay in Italy, to the innumerable available works on Platonistic subjects, as well as to the spirit of his age, and that he made as full a use of that knowledge as any poet of the sixteenth century in France.

APPENDIX

The following is a transcription of a discourse on *Fear* made by Desportes before the Académie du Palais. With the exception of a few sentences quoted by Jacques Lavaud in his *Philippe Desportes*[1], which have been set off by asterisks in this transcription, it has never been published. It is preserved in a manuscript volume containing ten discourses, all but two of which appear in Edouard Frémy's *l'Académie des derniers Valois*.[2] The first of these two is by an anonymous author and is on the subject of *Ambition*. The other is Desportes' discourse on *Fear*. The manuscript is the property of the Bibliothèque Nationale and is available under the catalogue number B.N., nouv. acq. franç. 4655, to anyone who wishes to see it.

The manuscript, in folio, is now in an eighteenth-century binding of red Moroccan leather, bearing the coat of arms of the king. It is approximately 15x22 cms in size. Pages 1-5 are blank; page 6 bears only the cipher R-1305; page 7, the catalogue number and the seal, Royale Bibliothèque. Only the right hand pages are numbered, and they are numbered chronologically. Desportes' discourse on *la Crainte* is found on pages 63-73 inclusive.

This manuscript lacks neatness and precision. Some insertions of words have been made above the normal line. The handwriting is fairly neat but difficult to decipher today. It is not that of Desportes, as is evident when one compares it with samples of Desportes' handwriting given in Lavaud.

In some places, where the text is marred so that some words are indistinguishable, blanks have been left in this transcription. When a reading is questionable, it is followed by a question mark.

Punctuation seems to be faulty. Colons are frequently used where we would use periods; commas are placed where they do not seem to belong, and omitted where they are needed.

Certain language peculiarities should be noted. *Ce* is frequently given as the spelling for the reflexive pronoun *se*. *Pour* is generally written *po*ʳ. *Notre* (nostre) and *votre* (vostre) are sometimes written *nre* and *vre*, respectively. *Qui* is sometimes used before such verbs as *faut* where *qu'il* would be called for today. In a few cases there is lack of agreement between subject and verb. Other sixteenth-century variations in orthography, familiar to everyone, need not be mentioned.

The sign // has been used to indicate the beginning and end of pages.

DE LA CRAINTE

Quelques anciens soulleyent dire que la crainte est le lyen de la parole, & de la raison, aduenant ordinairement a ceux qui sont trop supris de ceste passion, qu'ilz perdent l'office de la voyx, ou ce troublent et s'estõnent de telle sorte qu'ilz s'esgarent en leur pensée, & leur imagination: voyre bien souuant ilz oublient, & ne peuuent rien dire de ce qu'ilz veullent, ou qu'il ont premedité, et telz// accidens sont arriues quelque foys a des plus grans personnages et plus excellents orateurs: Come l'on dit qu'il aduint a Demostenes ayent a parler deuãt le Roy Phelipes de Macedoine, et a plusieurs autres que la presence des Roys, l'assemblée d'un Senat, ou la multitude d'un peuple a tellement estonez qu'ilz sont demeurez muetz, et n'ont aucunemẽt respondu a l'attente qu'on avoit d'eux; on ne treuuera donc pas estrange si deuant un si grãd Roy je m'estone, je suis confus, et par le changement de mon visage, & de ma voyx je mõstre la crainte & perturbation de mon esprit; au contraire Sire en ce subiet dont nous auons a parler, qui est la passion mesme de la crainte, tel lyen qui m'attache la langue, & l'estonemẽt qui m'assaut feront voyr parauanture plus clairement la force de ces effaitz que n'eüssent sceü toutes mes paroles mieux ordonnées// & plus exactement prononcées mais afin que nos dĩscours ne paroissent point monstreux n' ayent ni teste, ni bras, ni autre partye qui s'entretiene je seray constrainct de garder l'ordre accoustumé redisant parauanture les choses que vre magesté aura desia entendues, mais ce sera auec la plus grande brieueté & facillité que je pouray; nous auons veü par les lectures precedentes que toutes nos affections ce font en la puissance appetitive de nre ame et qu'elles regardent, vissent, & s'adressent a deux obietz, au bien, & au mal; a l'un po^r le suivre & pourchasser, a l'autre po^r l'euiter & fuir: Car naturellement nous suiuons les choses qui nous semblent bones & profitables, et fuions les mauuaises come celles qui nous peuuent nuire: Par ainsy donc naturellement ce qui nous semblera horible, mauuais, & nuisible, nous causera crainte, si nous auons opinion qui nous nuyse, & nous soit prochain, mesme si nous auons pensées qui ne se puissẽ euiter: mais po^r venir a la deffinition de la crainte. Je// diré que la crainte "n'est autre chose qu'une perturbation du cœur, & une tristesse née de l'imagination d'un mal prochain qui soit po^r nous apporter facherye ou destruction: Or tout ainsy qu'en l'attente d'un bien l'ame s'espanouit, s'allegre,

& s'esmeüt d'une certaine confience, ainsy de l'oppinion d'un
mal procede la terreur, & un rabayssement d'esprit qui nous
fait fuir: Voila donc deux affections differentes, la crainte
et la confience, l'une qui nous jrite & nous point, l'autre
qui nous retire & nous espouuante; mais de toutes les deux
la force les guide & les modere, remet & rassure la crainte,
et rabaisse & reprime la trop grāde confience; L'une & l'autre
de cez passions par l'excez ce changent, la crainte en timidité
& couardise, et la confience en audace & temerité; mais
sens m'arrester dauantage a chascune d'elles, et aux divisions
qui s'en sont faites, mesme par Demostene, qui en met six sortes,
je reviendray a mon subiet, disant auec St Augustin//
que la crainte ruisselle & prend son cours de ces deux sourgōs[3]
de perdre ce que nous aymons, ou n'acquerir pas ce que
nous desirons: or, est il tout certain que durant nostre vie
nous aymons tousiours quelque chose, nre ame ayent en soy
une puissance amoureuse et née po^r aymer, tout aussi qu'elle
en a pour sentir, entendre et retenir. Et la chose que nous
aymons mesme en la possedant nous n'en pouuons estre as-
surez; veü que tout ce qui est dessous la lune est sujet a
changement, mutation, et corruption: car mesme en aymant
Dieu qui est incorruptible, a cause de nos imperfections et
po^r la difficulté de ces comēdemens nous auons tousiours
crainte; De sorte que nous pouuons dire que les homẽs en
vivāt ne peuuent jamais estre delivrez de la crainte: mais
encore semble il qu'ilz ce deuroient bien contenter, et n'auroient
tant dequoi ce plaindre, si n'en estoient ——————— que d'une
sorte, au lieu qui s'en treuve infinies et dautant de façon que
leurs affections, leurs desirs, et leurs haynes sont differentes:
toutes lesquelles je m'essairé de reduire a deux genres, en
chefs principaux: "la premiere sera celle qui procede de
la nature et qui est distribuée, voyre qui est essentielle si
faut ainsy dire, en chasque nature des animaux; Aussy les//
theologiens appelle la crainte naturelle qui fait la separation
de l'ame, et du corps, et de la disipation de l'ame et disolution
du composé", laquelle est si naturelle, si coustumiere, et si
permissible que le fils de Dieu mesme, quand il vivoit entre
les hommes fremist, coñe on list aux sainctes lettres et a
l'jnstant de sa passion craignit la mort: "L'autre est
celle que nous concevons des advercitez, et des malheurs,
qui nous menassent, et nous sont prochains, lesquelz nous
estimons surpasser nos forces, ces deux sortes sont toutes deux

comprises en ceste diffinition, mais telles passions ont esté par la nature sagement doñées aux homes afin de prevoir et fuyr les choses nuisibles. Et les anciens l'ont tant estimée qui disoient la crainte, et la peine estre l'element de la vertu:" Les Efores en Lacedemone aupres de leur tribunal avoient fait bastir un temple a la crainte estimant qui//n'auoit rien qui peut mieux corriger une Republique: Solon disoit que tout ne pouuoit estre bien gouverné sans la crainte de la peine, et l'esperance du loyer: Aristote aussi a fort emplement traitté de ceste passion, monstrant quelles choses nous font plus ordinairement craindre, qui sont ceux qu'on craint, et coñe sont esmeüs les hoñes en la crainte, et dit entre autre qu'entre les maux et les perilz, que ceux sont les plus redoutez qui sont plus voysins et sont plus pres d'arriuer: ce que Virgil nous a bien voullu doñer a cognoistre en la persone d'Enée car coñe le vieillart Anchise son pere refusa d'abondoñer Troye plaine de flame, d'horreurs, de meütre, et de pillage, et qu'au contraire ce voullut enterrer soubz les ruines de sa ville, reprochant la couardisse a son filz, et a ceux qui n'alloient ce precipiter aux dangers, et a la mort. Enée po^r le forcer et l'arracher de ceste resolution, luy causer un espouuantement soudain, disoit tout a cette heure arrivera Pirus desgoustant//de tant de sang de Priam qu'il a massacré ayēt tuë le fils deuant les yeux du Pere, et le pere deuant les authelz, a la veüe des vieux: po^r que los maux prochains nous font craindre et nous espouuante daventage, comme aussy les signes et presages qui nous peuuent denoncer la veüe de ces maux, nos estoñent semblablement et nous esmeuuent, ainsy que les comettes, les tremblements de terre, les visions, les voyx jncertaines, les monstres, et les signes d'orage et de tourmente a ceux qui sont sur mer, le henissement des chevaux, voire la passion a ceux qui ont querellé, et brief toute sorte de marques qui peuuent doñer opinion des choses horible et nuisibles entre lesquelles//on peut bien mettre la haine et le courroux, ou le desdain de ceux qui ont puissance de nuire: Car s'il est ainsy que les actions de l'hoñe despendēt du voulloir et de la puissance, quand l'un et l'autre ce treuue en quelque un, lequel nous auons offencé certainement il y a grand occasion de craindre le mal, et le vangance prochaine, coñe quand nous avons fait desplaisir a gens riches plains d'eloquence, d'entendement ou d'authorité: Et surtout font craindre les hoñes de vertu, courageux, et

vallureux quand ils ont la puissance ou qu'ils sont offensez;
Ce que Ciceron veut signifier en une de ces epitres a Atticus
quand il monstre de craindre bien fort que Pompée out-
ragé de ces ennemis ne deviene cruel a sa patrie: Il montre
apres qu'il y a des sortes de gens qui ne craignent point//
c'est a sçavoir les desesperez, lesquels sont asseuréz qu'ils ne
peuuent faillir que mal ne leur arrive, et ceux qui pensent avoir
desià supporté et estre au comble des plus grandes engoises
et calamitez: Car au contraire ils souhaite la mort, et bien
souuent ce la donnent: Comme fist la malheureuse Didon
ce voyant abandonnée d'Enée et desesperant de pouuoir
souffrir les angoisses de son absence: Et peü apres elle ce
repent de n'avoir mis le feü dans ces vaisseäux de ne l'avoir
desmembré par pieces, et jetté dans la mer, de n'avoir fait
tuer ces gens, et son filz Ascagne po^r luy avoir fait manger:
puis elle dit qu'ay-je a craindre estant certaine de mourrir//
Mais je demeürerois trop si je me voullois arrester sur tous
points touchez par Aristote, ou si j'entreprenois toucher
particullierement de tant de craintes differentes, auxquelles
parasuanture nous fournissõs de boys et de matiere po^r les
alumer par nos trop desreglées et immoderées affections et
convoitises: Car pour aymer plus qui ne faut les grandeurs,
les richesses, les voluptez en ceste vie miserable nous tumbons
en des vains espouuentemens, craignãts d'estre privez des
choses qui nous sont cheres: Et de tant plus que nous les aymons ardenment aduient que plus sommes nous naurez, et
blessez de ceste passion, laquelle bien souuant est fauce, et
prise sans cause: Il faudroit po^r la moderation d'jcelle moderer cez autres affectiõs, n'aymer, ni hair trop. Sinon ce
qui veritablement seroit aymable, vertueux et bon, ou qui
seroit mauvais, vicieux et digne d'estre hay: Enquoy je se-
rois d'avis//d'ensuiure le conseil d'Epictete examinant bien
soigneusement les choses qui sont süres, et en notre puissance
come les artz, les sciences, les bonnes oppinions, les vertus, et
autres excellentes qualitez qui sont de substance incorruptible
et qui ne nous peuuent estre derobée: prenant garde d'autre
part de celles qui sont externes, et desquelles nous ne deuons
point faire d'estat, parce qu'elles despendent d'autry, et par
consequent nous ne deuons point tant mettre nre affection;
come nos œuvres, les biens de la fortune, les richesses, les
grandeurs et autres semblables qui regardẽt seulement le pire,
et la plus forte partie de nous: Car quand ceste immoderée

affection qu'on leur porte cessera, ou poʳ le moins sera reglée, ou moderée, que nous ne les aymions que cõme//il faut, la poignante crainte de les perdre, ce rebaissera et si la possession ne cesse du tout, elle ce moderera de beaucoup, laquelle autrement nous rendroit tousiours malheureux, et tourmentez: Seneque disoit si on craint autant que l'on peut, jamais il n'aura de borne ni di mesure a nos miseres: il faut que les choses fortuites despendent de nous, et non au contraire nous d'elles: afin que la continuelle crainte du mal aduenir ne nous oste pas le bien present: Beäucoup de choses nos font craindre plus qu'ils ne doiuent, beaucoup deuant qu'elles deücent, et beäucoup d'autres qui ne le deuroient pas du tout: ne soions donc point miserables deuant le temps, et n'accordons pas si facilement a nre opinion qui nous estoñe bien souuant poʳ ces choses qui ne sont point beaucoup a craindre: cõme ceux que la pouciere esmeüe par un troupeäu de bestes ou la rumour incertaine, ont mainte foys fait abandoñer//le camp: Celuy craint et ce tourmente plus qu'il n'est de besoing qui craint deuant qui soit necessaire: Je ne veux pas conseiller la negligence, et peü de soing. Car au contraire j'enseigne et conseille de considerer diligement et de bone heure, par une salutaire prevoience, a ce qui nous peut nuire, poʳ le destourner, enquoi la confience me semble plus propre que la crainte. qui nous fait a tous momens changer de conseil, et nous rend laches et paresseux: Aussi Ciceron appelle la parresse crainte de labeur et de travail, estant la propre des timides de perdre le courage, entendant qu'il faut entreprendre quelque acte laborieux: Et poʳ le moindre obstacle qui arrive ilz s'estonent et demeurent despourueüs de tout conseil: Car cõme dit Plutarque entre les maladyes et passions de l'ame, il y en a plusieurs qui ont//je ne sçay quoy de haut et d'esleué, et ni en a pas une, par maniere de dire, qui soit destituée du mouvement actif; mais c'est le comun blasme qu'on doñe a toutes passions qu'avec leur ayguillon actif, elles pressẽt et viollẽt si fort la raison, qu'elle la forcent, excepté la peur seule laquelle, desnué de raison, et d'assurance a un estourdissement, et allienassion du bon sens, estant cõme morte sans exploit, ni effet quelconque: Ce que je confirmerois par maints exemples et authoritez que j'omets poʳ n'estre trop long, me contentant de ces deux passages de Plaute qui monstre assez come elle nous asomme, & nous fait perdre toute cognoissance: Je suis, dit il, tout remply de peur que je ne sçay en quel lieu je suis, ni moy miserable ne puis mouuoir po᷊ la crainte qui est en moy: Et en un autre endroit: je ne suis ni mort ni vif et ne sçay ce que je deuiendré, ce que je feray, ni ou j'yré// tant je suis remply de peur. J'ay dit au commencement que la force estoit la moderation de cez deux passions la crainte et la confience et sembleroit que parlant de les moderer, je deüsse descourir de la force, ce que je ne veux faire, remettant a en traitter en son ranc: Je parleray seulement de cez craintes alentour desquelles la force n'opere point: Cõme est la crainte de l'jnfamie de la pouureté, des jniures, des tourmãs et autres semblables: Car la force n'agit qu'a l'entour de choses qu'il faut quelque fois craindre et quelque fois non, cõme la crainte d'jnfamie et de deshoneür procedãt d'aucun malfaict, par raison est tousiours a craindre: Par ainsy la force ne la regarde point, mais les autres craintes de la pauureté, de la prison, de l'exile, et//des tourmens, pourueü qu'elle n'arrive point par nre faute, pource que ce sont choses externes et qui ne sont pas en notre puissance, si nous voulons croire les Stoiciens et ceux mesme de nre religion, ce ne sont point choses qu'il faille craindre, ni qui soient mauuaises, ni vicieuses puis qu'elles arrivent quelque fois, aux plus gens de bien: Et celuy qui les supporte avec un esprit moderé ne ce dira pas fort, fais temperat, et magnanine: Il est vray que si pauureté, jniure, ou tourment, nous arrive par nre faute, elle sont a blasmer et a craindre: Et ceste crainte de deshonneur procedant du malfaict, est celle qui faut principallement euiter, suiuant la maxime d'Jsocrate qu'on doit plus tost craidre l'ignominie que le peril: Aussy Platon dit en premier livre des loyx qu'il y a deux choses qui//font naistre la victoire l'audace envers ces ennemis et la crainte d'infamie envers cez amis: Tertullien dit que la crainte est le fondement de salut: C'est ceste crainte-la po᷊ laquelle nous ne deuons point craindre toute sorte de perilz, ni perte de richesse, de faveurs et d'authoritez, ni la mort mesme quand il en sera besoing, ne treuuant rien de facheux ni horrible que ce qui est deshoneste, et vicieux: Quand nous serons arriuez a ceste perfection, alors serons nous deliurez par un repos d'esprit, de tant de tourmens, et de defraieurs continuelles qui ne nous abandonnent jamais si nous laissons aller a l'opinion, nous estonant des coups de la fortune qui ne nous doit point fere de peur quand nous serons bien armez et ramparez de la vertu, laquelle les Stoitiens ont dit estre ——— de cognoistre les//choses qui faut, ou ne faut pas craindre: Ceux qui redoute si fort la pauureté qui ni a vice, ou trahisson qui ne comettent po^r s'enricher: qu'ilz regardent Epaminondas, qu'ils contemple Fabricius, cest excellēt capitaine Romain desdaignant les richesses: Celuy qui boira en public dans des vaiseäux de terre, ne se soucira d'en avoir d'or: Ceux qui briguent les honneurs et authoritez qui ce represente Sextus refusant ceux qui luy estoient offerts de Jules Cesar: Jugant bien sagement que tout ce qui nous estoit donné, nous pouuoit estre aussy osté: S'il redoute l'exil, qu'ils voyent que le banissement de Diogene donna commencement a la Philosophie: S'ilz craignent le feü qu'ils jettent l'œyl sur sur Mutius Ceuola [Mucius Scaevola] qui courageusement ce brusla la main et le bras: s'ils craignent le venin, qu'ils suiuent l'exemple de Socrate, qui le prist sans s'estoñer: Atilius Regule// ne craint pas la croix, ni les tourmens, et Caton ce tua luy mesme voiant mourir sa republique: Mais peut estre deuois je obmettre cez exemples, po^r la diversité des opinions qui sont entre les hoñes, les uns soustenāt que ce Caton, Brute, Cassie et Lucrece Romaine, et tant d'autres persoñages qui se sont tuez pour ne suruiure apres leur patrie, pour ne tomber entre les mains de leurs ennemis, ou po^r la juste douleur d'un deshonneur receü, ont faict acte, d'hoñes forts: Les autres au contraire assurent que telles viollences deuoit plus tost estre attribuées a la crainte et a la timidité, estant signe d'un courage lache et craintif de ce tuer pour fuir les adversitez: Veü qu'en tous temps, et en toute fortune il y a tousiours lieu po^r la vertu: Mais ces debats demanderoit plus de temps qu'il ne nous est permis, po^r les raisons qui s'allegent d'une part// et d'autre "je ne m'estendré plus loing po^r mettre fin a ce discours sans m'arrester a la nature, aux effaitz et aux exemples de l'audace et de la timidité desquelz je remetz a parler a quand nous discourrōs de la force, Je recouvrerez a dire que puis que la crainte n'est autre chose qu'une opinion, & une attente du mal, celuy qui s'assure qu'aucun mal ne luy peut arriver sera franc de toute crainte: Or est il que l'hoñe juste & vertueux ne doit point estimer qu'il y ayt aucun mal en la vie que l'offence, & le peché et par consequēt ne doit point avoir de peur que rien luy puisse arriver d'horrible que merite d'estre craint:" Car coñe disoit Horace si tout le monde tombe par piece que les ruines en la frapant & l'assomant le treuueroit sans peur et sans crainte:

Si Totus Illabatur Orbis Impavidum Feriēt Ruinae.[4]

NOTES

CHAPTER I

1. See note 14, Introduction.
2. *The French Academies of the Sixteenth Century* (London: The Warburg Institute, 1947), p. 20.
3. See Jules Alexandre Clerval, *Ecoles de Chartres* (Paris: A. Picard et fils, 1895), p. 29.
4. *Ibid.*, p. 118.
5. Frances Yates, *op. cit.*, p. 87.
6. Jules Alexandre Clerval, *op. cit.*, pp. 250 ff.
7. (London: J. M. Dent & Co., 1902), p. 286.
8. Lavaud, *op. cit.*, p. 5.
9. *Histoire de la poésie française* (Paris: Boivin et Cie, n. d.), I, 96.
10. This work was written between 1514 and 1518 and published in Venice in 1528. It was translated into French by Jacques Colin in 1537.
11. *Op. cit.*, p. 96,
12. Lavaud, *op. cit.*, p. 8.
13. *Ibid.*, p. 437.
14. Henri had had as tutor Jacques Amyot, the celebrated Hellenist, churchman, scholar, and translator of the works of Plutarch into French. The following is a letter from Amyot to Pontus de Tyard, one of the king's protégés and readers: "Monsieur de Bissy, ie fus bien aise, laultre iour que ie receu vostre lettre du 27 d'aoust, dentendre lhoneste occupation que prent le Roy de vous ouyr discourir de la constitution & mouuement du ciel, & que vous aiez trouué par experience ce quaultre fois ie vous en auois dit touchant la capacité de son entendement, laquelle il tient du Roy Françoys, son grand pere, desireux dapprendre & entendre toutes choses haultes & grandes. Iay eu lhonneur de luy auoir monstré les premieres lettres, mais ie ne manié iamais esprit denfant qui me samblast plus propre subiect pour en faire quelque iour vn bien sçauant homme, s'il eust continué en la façon destudier que ie luy auois commancée: car, oultre les parties de lentendement quil a telles que lon les scauroit desirer, il a la patience douyr, de lire & descrire, ce que son grand pere nauoit pas."
Quoted by Marty-Laveaux in the *Notice* of his edition of *Les Œuvres poétiques de Pontus de Tyard* (Paris. Alphonse Lemerre, 1875), pp. xxii-xxiii.
15. Pierre de L'Estoile, *Mémoires-Journaux de...* (Paris: Librairie des Bibliophiles, 1875-83), *passim*.
16. Théodore-Agrippa d'Aubigné, *Œuvres complètes de...* (Paris: A. Lemerre, 1873-92), *passim*.
17. Philippe Desportes, *Œuvres de...*, ed. Alfred Michiels (Paris: Adolphe Delahays, 1858), p. 456. This edition is divided into the following books: *Diane I: Diane II; Les Amours d'Hippolyte; Cléonice; Elégies I; Elégies II; Imitations de l'Arioste; Diverses Amours; Bergeries et Masquarades; Epitaphes; Prières et autres Œuvres Chrestiennes.* Hereafter reference to Michiels' biography of Desportes or to the works of the poet

in this edition will simply be to Michiels or to some particular book of poems.

18. These poems are. La terre nagueres glacee. . . (*Diane II*, "Complainte," p. 84); Las que nous sommes miserables. . .(*Diverses Amours*, "Chanson," p. 416); Ah Dieu! que c'est un estrange martire. . .(*Div. Am.*, "Dialogue," p. 380).

19. Lavaud, *op. cit.*, p. 72.

20. In the *Avant-propos* of his book, *Le Pétrarquisme en France au XVIe siècle* (Montpellier: Coulet et fils, 1909), Joseph Vianey points out that there were three such waves: that which affected the works of Marot and Saint-Gelais; that which began in 1549 with Du Bellay's *Olive;* and that of which Desportes is the greatest representative. Platonism had also enjoyed several periods of popularity.

21. *Op. cit.*, p. 80.

22. *Ibid.*, p. 41.

23. Pierre Champion says in his "Henri III et les écrivains de son temps," *Bibliothèque d'Humanisme et Renaissance* (Paris: Librairie E. Droz, 1941), I, 52, that a favorite topic of conversation between these two men was Aristotle's *Poetica*, of which Louis Le Roy had made a translation in French especially for Henri.

24. See Edouard Frémy, *L'Académie des derniers Valois* (Paris: Ernest Leroux, 1887), pp. 96-98.

25. See Frances Yates, *op. cit.*, p. 152-53.

26. *Op cit.*, pp. 64-65.

27. This poem is reproduced in Michiels, p. 491. A few lines of it follow:
Orpheus hinc ieras alter, testudine mulcens
Clyaneæ cautis sibi concurrentia saxa:
Teque lyram pulsante tuus novus alter Iason
Henricus rediit, glaciali sospes ab Arcto,
Magna viæ refersens sibi præmia parta suisque,
Ipse duplex regnum, duplicem sua turba favorem.
Hos inter primum tibi Musa fidelis honorem
Jure dedit, sibi quem non æmulus occupet alter.

28. Quoted by Frémy, *op. cit.*, p. 86.

29. *Op cit.*, p. xlv.

30. See *The Universe of* . . ., ed. John C. Lapp (Ithaca: Cornell U. Press, 1950), p. xxii.

31. Yates, *op. cit.*, p. 111.

32. *Ibid.*, p. 124.

33. *Op cit.*, p. 126.

34. Quotation from *Bibliographie et Prosographie des rois de France*, 1583. See *op. cit.*, p. 65.

35. *Op cit.*, I, 458.

36 See *Œuvres complètes de* . . ., ed. Paul Laumonier (Paris: Hachette et Cie, 1914-19), III, 193-94.

37. See Yates, *op. cit.*, p. 276.

38. See ed. Maizeaux (Amsterdam: P. Brunel *et al*, 1740), II, 730 ff.

39. This poem—*Aventure première*, Michiels, p. 307 ff.—records a love tryst of three young princes and three princesses, still in their teens, in an out of the way corner of the palace.

40. André Lévêque, *Histoire de la civilization française* (New York: Henry Holt, 1940), p. 123.

41. Both Epernon and Joyeuse were made dukes, and the latter was married to a sister of the queen.

42. The following is from a *pasquil* recorded by L'Estoile, *op. cit.*, pp. 38 ff.:

>Le Roy estoque ses mignons,
>Les fait de son lit compagnons
>Et puis laisse ceste maniere,
>Pour enfoncer sa belle-mere.
>
>. . . . .
>Tu ne vis jamais tant de choses
>Qui dedans Paris sont encloses!
>
>. . . . .
>Que ce sont de beaux compagnons
>Que le Roy et tous ses mignons!
>Ils ont le visage un peu palle,
>Mais sont-ils femelle ou masle?
>Car ils servent tous d'un mestier.

43. Quoted by James A. Notopoulos, *The Platonism of Shelley* (Durham: Duke U. Press, 1949), p. 102.

44. See his *The Philosophy of Marsilio Ficino*, trans. into English by Virginia Conant (New York: Columbia U. Press, 1943), chap. XIII, passim.

45. Fictitious names given to two of the ladies sung by Desportes.

46. The maréchale de Retz.

47. Lavaud, *op. cit.*, p. 131.

48. *Epitaphes*, p. 483.

49. *Op. cit.*, p. 43.

50. *Epitaphes*, pp. 480-81.

51. *Diane II*, sonnet 64.

52. Lavaud, *op. cit.*, p. 242.

53. Faguet says, *op. cit.*, p. 97: "Desportes couvrit de ses ailes le jeune débutant, le convertit au catholicisme, c'est-à-dire à la monarchie et à la cour et s'en fit un ami qui fut toujours fidèle et qui du reste lui fit honneur."

54. See Lavaud, op cit., p. 334, quoted from Du Perron, *Les Diverses Œuvres de l'illustrissime cardinal Du Perron* (Paris: A. Estienne, 1622), p. 650.

55. *Ed. cit.*, p. xl.

56. See Lauvaud, *op. cit.*, p. 329, quoted from Jacques-Auguste de Thou, *Mémoires* (Paris, 1838), pp. 321-22.

57. Ibid., p. 378, quoted from Guillaume de Baïf, *Le Faict du proces de Baif*. . .(Fontainebleau, 1609), pp. 6-7.

58. See Maturin Régnier, *Œuvres complètes de* . . ., ed. Plattard (Paris: F. Roches, 1930), p. 24.

59. See Michiels, pp. 527-33.

60. See the marquis de Racan's *Vie de Malherbe* (Paris: Thiboust et Esclasson, 1672), p. 11.

61. See F. Brunot, *La Doctrine de Malherbe d'après son Commentaire sur Desportes* (Paris: G: Masson, 1891), pp. 82-84.
62. See Frémy, *op. cit.*, p. 104-5.
63. See ed. of Loeb Classical Library (New York: G. Putnam & Sons, 1920), I, x, 30-33.
64. Unpubl. Ph.D. dissertation (Yale University, 1948), I, 21-22.
65. See Constantin Photiades, *Ronsard et son luth* (Paris, 1925), p. 20.
66. See Lapp ed. of his *Universe* (Ithaca: Cornell U. Press, 1950), p. xxvii.
67. See Frémy, *op. cit.*, pp. 39-40.
68. *Op. cit.*, p. 7.
69. *Op. cit.*, p. 243.
70. Fernand Baldensperger in his "Siège de Rouen (1591-92) et son importance pour l'information de Shakespeare," *Comparative Literature Studies*, III (1941), suggests that the coterie of Marguerite de Navarre at Nérac was of interest to the English poet. It will be remembered too that *Love's Labour's Lost* has to do with a group of men who form a sort of *academe* and go into a solitary spot for the purpose of contemplation. See in particular Act I, scene i, 11. 71-85.
71. The most important of these groups were: *Congrégation des Pénitents de l'Annonciation de Notre Dame*, which placed its stress on the importance of music; *Ordre du Saint-Esprit*, which applied romantic and chivalric rules of the medieval military and knightly orders to the ills of the times, and entertained its initiates for two days with concerts; *Maison de Charité*, an orphanage, school, and hospital, where the orphans were instructed in ways to relieve the sick and the poor; *Confrérie de Sainte Cécile*, an association for the cultivation of religious music; *Confrérie d'Hieronymites*, whose members wore the habits of friars and spent their time in contemplation.
72. See Yates, *op. cit.*, p. 161.
73. See Michiels, p. 529.
74. See Lavaud, *op. cit.*, p. 474, quoted from *Bulletin de la Société de l'histoire du Protestantisme français*, XLV (1896), 199.
75. Sainte-Beuve said of our poet: "Plus on regarde dans la vie de Desportes, plus on y trouve d'abbayes." See William A Nitze and Preston Dargan, *A History of French Literature* (New York: Henry Holt, 1938), p. 188. At one time Desportes held the abbeys of Tiron, Josaphat, Vaux-de- Cernay, and Bonport.
76. See Lavaud, *op. cit.*, p. 383.
77. *Ibid.*, p. 437.
78. *Ibid.*, p. 439, quoted from the *Lettre de Pomponne à Bévilliers sur la mort de son frère*, B. N., ms, fr. 15894, fol. 611.
79. *Ibid.*, p. 409, quoted from Scévole de Sainte-Marthe, *Eloges des hommes illustres*...(Paris: A. de Sommaville et A. Courbé, 1644), p. 527.
80. *Ibid.*, 418. Lavaud points out, pp. 410 ff., that the good abbé was very liberal in permitting the humanists and scholars of his day to make use of his library.
81. *Œuvres complètes de* . . ., ed. Paul Laumonier (Paris A. Lemerre, 1914-19), VI, 23.
82. *Ibid.*, I, 295.

83. *Amours d'Hippolyte,* p. 130.
84. Brunot, *op. cit.,* p. 237
85. (Oxford: The Clarendon Press, 1910), p. 212.
86. Lavaud says, *op. cit.,* p. 179: "Au total, sur 631 pièces que contient l'édition Michiels, 191 ont été prises chez les Italiens ou les Espagnols."
87. (Cambridge, Mass: Harvard U. Press, 1942), pp. 261-62.
88. The following works have been devoted to the subject:
Anonymous, *Rencontre des Muses de France et d'Italie* (Lyon, J. Roussin, 1604).

C. B. Beall, "Un Echo de Guinicelli dans Philippe Desportes," *Modern Language Notes,* LVII ((1942), 429 ff.

————, "La Fortune du Tasse en France," *Studies in Literature and Philosophy,* IV (1942).

Alice Cameron, "Desportes et Ariosto; Additional Sources in the Orlando and the Liriche," *MLN,* L (1935), 174-78.

————, "Notes on Desportes and Du Bellay; with Text of the Poem *Complainte,*" *MLN,* L (1935), 378-80.

Al Cioranescu, *Les Imitations de l'Arioste de Philippe Desportes* (Paris: 1936).

R. J. Clements, "Desportes and Petrarch," *Romanic Review,* XXXVI (1945), 103-12.

F. Flamini, *Studi di storia letteraria italiana e straniera* (Livorno: Tip. di R. Giusti, 1895), pp. 347 ff.

François Grudé, sieur de La Croix du Maine, *Les Bibliothèques françoises de La Croix du Maine et de Du Verdier* (Paris: Saillant et Nyon, 1772-73), II, 239-42.

J. Hutton, "Three Notes on French Authors: Desportes, Guéroul, Ronsard," *MLN,* LV (1940), 579-81.

L. E. Kastner, "Desportes et Angelo di Costanzo," *Revue d'Histoire Littéraire* (1908), 113 ff.

————, "Desportes et Guarini," *RHL,* 1910, pp. 124 ff.

Gustave Lanson, "Etudes sur les rapports de la littérature française et de la littérature espagnole au XVIIe siècle," *RHL,* 1897, pp. 61-72.

E. G. Matthews, "Gil Polo, Desportes and Lyly's *Cupid and my Campaspe,*" *MLN,* LVI (1941), 606-7.

Marcel, Raymond, *L'Influence de Ronsard sur la poésie* (Paris: H. Champion, 1927), II, 78-109.

J. G. Scott, "Encore un imitateur de Desportes," *Revue de la littérature comparée,* V (1925), 471-73.

F. Torraca, *Gl'imitatori stranieri di Jacopo Sannazaro* (Rome Loescher, 1883), pp. 36 ff.

H. Vaganay, "Du nouveau sur Desportes: Desportes et Malherbe," *Bulletin du Bibliophile,* 1928, pp. 502-506.

J. Vianey, *Le Pétrarquisme en France au XVIe siècle* (Paris: Coulet et fils, 1909), chap. III ff.

————, "Un Modèle de Desportes non-signalé encore: Pamphilo Sasso," *RHL,* X (1903), 277-82.

————, "Une Rencontre des Muses de France et d'Italie demeurée inédite," *RHL,* 1906, pp. 92-100.

89. Michiels, pp. 527-33.

CHAPTER II

1. A distinction will be made between Platonism and Neoplatonism only when necessary to the clear understanding of the subject matter under consideration.
2. *Op. cit.*, p. 13.
3. The word "naifvement" here refers to the divine inspiration of the poet and was commonly used with this meaning by Renaissance poets.
See R. J. Clements, *op. cit.*, chap. V, *passim*.
4. *Op. cit.*, p. 111.
5. Hereafter when reference is made to one of the dialogues of Plato its title alone will be given. Quotations from Plato are from the Benjamin Jowett translation, *The Dialogues of Plato* (New York: Random House, 1937), in which the pagination follows that of Stephanus (Henri Estienne).
6. *Timaeus*, 27, 28, 48.
7. *Ibid*, 29.
8. *Ibid.*, 30.
9. *Republic*, X, 597.
10. *Timaeus*, 40.
11. *Ibid.*, 48.
12. *Ibid.*, 48.
13. *The Holy Bible*, Douay version (New York: P. J. Kennedy & Sons, 1948), Genesis 1:1-2.
14. I am indebted to Dr. Paul Friedlander for pointing out "a remarkable fusion (not confusion) of the two," and for other valuable suggestions in the interpretation of these lines.
15. Sonnet 7; imitated from the Italian poet Copetta. See J. Vianey, *Le Pétrarquisme en France au XVIe siècle* p. 304.
16. *Timaeus*, 28-29.
17. Thomas H. Billings, *The Platonism of Philo Judaeus* (Chicago: U. of Chicago Press, 1919), p. 27. Also see note 10 of the Introduction.
18. Ode, pp. 509 ff.
19. P. lxxxi.
20. *Op. cit.*, p. 148.
21. *Timaeus*, 31, 32, 52, 53.
22. *Diane I*, pp. 50-53.
23. 29-30.
24. 197.
25. *Diane I*, pp. 50-53.
26. *Ibid*.
27. See note 25.
28. 28-29, 32.
29. See note 15.
30. *Diane I*, sonnet 51.
31. See his *Universe, ed. cit.*, p. 54.
32. *Ibid.*, p. 8.
33. *Timaeus*, 34.
34. Ode, pp. 509 ff.
35. *Amours d'Hippolyte*, pp. 134-36.
36. *Œuvres chrestiennes*, pp. 509-12.

37. *Amours d'Hippolyte*, pp. 172-73.
38. *Timaeus*, 29-30.
39. *Gorgias*, 468.
40. *Timaeus*, 49.
41. *Amours d'Hippolyte*, pp. 134-36.
42. *Timaeus*, 38.
43. Chaps. I and II.
44. *Timaeus*, 28, 37, 38.
45. *Diane I*, pp. 50-53.
46. *Ibid.*, sonnet 41.
47. *Timaeus*, 32.
48. *Diane I*, pp. 50-53.
49. *Timaeus*, 32-33.
50. *Ibids.*, 31-32.
51. See Cicero, *De republica*, VI; Plutarch, *De musica;* Macrobius, *Commentary on Cicero's Somnium Scipionis*, ii, 1. 1-8; Ficino, *Commentary on Plato's Symposium* (Jaynes' trans.), pp. 174 ff. and 181; Leone Ebreo, *Dialoghi d'amore*, second dialogue; Du Bellay, *Hymne de la surdité*, ed. Marty-Laveaux, II, 404.
52. 617.
53. *Amour d'Hippolyte*, sonnet 78.
54. Aristotle did not believe in the harmony of the spheres.
55. *Paradiso*, Canto primo, vv. 76-84.
56. See *Republic*, *II*, 376; *Timaeus*, 28.
57. *Timaeus*, 41.
58. 79.
59. *Ethics*, Book I, chap. 7.
60. "The Platonism in Pontus de Tyard's *Erreurs Amoureuses*," *Modern Philology*, XXXV (1937), 151.
61. *Enneads*, I, ii, 6. See Grace H. Turnbull, *The Essence of Plotinus;* extracts. . .based on trans. by Stephen Mackenna (New York: Oxford U. Press, 1934).
62. Trans. by W. V. Cooper, ed. Temple Classics (London: J. M. Dent, 1940), p. 82.
63. *Le Rime de Francesco Petrarca* (Firenze: Barbéra, 1882), "Sonneti e canzoni in vita di Madonna Laura," sonnet 10.
64. Girolamo Benivieni, *Canzone dell'amore divino* (Ode of Love), as reproduced in *Modern Philology*, VIII (1911), 545-60.
65. See Abel Lefranc, *Grands écrivains français de la Renaissance*, "Marguerite de Navarre et le Platonisme de la Renaissance," pp. 1 ff.
66. *Les dernières poésies de* . . ., ed. A. Lefranc (Paris: Colin, 1896), p. 296.
67. Ed Michel François (Paris: Garnier frères, 1942), pp. 151-52.
68. 509.
69. *Epitaphes*, pp. 487-89.
70. *Prière en form de confession*, pp. 514-17.
71. *Œuvres chrestiennes*, Sonnets spirituels, 2; imitated from the Italian Daniello. See J. Vianey, *Le Pétrarquisme en France* . . . p. 304.
72. (Paris: Boivin & Cie, 1928), chap. VIII.

73. *Amours d'Hippolyte*, pp. 172-73.
74. *Œuvres chrestiennes*, pp. 498-99.
75. 40 ff.
76. *The City of God*, trans. by Marcus Dods (New York: Modern Library, 1950), Book Fourth, p. 132. See also Book Twelfth, chaps. XXV, XXVI.
77. *Elégies I*, Elégie 2.
78. See *Apology*, 27 ff.
79. See *Statesman*, 271.
80. See *Symposium*, 202.
81. See *Phaedo*, 108.
82. *Timaeus*, 41.
83. *Diane I*, pp. 48-50.
84. P. 470.
85. Sixth Speech, chap. III, pp. 184 ff.
86. 899.
87. 41.
88. *Diane I*, pp. 48-50.
89. *Phaedrus*, 246.

CHAPTER III

1. 34.
2. *Ibid.*, 41.
3. *Ibid.*
4. *Ed. cit.*, Fourth Speech, chaps. III-IV.
5. *Elégies I*, Elégies 2.
6. *Amours d'Hippolyte*, pp. 175-77.
7. *Œuvres chrestiennes*, pp. 514-17.
8. 42.
9. 961.
10. Bréhier, *op. cit.*, chap. IV, *passim*.
11. See Introduction to *Saint Thomas Aquinas* (New York: Modern Library, 1848), Question lxxix, First Article, p. 336.
12. *Diane II*, pp. 113-14.
13. *Amours d'Hippolyte*, pp. 124-25.
14. See Bréhier, *op. cit.*, chap. III, *passim*.
15. *Diane I*, sonnet 41.
16. 511.
17. 184, 201 ff.
18. 510-11.
19. *Diane I*, pp. 53-57; imitated from Petrarch, *ed. cit.*, "Sonetti e canzoni in morte di Madonna Laura, canzone 7.
20. 42.
21. *Diane I*, pp. 66-67; imitated from Tansillo. See Flamini, *Studi di storia letteraria*...(Livorno, 1895), p. 359.
22. *The Platonism of Joachim Du Bellay* p. 32. Also see Dante's' *Paradiso*, IV, 49 ff.
23. Canto quinto.
24. P. 470.

NOTES 165

25. *Epitaphes*, p. 472.
26. 247, 248, 250.
27. *Enneads*, IV, iii, 7.
28. *Ibid.*, 20.
29. *Ibid.*, 6.
30. See *Phaedrus*, 246, 248, also for treatment of wings of soul.
31. *Enneads*, IV, viii, 1; also see *Gorgias*, 493; *Cratylus*, 400; *Republic*, VII, 514.
32. *Dernières poésies*, ed. Lefranc, pp. 121 ff.
33. *Epitaphes*, pp. 487-89.
34. *Œuvres chrestiennes*, sonnet 18; imitated from Petrarch, "Sonetti e canzoni in morte di Madonna Laura," sonetto 85.
35. *Elégies I*, Elégie 5.
36. 253 ff.
37. *Amours d'Hippolyte*, sonnet 65.
38. 246, 251.
39. Psalms of David, CXXXIX, 8-10.
40. *Rime, ed. cit.* "In morte di Madonna Laura," Canzone VII, pp. 344 ff.
41. *Rime di Michelangelo Buonarroti*, ed. Biagioli (Paris: Presso l'Editore, 1821), sonnet 22.
42. *Diane I*, pp. 53-57. See chap. III, note 19.
43. *Cléonice*, sonnet 17; imitated from Costanzo. See J. Vianey, *op. cit.*, p. 197.
44. *Ibid.*, sonnet 25; imitated from the Italian Costanzo. See J. Vianey, *op. cit.*, p. 197.
45. *Ibid.*, sonnet 26.
46. *Amours d'Hippolyte*, pp. 124-25.
47. *Ibid.*, sonnet 78.
48. *Cleonice*, sonnet 94; imitated from Bernardo Tasso. See Lavaud, *op. cit.*, pp. 267-82.
49. 41.
50. 81.
51. 249.
52. *Op. cit.*, pp. 93-94.
53. *Ed. cit.*, sonnet 7.
54. *Commentary on the Symposium*, Fourth Speech, chap. IV.
55. *Ibid.*, pp. 205 ff.
56. *The Philosophy of Love* (Dialoghi d'Amore), trans. by F. Friedeberg-Seeley and Jean H. Barnes (London: The Soncino Press, 1937), p. 391.
57. *Dernières poésies, ed. cit.*, Livre second, fol. 285.
58. *Œuvres poétiques de* . . ., ed. Ferdinand Gohin, (Paris: Edouard Cornély, 1909), pp. 89-90. He is even more specific concerning this phenomenon in his *Parfaicte Amye*, pp. 48 ff.:

> Il nous souvient de la saison passée,
> De la Beaulté, qu'au ciel avons laissée.

59. *Diane I*, pp. 48-50.
60. *Ibid.*, pp. 53-57. See chap. III, note 19.

CHAPTER IV

1. 439.
2. 249.
3. *Phaedo*, 65.
4. *Ibid.*, 76.
5. 28.
6. See Jules Alexandre Clerval, *Les Ecoles de Chartres au moyen âge* (Paris: A. Picard et fils, 1985), p. 117.
7. Ed. Temple Classics (London: J. M. Dent, 1940), p. 78.
8. *Rime, ed. cit.*, "In vita di Madonna Laura," sonnet 108.
9. First Speech, chap. III, p. 127.
10. *Op. cit.*, sonnet 11.
11. V.-L. Saulnier, in his recent exhaustive study of Scève and his works, *Maurice Scève* (Paris: Klinksieck, 1949), pp. 163 ff., says that Scève's *Délie* is not just literature, and he agrees to the basic Platonism of the sentiments expressed. However, he adds: "En résumé, la Délie de Scève n'est pas l'Idée, ni la Délia de Thibulle, mais la Délie de Virgile, c'est-à-dire, Diane, la déesse rebelle à l'amour, lumineuse, sœur du Jour. Tels sont les sens et le symbole du pseudonyme." It is interesting to see him comparing the Délie of Scève to Diane, since the first two books of Desportes' poetry were addressed to a lady who was given the name of Diane.
12. Ed. Michel François (Paris: Garnier frères, 1942), XIV Nouvelle.
13. *Op cit.*, p. 46.
14. *The Works of Guillaume De Salluste Sieur Du Bartas*, ed. Holmes, Lyons, and Linker (Chapel Hill: U. of North Carolina Press, 1935), II, 257.
15. *Ibid.*, III, 24.
16. *Ibid.*, III, 14.
17. *Diane II*, sonnet 67.
18. *Amour d'Hippolyte*, sonnet 65.
19. *Cléonice*, sonnet 94. See chap. III, note 48.
20. *Elégies I*, Elégie 7; imitated from Guinicelli. See C. B. Beall, "Un Echo de Guinicelli dans Philippe Desportes," *MLN*, LVII (1942), 429.
21. *Timaeus*, 51.
22. *Enneads*, V, viii, 1.
23. (New York: Phaidon Publishers, Inc., 1951), pp. 222-27.
24. *Op. cit.*, sonnet 1; see also Clements, *op. cit.*, p. 245.
25. *Cléonice*, sonnet 16; see also Clements, *op. cit.*, p. 245.

CHAPTER V

1. *The Art of Courtly Love*, trans. John Jay Parry (New York: Columbia U. Press, 1941), Book I, chaps. I-V.
2. (New York: F. S. Crofts & Co., 1938), pp. 171-73.
3. *Ed. cit.*, note 1, pp. 6 ff.
4. *Ibid.*, p. 3.
5. *Ibid.*, p. 12.
6. Guinicelli's great poem is: *Al cor gentil ripara sempre Amore*.
7. So designated first by Dante in his *Purgatorio*, Canto XXIV, v. 57.

Concerning Guinicelli and the *dolce stil nuovo*, see C. H. Grandgent, *Dante* (New York: Duffield & Co., 1916), pp. 132 ff.

8. See *Tutte le opere di Dante Alighieri* (Oxford: Nella Stamperia dell'Università, 1904). In the *Convivio*, pp. 238 g., the lady is thus described, Trattato terzo, Canzone seconda:

> In lei discende la virtù divina,
> Sicome face in angelo che'l vede;
>
> . . . .
> Di costei si può dire:
> Gentil è in donna ciò che in lei si trova;
> E bello è tanto, quanto lei simiglia.
>
> . . . .
> Cose appariscon nello suo aspetto,
> Che mostran de' piacer del Paradiso;
> Dico negli occhi e nel suo dolce riso,
> Che le vi reca Amor com' a suo loco.
>
> . . . .
> Sua beltà piove fiammelle di fuoco,
> Animate d'un spirito gentile,
> Ch'à creatore d'ogni pensier buono;
> E rompon come tuono
> Gl'innati vizi, che fanno altrui vile.

Dante goes on to say, "Whereas, inasmuch as wondrous things are perceived in her under the bodily aspect. . .it is manifest that her form, to wit her soul, which guides the body as its proper cause, miraculously receives the gracious excellence of God. . .this lady has been endowed and ennobled by God." This translation is taken from the Temple Classics ed. of *The Convivio of Dante Alighieri*, p. 170.

9. Charles S. Singleton, in his *Essay on the Vita Nuova* (Cambridge: Harvard U. Press, 1949), p. 67, quotes from Petrarch's *Secretum* as follows: "I can only say that whatever I am I owe to her [Laura]. And if I have any portion of fame or glory, I should never have attained it had she not cultivated with her very noble afffections the seed of virtue which nature had planted in my breast. She recalled my youthful mind from all unworthy things and . . . forced it to look on lofty things . . . What other desire did I have in youth if not to please her alone who had so pleased me? And in order to do this you know to what labors I yoked myself, scorning a thousand lascivious and voluptuous things."

For an exhaustive study of the Platonism of Petrarch, see Robert V. Merrill, "Platonism in Petrarch's *Canzoniere*," *Modern Philology*, XXVII 1929-30), 165-73.

10. *Rime, ed. cit.*, "In vita di Laura," Canzone 7, p. 79.

11. *Ibid.*, sonnet 122, p. 172.

12. See Paul Oscar Kristeller's *The Philosophy of Marsilio Ficino* (New York: Columbia U. Press, 1943), pp. 286-88.

13. *The Platonism of Shelley*, p. 101.

14. To mention only the more prominent participants in the discussions which take place in the better known dialogues, there were: Socrates, Timaeus, Parmenides, Lysis, Phaedrus, Craytlus, Ion, Agathon, Pausanias, Eryximachus, Aristophanes, Meno, Crito, Glaucon.

15. The most important collections of Italian *Rime* known to the men of Desportes' age were (see Lavaud, *op cit.*, pp. 178 ff.): *Rime diverse di molti eccellentiss. auttori nuovamente raccolte*, Libro primo (Venice: Gabriel Giolito, 15 45); *Rime di diversi nobili poeti toscani, raccolte da M. Dionigi Atanagi*, Libro primo (secondo)...(Venice: Lodovico Avanzo, 1565); *I Fiori delle rime de' poeti illustri, nuovamente raccolti e ordinati da Girolamo Ruscelli*...(Venice: Giovanbattista e Melchior Sessa, 1569); *Rime de gli illustrissimi sig. Academi Eterei* (Ferrara, 1567); *Rime scelte*—better known as *Recueil de Dolce* (?).

16. *Phaedrus*, 251.
17. *Ibid.*, 251 ff.
18. *Symposium*, 183.
19. See Holmes, *op. cit.*, p. 170.
20. Sappho says: "Now Love masters my limbs and shakes me, fatal creature, *bitter-sweet*." See *Sappho*, trans. H. T. Wharton (London: John Lane, 1895), p. 96.
21. *Republic*, VII.
22. *Amour d'Hippolyte*, sonnet 40.
23. *Phaedrus*, 251.
24. *Diane I*, sonnet 55; imitated from Tebaldeo. See Vianey, *op. cit.*, p. 231.
32. *Elégies I*, Elégie 1.
26. See Robert V. Merrill, *The Platonism of Joachim Du Bellay*, pp. 136 ff.
27. *Ibid.*, pp. 11-44.
28. See Lavaud, *op. cit.*, p. 6.
29. Baldassare Castiglione, *The Book of the Courtier*, trans. Sir Thomas Hoby (London: J. M. Dent, 1948), pp. 306-7.
30. Lavaud, *op. cit.*, p. 131.
31. *Diverses Amours*, pp. 372-73.
32. *Elégies I*, Elégie 1.
33. Lavaud, *op. cit.*, p. 5.
34. Mention has been made of the sonnets dedicated to the memory of Claude de Laubespine.
35. 199-201.
36. *Enneads*, III, v. 1.
37. *Commentary on the Symposium*, ed. cit., First Speech, chap. IV, p. 130.
38. Castiglione, *op. cit.*, p. 303.
39. *Œuvres poétiques*, ed. cit., pp. 13-14.
40. *Diane I*, pp. 50-53.
41. *Amours d'Hippolyte*, pp. 172-73.
42. *Diverses Amours*, p. 397.
43. 209 ff.
44. *Diane I*, pp. 50-53. This poem is the most complete expression of Platonism to be found in the works of Desportes. The first part, having to do with the creation, seems to be drawn from the *Timaeus;* the second part, having to do with love, from the *Symposium.*
45. Pp. 476-77.
46. 251.

47. *Diane II*, pp. 78 ff.
48. *Ed. cit.*, p. 13.
49. 244 ff.
50. Seventh Speech, chap. XIII.
51. *Ibid.*, chap. XV.
52. *Parfaicte Amye, ed. cit.*, p. 73.
53. *Amours d'Hippolyte*, sonnet 65.
54. 251.
55. *Cléonice*, sonnet 79.
56. *Elégies I*, Elégie 14.
57. *Diverses Amours*, pp. 373-75.
58. *Ibid.*, pp. 407-08.
59. *Diane I*, sonnet 65.
60. Poetic fury will be discussed at much greater length in the section of this work devoted to poetry.
61. *Diane I*, pp. 50-53.
62. *Œuvres chrestiennes*, sonnet 3.
63. *Diverses Amours*, sonnet 39.
64. *Œuvres chrestiennes*, p. 509.
65. 197.
66. 201 ff.
67. *Enneads*, III, v, 4.
68. *Ibid.*, I, ii, 1.
69. *Parfaicte Amye, ed. cit.*, p. 49.
70. *Amours d'Hippolyte*, pp. 173-75.
71. *Cléonice*, sonnet 26.
72. *Amours d'Hippolyte*, pp. 134-36.
73. *Diane I*, pp. 60-61.
74. 180 ff.
75. *Diane II*, sonnet 58.
76. *Amours d'Hippolyte*, pp. 152-53.
77. 182-83.
78. *Diverses Amours*, sonnet 8; imitated from Ragnina. See J. Vianey, "Une Rencontre des Muses de France et d' Italie demeurée inédite," *RHL*, 1903, pp. 92-100.
79. 212.
80. *Amours d'Hippolyte*, pp. 130-31.
81. *Ed. cit.*, p. 65.
82. *Elégies I*, Elégie 7; imitated from Guinicelli. See C. B. Beall, "Un Echo de Guinicelli dans Philippe Desportes," *MLN*, LVII (1942), 429.
83. *Œuvres de . . .*, ed. Abel Lefranc (Paris: Champion, 1913-31), II, 430-31.
84. *Elégies I*, Elégie 6.
85. *Epitaphes*, p. 484.
86. *Elégies II*, pp. 307-15.
87. *Diane I*, sonnet 50.
88. *Cléonice*, sonnet 92.
89. 65-66.
90. 207.
91. *Bergeries*, pp. 447-48.

92. *Cartels et Masquarades*, pp. 459-60.
93. *Cléonice*, sonnet 94; imitated from Bernardo Tasso. See Lavaud, *op. cit.*, p. 267.
94. *Elégies I*, Elégie 7. See note 82 above.
95. *Amours d'Hippolyte*, sonnet 59.
96. *Diverses Amours*, pp. 391-95.
97. *Cartels et Masquarades*, pp. 457-58.
98. *Bergeries*, pp. 442-43.
99. 45 ff.
100. 508.
101. *Tutte le opere di Dante Alighieri*, ed. cit., p. 216.
102. *Rime*, ed. cit., "In vita di Madonna Laura," sonnet 3.
103. *Commentary on the Symposium*, ed. cit., Sixth Speech, chap. II, p. 183.
104. *Amours d'Hippolyte*, sonnet 61.
105. *Ibid.*, pp. 172-73.
106. Fourth Book, p. 304.
107. *Diane I*, sonnet 56.
108. 401.
109. *Enneads*, I, vi, 1.
110. *Cléonice*, sonnet 3; imitated from Torquato Tasso. See Vianey, *Le Pétrarquisme en France*. . ., p. 204.
111. *Cléonice*, sonnet 94; imitated from Bernardo Tasso. See Lavaud, *op. cit.*, p. 267.
112. 190-91.
113. *Comparative Literature*, I (1949), 97-112.
114. *Op. cit.*, Vol. I, Book I, chap. VIII, pp. 89-90. Dr. Merrill does not mention this appearance of the myth, although he develops the history of the myth prior to the Pléiade.
115. *Derniéres poésies*, ed. cit., p. 217.
116. *Ed. cit.*, VIIIe nouvelle.
117. *Œuvres poétiques*, ed. cit., "L'Androgyne de Platon," pp. 85-95.
118. *Elégies I*, Elégie 9.
119. *Diverses, Amours*, sonnet 8.
120. *Diane II*, sonnet 66.
121. *Ibid.*, sonnet 68; imitated from Costanzo. See Vianey, *Le Pétrarquisme en France*. . . , p. 238.
122. *Ibid.* pp. 113-14.
123. *Amours d'Hippolyte*, pp. 123-24.
124. *Ibid.*, pp. 140-41.
125. *Elégie I*, Elégie 16.
126. See Appendix.
127. 182.
128. See Héroët, *Œuvres poétiques*, ed. cit., p. 19, note 1.
129. *Ibid.*
130. *Ibid.*, p. 19, ll. 283-85.
131. *Elégies I*, Elégie 7.
132. *Ibid.*, Elégie 18.
133. 196-97.
134. *Parfaicte Amye*, ed. cit., p. 13.

135. *Diane II*, pp. 78-79.
136. *Amours d'Hippolyte*, pp. 159-61.
137. 253.
138. *Commentary on the Symposium*, ed. cit., Second Speech, chap. VIII, p. 144.
139. P. 76.
140. *Amours d'Hippolyte*, pp. 159-61.
141. *Statesman*, 271, 272; *Laws*, IV, 713; *Cratylus*, 398.
142. *Statesman*, 273, 274.
143. *Laws*, IV, 713, 714.
144. *The Platonism of Joachim Du Bellay*, p. 27.
145. *Elégies I*, Elégie 9.
146. *Diane I*, sonnet 37; imitated from Sasso. See Vianey, *Le Pétrarquisme en France*, p. 228.
147. *Cartels et Masquarades*, p. 460.

CHAPTER VI

1. *Symposium.* 177.
2. *Lyra Graeca* (New York: G. P. Putnam's sons, 1922), II, 183 ff. See also p. 401 for mention of this goddess by Alcaeus; and Vol. II, p. 197 for mention of her by Anacreon.
3. "Eros," *Journal of Philosophy*, XXXI, pp. 337-45.
4. *Symposium*, 203.
5. *Ibid.*, 178.
6. *Loc. cit.*
7. Love is here identified as the son of Aphrodite—the Latin Venus—which is the rôle most amatory poets assign him.
8. *Symposium*, 180.
9. *Ibid.*, 195 ff.
10. *Ibid.*,
11. See Lisle Cecil John, *The Elizabethan Sonnet Sequences* (New York: Columbia U. Press, 1938), chap. II, *passim*. These works were rediscovered during the period of the Renaissance. The former was published in Italy in 1494 and influenced the concepts of Telbaldeo and Chariteo, who in turn had great influence on the Pléiade in general and on Desportes in particular. The latter was published in France by Henri Estienne in 1554 and translated into French by Remy Belleau and published again in 1556.
12. *Ibid.*
13. See particularly first part by Guillaume de Lorris.
14. See Charles S. Singleton, *An Essay on the Vita Nuova* (Cambridge, Mass.: Harvard U. Press, 1949), pp. 48 ff.
15. *Diane I*, pp. 53-57.
16. *Amours d'Hippolyte*, pp. 140-41.
17. *Ed. cit.*, p. 125.
18. *Diane I*, pp. 50-53.
19. *Lysis*, 216.
20. 178.
21. *Diane I*, pp. 50-53.

22. *Elégies I*, Elégie 9.
23. *Ibid.*, Elégie 5.
24. *Diane I*, pp. 50-53.
25. *Roland furieux*, pp. 324 ff; inspired by Ariosto. See Lavaud, *op. cit.*, pp. 31 ff.
26. *Cartels et Masquarades*, pp. 459-60.
27. *Elégies I*, Elégie 9.
28. *Cartels et Masquarades*, pp. 460-61.
29. *Diverses Amours*, pp. 405-07.
30. *Bergeries*, pp. 451-52.
31. *Elégies I*, pp. 287-91.
32. The "lourde et pesante masse" here spoken of is the state of chaos existing before the creation.
33. *Diane I*, pp. 61-65; imitated from an unknown Italian poet. See Lavaud, *op. cit.*, note 5, p. 179.
34. *Ibid.*, pp. 50-53.
35. V, 731.
36. *Cléonice*, sonnet 73.
37. *Phaderus*, 252.
38. *Diane I*, sonnet 6; inspired by Ariosto. See Lavaud, *op. cit.*, p. 179.
39. *Diane I*, pp. 50-53.
40. *Ibid.*, I, pp. 53-56. See chap III, note 19.
41. *Ibid.*, pp. 50-53.
42. *Symposium*, 196.
43. *Diane I*, pp. 50-53.
44. *Diane II*, sonnet 1.
45. *Diverses Amours*, pp. 408-11.
46. *Ibid.*, sonnet 10.
47. *Ibid.*, p. 430.
48. See Lisle Cecil John, *op. cit.*, chap. II, *passim*.
49. *Phaedrus*, 255; also see Robert V. Merrill, "Eros and Anteros," *Speculum*, XIX (1944), 265-84.
50. *Œuvres poétiques*, ed. cit., pp. 96-99.
51. *Amours d'Hippolyte*, sonnet 65.

CHAPTER VII

1. 216
2. *Symposium*, 211-12.
3. *Hesiod, the Homeric Hymns and Homerica* (New York: G. P. Putnam's Sons, 1920), pp. 407 ff.
4. *Tutte le opere, ed. cit.*, "Vita Nuova," sonnet 16, p. 224.
5. *Rime, ed cit.*, "In vita di Madonna Laura," sonnet 162.
6. Second Speech, chap. II, p. 133.
7. *Ibid.*, Fifth Speech, chap. II, p. 167.
8. *The Book of the Courtier, ed. cit.*, Fourth Book, p. 310.
9. *Rime, ed. cit.*, sonnet 44.
10. Second Speech, chap. IX, p. 147.
11. See Walter Pater, *The Renaissance* (London: Macmillan & Co., 1920), pp. 73 ff., and John Addington Symonds, *The Life of Michelangelo Buonarroti* (New York Modern Library, 1928), pp. 381 ff.

12. See Fernand Baldensperger, *Les Sonnets de Shakespeare* (Berkeley: U. of California Press, 1943), pp. vii-ix, 367-70.
13. See Lavaud, *op. cit.*, pp. 39-43.
14. This youth was fatally wounded in a duel, and during the days while he lingered between life and death the king, Henri III, did not leave his bedside.
15. *Epitaphes*, p. 476.
16. *Elégies I*, Elégie 17.
17. *Symposium*, 211-12.
18. *Diane II*, sonnet 24.
19. 25.
20. *Epitaphes*, sonnet 3, pp. 484-85.
21. *Amours d'Hippolyte*, pp. 171-72.
22. *Epitaphes*, p. 477.
23. *Amours d'Hippolyte*, sonnet 18; imitated from Tebaldeo. See Vianey, *Le Pétrarquisme en France...*, p. 230.
24. *Amours d'Hippolyte*, pp. 123-24.
25. *Ibid.*, sonnet 65.
26. *Elégies I*, Elégie 7. See chap. IV, note 20.
27. *Œuvres chrestiennes*, sonnet 18; imitated from Petrarch. See Flamini, *op. cit.*, p. 353.
28. Psalms, 89: 4.
29. *Ibid.*, Ecclesiastes, 1, v. 2.
30. *Œuvres chrestiennes*, sonnet 2. The sentiments expressed in this sonnet resemble those expressed by Du Bellay in his most famous sonnet—see sonnet 113 of *l'Olive*—*Œuvres françoises de Joachim du Bellay*, ed. Marty-Laveaux, I, 137. However, since Desportes rarely borrowed from other French poets, it is more likely that he, like Du Bellay, went to the Italian poet, Daniello, for his inspiration:

>Se'l viver nostro è breve oscuro giorno
>Press' a l'eterno, e pien d'affanni e mali;
>Et più veloci assai che venti, o strali
>Ne vedi ir gli anni, e piu non far ritorno
>Alma; che fai? che non ti miri intorno
>Sepolta in cieco error tra le mortali
>Noiose cure? e poi ti son date ali
>Da volar a l'eterno alto soggiorno,
>Scuoti le trista ch'é ben tempo homai
>Fuor del visco mondan ch'e si tenace,
>E le dispiega al ciel per dritta via;
>Ivi é quel sommo ben ch'ogni huom desia;
>Ivi'l vero riposo; ivi la pace
>Ch 'indarno tu quagiu cercando vai.

See also Robert V. Merrill, *The Platonism of Joachim Du Bellay*, pp. 41-42.
31. *Amours d'Hippolyte*, pp. 171-72.
32. *Cléonice*, sonnet 18.
33. *Ibid.*, sonnet 25; imitated from Costanzo. See Vianey, *op. cit.*, p. 197.
34. *Ibid.*, sonnet 35; imitated from Costanzo. See Vianey, *op. cit.*, p. 238.

CHAPTER VIII

1. 249.
2. *Amours d'Hippolyte*, sonnet 8.
3. *Ibid.*, sonnet 1; imitated from Sannazaro. See La Croix du Maine and Du Verdier, *Les Bibliothèques françoises de* . . . (Paris: Saillant and Nyon, 1772-73), III, 207. It was doubtless to this sonnet that Ronsard made reference when he said:

> Lecteur, je ne veux estre escolier de Platon
> . . . .
> Ny volontaire *Icare* . . .
> Perdus pour attenter une sotise estreme.

See chap I, note 82.

4. 222.
5. See Nesca A. Robb, *Neoplatonism of the Italian Renaissance* (London: George Allen & Unwin Ltd., 1935), chap. VIII, *passim*.
6. *Rime, ed.cit.*, sonnet 12.
7. *Cléonice*, sonnet 16; imitated from Michelangelo. See Vianey, *op. cit.*, p. 237.
8. *Ibid.*, sonnet 41; imitated from Costanzo. See Vianey, *Le Pétrarquisme on France* . . . p. 237.
9. *Elégies I*, Elégie 8.
10. *Diverses Amours*, p. 407-08.
11. *Bergeries*, pp. 440-42. Except for the lines quoted there is nothing in his poem which can be related to truly Platonic concepts, for it is probably the most erotic of the works of Desportes, and as such is very rare. Inspired from Jean Second. See Lavaud, *op. cit.*, p. 131.
12. *Op cit.*, chap. III, *passim*.
13. 209.
14. *Elégies I*, Elégie 10.
15. *Cléonice*, sonnet 92.
16. *Symposium*, 208.
17. *Diverses Amours*, sonnet 8; imitated from Ragnina. see Vianey, *Le Pètrarquisme en France* . . . , p. 96.
18. *Epitaphes*, sonnet 1, p. 484.
19. *Ibid.*, pp. 487-89
20. 251.
21. *Diane I*, sonnet 7; imitated from Tebaldeo. See Vianey, *Le Pétrarquisme en France* . . . , p. 231.
22. 251.
23. *Diane I*, sonnet 43; imitated from Petrarch, *Rime, ed. cit.*, "In vita di madonna Laura," sonnet 22.
24. *Symposium* 212.
25. *Diverses Amours*, sonnet 9.
26. *Cléonice*, sonnet 36; imitated from Veniero. See Vianey, *Le Pétrarquisme en France*, p. 236.
27. *Symposium*, 196.
28. *Diane I*, pp. 50-53.
29. *Ibid.*
30. Sixth Speech, chap. XI, p. 204.

31. See *The Platonism of Joachim Du Bellay*, p. 145; also see *Enneads* III, 5.
32. See Holmes, *op. cit.*, p. 172.
33. See the section on Chartres in Henry Adams' *Mont-Saint-Michel and Chartres* (1904).
34. *Symposium*, 204.
35. *Rime, ed. cit.*, "In vita di Laura," sonnet 162.
36. *Ibid.*, sonnet 180.
37. *Rime, ed. cit.*, sonnet 15.
38. *Cléonice*, sonnet 76; imitated from Guarini. See Lavaud, *op. cit.*, p. 283.
39. *Amours d'Hippolyte*, sonnet 17.
40. *Cléonice*, sonnet 9.
41. *Ibid.*, sonnet 46. Lavaud, *op. cit.*, p. 202, speaks of these lines as being of almost perfect purity, the most beautiful perhaps of all those in the works of Desportes.
42. *Ibid.* sonnet 3; imitated from Torquato Tasso. See Vianey, *Le Pétrarquisme en France...*, p. 204.
43. *Diane I*, pp. 48-50.
44. *Ibid.*, pp. 50-53.
45. *Amour d'Hippolyte*, pp. 123-24.
46. *Cléonice*, sonnet 7.
47. *Ibid.*, sonnet 38.
48. *Amours. d'Hippolyte*, pp. 127-28.
49. *Diane I*, sonnet 25.
50. *Ibid.*, sonnet 38.
51. *Amours d'Hippolyte*, pp. 123-24.
52. Seventh Speech, chap. X, p. 228.

CHAPTER IX

1. *Republic*, III, 398.
2. *Protagoras*, 326; *Laws*, VII, 810.
3. *Protagoras*, 347.
4. *Laws*, VII, 817.
5. 214
6. 244
7. 533.
8. 22.
9. See *The Works of Aristotle*, trans. under editorship of W. D. Ross (Oxford: Clarendon Press, 1930), *Poetica*, chap. IV, 1448b.
10. *Ibid.*, chap. XVII, 1445a.
11. See *Complete Works of Horace*, ed. Caspar J. Kraemer (New York: Modern Library, 1936), *The Art of Poetry*, pp 397 ff.
12. See ed. Felix Gaiffe (Paris, 1910), Livre I, chap. I.
13. See Frances Yates, *op. cit.*, p. 80.
14. See Robert J. Clements, *Critical Theory* . . . , chap. V, *passim*.
15. *Ed. cit.*, Part II, chap. IV. The words "Lis doncques et relis . . . " come from Horace, *ed. cit.*, p. 406: "Do you, my friends, study the Greek masterpieces; thumb them day and night."

16. *Ibid.*
17. See Robert V. Merrill, *The Platonism of Joachim Du Bellay*, pp. 91 ff.
18. See Edouard Frémy, *op. cit.*, p. 231.
19. See Frances Yates, *op. cit.*, p. 129.
20. *Imitations de l'Arioste*, pp. 336-52.
21. *Diane I*, pp. 50-53.
22. 196.
23. *Diverses Amours*, pp. 413-14.
24. *Diane* II, sonnet 75.
25. *Diverses Amours*, pp. 428-29.
26. *Symposium*, 205 ff.
27. See *ed. cit.*, Odes IV, 8.
28. *Ibid.*, III, 30.
29. *Divina Commedia, ed. cit.*, Canto XXV, lines 55-56.
30. See Clements, *op. cit.*, p. 46.
31. *Œuvres complètes de* . . . , ed. P. Laumonier (Paris: Lemerre, 1914-19), II, 462.
32. *Ibid*, VI, 23, "A Philippe des-Portes, Chartrain."
33. Quoted by Lavaud, *op. cit.*, p. 477, from Scévole de Sainte-Marthe, *Œuvres de* . . . (Paris, 1579), fol. 162.
34. *Op. cit.*, pp. 141-42.
35. *Amours d'Hippolyte*, pp. 124-25.
36. *Diane* I, sonnet 1.
37. X, 617.
38. *Cléonice*, sonnet 1.
39. *Ibid.*
40. 47 ff.
41. III, 404, 410.
42. IV, 424.
43. II, 659.
44. *Ed. cit.*, Third Speech, chap. III, pp. 150-51.
45. *Op. cit.*, pp. 308 ff.
46. Quoted by Yates, *op. cit.*, p. 106, from "Remonstrances de Monsieur Du Faur de Pibrac, du xxiii Novembre 1572," printed in *Harangues et actions publiques des plus rares esprits de nostre temps* (Paris, 1609), pp. 777-83.
47. *Op. cit.*, p. 237.
48. *Cartels et Masquarades*, pp. 460-61.
49. See Yates, *op. cit.*, p. 269.
50. See chap. I, note 18, for his poems put to music by La Grotte. Others have been published in Yates, *op. cit.*, pp. 334 ff., and in D. P. Walker's "The Influence of *Musique mesurée à l'Antique* Particularly on the Airs de Cour of the Early Seventeenth Century, "*Musica Disciplina*, II (1948), 142-163. Of the Desportes songs which he reproduces, Walker says that the "rhythm resembles that of *musique mesurée* except that it is not based on a metrical scheme."
51. *Œuvres complètes de Pierre Ronsard, ed. cit.*, "Sonnets pour Hélène." II, 42.
52. *Cléonice*, sonnet 94; imitated from Bernardo Tasso. See Vianey, *Le Pétrarquisme en France* . . . , p. 238.

53. *Diverses Amours*, pp 413-14.
54. Ibid., p. 427.
55. *Amours d'Hippolyte*, sonnet 15.
56. See Clements, *op. cit.*, p. 44.
57. *Ibid.*, p. 150 ff; Clements gives a brief sketch of the history of the swan motif in antiquity. See also D'Arcy Thompson, *A Glossary of Greek Birds* (London: 1936), p. 184.
58. 85.
59. See R. V. Merrill, *The Platonism of Joachim Du Bellay*, pp. 87-90.
60. *Œuvres de* . . . , *ed cit.*, Book III, chap. xr, pp. 160-61.
61. *Œuvres de* . . . *ed. cit.*, I, 163.
62. See Yates, *op. cit.*, p. 150
63. *Diane I*, sonnet 34; imitated from Sasso. See Vianey, *Le Pétrarquisme en France* . . . , p. 228.

CHAPTER X

1. *Symposium*, 206.
2. See the *Protagoras* and the *Meno*, *passim*.
3. *Enneads*, *ed. cit.*, I, vi, 8.
4. *Ibid.*, I, iii, 2.
5. *Ibid.*, 7.
6. *The City of God, ed. cit.*, Book IV, p. 128.
7. *Introduction to Saint Thomas Aquinas*, ed. Anton C. Pegis (New York: Modern Library, 1948), Question xlix, p. 544.
8. *Ibid.*, Question lv, p. 560.
9. *Ibid.*, p. 581.
10. *Ibid.*, p. 582.
11. Sometimes written *Convito*, but found as above in both the Italian version (Oxford: Nella stamperia dell'Università, 1904) and in the Temple Classics trans. (London: J. M. Dent, 1940).
12. Ed. Temple Classics, pp. 309 ff. Dante takes this definition from Aristotle's *Physics;* see *Works of Aristotle*, ed. Ross (Oxford, 1930), II, 247b.
13. *Ibid.*, pp. 320 ff.
14. See Paul Oskar Kristeller, *op. cit.*, chap. XIV, *passim*.
15. Wm. A. Nitze, in his article " 'Vertu' as Patriotism in Corneille's *Horace*," *PMLA*, LXV (Dec., 1952), 1168-69, quotes the following lines from Spencer's *Faerie Queene*, Book 1, Canto V, and says they are a "noble expression of the Renaissance faith in the active life . . . thoroughly in the spirit of Castiglione's *The Courtier*":
> The noble hart, that harbours vertuous thought
> And is with child of glorious great intent,
> Can neuer rest vntill it forth haue brought
> Th' eternall brood of glorie excellent.
16. Lavaud, *op. cit.*, p. 317.
17. *Ibid.*, pp. 244 ff.
18. See Frémy, *op. cit.*, pp 221 ff.; also Bibliothèque Nationale, nouv. acq. franc. 4655. A discourse by Desportes on *la Crainte* from the hitherto unpublished manuscript of the Bibliothèque Nationale has been transcribed

and placed in the Appendix of this study. It will be treated in the following chapter.

19. See Frémy, *op. cit.*, pp. 231 ff.
20. See Lavaud, *op. cit.*, p. 246, note 4.
21. See Frémy, *op. cit.*, pp. 221 ff.
22. *Ibid.*, p. 233.
23. *Ibid.*, p. 235.
24. *Ibid.*
25. *Phaedo*, 79-80.
26. *Republic*, IV, 435-42.
27. See Frémy, *op. cit.*, p. 236.
28. *Ibid.*
29. *Philebus*, 59.
30. Frémy, *op. cit.*, p. 237.
31. *Ibid.*
32. *Phaedo*, 65.
33. *Republic*, VI, 490.
34. *Supra* pp. 2 and 21.
35. See Lavaud, *op. cit.*, pp. 444 ff.
36. See George Depue Hadzsits, *Lucretius and His Influence* (New York: Longmans, Green and Co., 1935), chap. XI, *passim*.
37. The "carpe diem" theme of Horace was dear to Ronsard, who championed the moral virtues, as against the intellectual ones.
38. See Gilbert Highet, *The Classical Tradition* (New York & London: Oxford U. Press, 1949), *passim*. Seneca really came into his own in France only toward the end of the sixteenth century with Montaigne and the dramatic theorists.

CHAPTER XI

1. IV, 435-42.
2. X, 896.
3. *Republic*, IV 441.
4. *Meno*, 77.
5. *Protagoras*, 358.
6. *Ibid.*, 349, 359.
7. X, 904.
8. I, 646.
9. *Ibid.*, 469. The Jowett translation of this reads: "What is there which so surely gives victory and safety in war? For there are two things which give victory—confidence before enemies, and fear of disgrace before friends."
10. IV, 429.

CHAPTER XII

1. *Musica Disciplina*, II (1948), 259-60.
2. See Lavaud, *op. cit.*, pp. 475 ff.
3. (Paris: Librairie Delagrove, 1943), pp. 137-38.

4. See Ferdinand Brunot, *La Doctrine de Malherbe d'après son Commentaire sur Desportes* (Paris: G. Masson, 1891), pp. 121 ff.

5. Malherbe's *Commentaire,* in the form of marginal notes on the *Premieres œuvres* of Desportes, is well known. See Brunot, op. cit., pp. 88 ff.

APPENDIX

1. *Op. cit.,* pp. 248-49.
2. *Op. cit.,* pp. 221 ff.
3. This is doubtless an early spelling of the word *surgeon.*
4. Desportes seems to be quoting from memory the following words of Horace, *Odes,* Book III, Ode, iii, lines 7-8: "Si fractus inlabatur orbis, impavidum ferient ruinae" ("Were the vault of heaven to break and fall upon him, its ruins would smite him undismayed"). The fact that he change "fractus" to "totus" does not change the sense of the quotation appreciably. The *n* in the word "inlabatur" may have become *l* through assimilation. On the other hand the discrepancies in the manuscript are more probably the fault of a scribe than of Desportes.

GENERAL BIBLIOGRAPHY

Bayle, Pierre. *Dictionaire historique et critique.* Edition by Des Maizeaux. Amsterdam: P. Brunel, 1740. 4 vols.

Billings, Thomas H. *The Platonism of Philo Judaeus.* Chicago: U. of Chicago Press, 1919. 103 pp.

Boodin, J. E. "Cosmology in Plato's Thought," *Mind,* XXXVIII (Oct., 1929), 489-505; XXXIX (Jan., 1930), 61-71.

Burckhardt, Jacob Christoph. *The Civilization of the Renaissance in Italy.* Translated by G. C. Middlemore. New York: Harper and Bros., 1929. 640 pp.

Chamard, Henri. *Histoire de la Pléiade.* Paris: H. Didier, 1939. 4 vols.

———. *Les Origines de la poésie française.* Paris: E. de Boccard, 1932. 307 pp.

Champion, Pierre. "Henri III et les écrivains de son temps," *Bibliothèque d'humanisme et renaissance,* I (1941), 43-172.

Charbonnel, J.-Roger. *La Pensée italienne au XVIe siècle et le courant libertin.* Paris: E. Champion, 1919. 720 pp.

Comte, C. and P. Laumonier. "Ronsard et les musiciens de XVIe siècle," *Revue de l'histoire littéraire francaise,* VII (1900), 341 ff.

De Graff, T. B. "Plato in Cicero," *Classical Philology,* XXXV (April, 1940), 143-53.

Demos, R. "Eros," *Journal of Philosophy,* XXXI (June, 1934), 337-345.

Denys (Saint . . . the Areopagite). *Œuvres de . . .* Edition by Monseigneur Darboy. Paris: Maison de la Bonne Presse, 1887.

Egger, Emile. *L'Hellenisme en France.* Paris: Didier et Cie, 1869. 2 vols.

Fletcher, Jefferson B. "Benivieni's *Ode of Love* and Spencer's *Fowre Hymes,*" *Modern Philology,* VIII (1911), 545-60.

———. "A Survey in Renaissance Mysticism: Spencer's *Fowre Hymes,*" *PMLA,* XXVI (1911), 452-75.

Gilson, Etienne. *The Philosophy of St. Thomas Aquinas.* Translation by Ed. Bullough. Cambridge, Eng.: W. Heffer & sons, ltd., 1924. 287 pp.

Grandgent, C. H. *Dante.* New York: Duffield & Co., 1916. 397 pp.

Guthrie, Wm. K. C. *Orpheus and Greek Religion.* London: Methuen & Co., ltd., 1935. 287 pp.

Haight, Elizabeth H. *Apuleius and His Influence.* New York: Longmans, Green & Co., 1927. 190 pp.

Handschin, Jacques. "The 'Timaeus' Scale," *Musica Disciplina,* IV (1950), 3-42.

Hastings, James. *Dictionary of the Bible.* New York: Charles Scribner's sons, 1920. 992 pp.

Hauvette, H. *Littérature italienne.* Paris: Librairie Armand Colin, 1906. 518 pp.

Headlam, Cecil. *The Story of Chartres.* London: J. M. Dent, 1902. 361 pp.

Hermes (Trismégiste). *Cinq livre de . . .* Edition by Louis Ménard. Paris: Perrin et Cie, 1925. 280 pp.

Hutton, J. "Three Notes on French Authors: Desportes, Guérould, Ronsard," *Modern Language Notes*, LV (1940), 579-81.
Inge, William Ralph. *The Philosophy of Plotinus*. New York: Longmans, Green & Co., 1929. 2 vols.
John, Lisle Cecil. *The Elizabethan Sonnet Sequences*. New York: Columbia U. Press, 1939. 278 pp.
Jules-Bois, H. A. "Vision of Eternal Joy: Plato & Confessions of St. Augustine," *Commonweal*, XII (July, 1930), 339-41.
Kantorowicz, E. H. "Plato in the Middle Ages," *Philosophical Review*, LI (May, 1942), 312-23.
Kerr, W. A. R. "Antoine Héroët's Parfaite Amye," *PMLA*, XX (1904), 567-83.
———. "Le Cercle d'amour," *PMLA*, XIX (1904), 33-63.
———. "The Pléiade and Platonism," *Modern Philology*, V (1908), 407-21.
Klibansky, Raymond. *The Continuity of the Platonic Tradition during the Middle Ages*. London: Warburg Institute, 1939. 58 pp.
Labé, Louise. *Louise Labé, sa vie et son œuvre*. Edition by Dorothy O'Connor. Paris, 1926.
Lanson, Gustave. "Etude sur les rapports de la littérature française et de la littérature espagnole au XVIIe siècle," *RHL* (1897), 61-72.
———*Histoire de la littérature française*. Paris: Hachette et Cie, 1896. 1166 pp.
Lee, Sidney. *The French Renaissance in England*. Oxford: Clarendon Press, 1910. 494 pp.
Lefranc, Abel. *La Vie quotidienne au temps de la renaissance*. Paris, Hachette et Cie, 1938. 253 pp.
Lewis, Clive S. *The Allegory of Love*. London: H. Milford, 1938. 378 pp.
Lipardi, Angelo. *The Dolce Stil Nuovo According to Lorenzo de' Medici*. New Haven: Yale U. Press, 1936. 348 pp.
Medici, Lorenzo de' . . . *Poesie volgari di Lorenzo de' Medici*. Edition by Janet Ross and Edward Hutton. Edinburgh: J. M. Dent, 1912. 2 vols.
Ménard, Louis. *Hermès Trismégiste*. Paris: Perrin et Cie, 1925. 280 pp.
Merrill, Robert V. "Eros and Anteros," *Speculum*, XIX (1944), 265-84
———. "Platonism in Petrarch's Canzoniere," *Modern Philology*, XXVII (Nov., 1929), 161-74.
———. "Platonism in Pontus de Tyard's *Erreurs armoureuses*," *Modern Philology*, XXXV (Nov., 1937), 139-58.
———. "The Pléiade and the Androgyne," *Comparative Literature*, I (1949), 97-112.
Mirandola, Giovanni Pico della . . . *A Platonick Discourse upon Love*, . . . *in Explication of a Sonnet by Hieronymo Benivieni*. Edition by Edmund G. Gardner. Boston: The Merrymount Press, 1914. 83 pp.
Mott, Lewis F. *The System of Courtly Love*. Boston: Ginn and Co., 1896. 153 pp.
Nock, A. D. "Eros the Child," *Classical Review*, XXXVIII (Nov., 1924), 152-55.

Notopoulos, James A. *The Platonism of Shelley.* Durham: Duke U. Press, 1949. 671 pp.

———. "Symbolism of the Sun and Light in the *Republic* of Plato," *Classical Philology*, XXXIX (July-Oct., 1944), 163-72; 223-40.

Ogle, M. B. "The Origin and Tradition of Literary Conceits," *The American Journal of Philology*, XXXIV (1913), 125-52.

Olmstead, Everett W. *The Sonnet in French Literature and the Development of the French Sonnet Form.* Ithaca: Cornell U. Press, 1897. 207 pp.

Omont, Henri. "Essai sur les débuts de la typographie grèque à Paris," *Mémoires de la société de l'histoire de Paris*, XVIII (1891), 1-72.

Parent, J. M. *La Doctrine de la création dans l'école de Chartres.* Paris: Librairie Philosophique J. Vrin, 1938. 221 pp.

Patch, Howard R. *The Goddess Fortuna in Mediaeval Literature.* Cambridge: Harvard U. Press, 1927. 200 pp.

Pater, Walter H. *Plato and Platonism.* London: Macmillan & Co., 1920. 282 pp.

———. *The Renaissance.* New York: Modern Library, 1919. 199 pp.

Patterson, W. F. "French Poetic Theory," *University of Michigan Publications in Language and Literature*, XIV, XV (1925), 1-978; 1-523.

Picot, Emile. *Les Français italianisants au XVIe siècle.* Paris: H. Champion, 1906-7. 2 vols.

Pieri, Marius. *Le Pétrarquisme au XVIe siècle: Pétrarque et Ronsard, ou l'influence de Pétrarque sur la Pléiade Française.* Marseille: Lafitte, 1896. 342 pp.

Plutarch. *Moralia.* Translation by Frank C. Babbitt. New York: C. P. Putnam's sons, 1927. 14 vols.

Putnam, Samuel. *Marguerite de Navarre.* New York: Coward-McCann, 1935. 374 pp.

Quintilianus, Marcus Fabius. *Institution oratoria.* Translation by H. E. Butler. New York: G. P. Putnam's sons, 1920. 4 vols.

Rathéry, Edme-Jacques. *Influence de l'Italie sur les lettres français.* Paris, 1853, 200 pp.

Robb, Nesca A. *Neoplatonism of the Italian Renaissance.* London: George Allen & Unwin, Ltd., 1935. 315 pp.

Rota, Berardino. *Delle rime del S. Berardino Rota.* Naples, 1572. 2 vols.

Sainte-Beuve, Charles-Augustin. *Tableau historique et critique de la poésie française et du théâtre français au XVIe siècle.* Paris: Charpentier et Cie, 1869. 499 pp.

Saitta, Giuseppe. *La filosofia di Marsilio Ficino.* Messina: G. Principato, 1923. 285 pp.

Sanctis, Francesco de . . . *History of Italian Literature.* New York: Harcourt, Brace & Co., 1931. 2 vols.

Sandys, John Edwin. *A History of Classical Scholarship.* Cambridge: University Press, 1903-8. 3 vols.

Saulnier, V.-L. *Maurice Scève.* Paris: Klinksieck, 1949. 2 vols.

Scève, Maurice. *Œuvres poétiques complètes de . . .* Paris: Garnier frères, 1927. 333 pp.

———. *Microcosme.* Lyon: Jean de Tournes, 1562.

Scott, J. G. "Encore un imitateur de Desportes," *Revue de littérature comparée*, V (July, 1925), 471-73.

———. *Les Sonnets Elisabéthains*. Paris: Champion, 1929. 343 pp.

Sears, Helen L. "The Concepts of Fortune and Fate in the Comedia of Lope de Vega." Unpublished Ph. D. dissertation. University of California, 1948. 505 pp.

Shorey, Paul. *Platonism Ancient and Modern*. Berkley: U. of California Press, 1938. 259 pp.

———. *The Unity of Plato's Thought*. Chicago: U. of Chicago Press, 1903. 88 pp.

Siegel, Paul N. "The Petrarchan Sonneteers and Neo-Platonic Love," *Studies in Philology*, XLII (1945), 165-82.

Singleton, Charles S. *An Essay on the Vita Nuova*. Cambridge: Harvard U. Press, 1949. 149 pp.

Smeaton, Wm. H. *The Medici and the Italian Renaissance*. New York: C. Scribner's sons, 1901. 286 pp.

Stevens, Linton C. "How the French Humanists of the Renaissance Learned Greek," *PMLA*, LXV (Mar., 1950), 241-48.

Symonds, John A. *The Life of Michelangelo Buonarroti*. New York: Modern Library, 1928. 544 pp.

———. *Renaissance in Italy*. London: Smith, Elder & Co., 1914. 495 pp.

Taylor, A. E. "Note on Plato's Astronomy," *Classical Review*, XLIX (May, 1935), 53-56.

———. *Plato, the Man and his Work*. London: Methuen & Co., Ltd., 1949. 562 pp.

Thompson, D'Arcy. *A Glossary of Greek Birds*. London: Oxford U. Press, 1936.

Tilley, A. *The Literature of the French Renaissance*. Cambridge: University Press, 1904. 2 vols.

Tillyard, E. M. W. *The Elizabethan World Picture*. New York: Macmillan Co., 1944. 108 pp.

Torre, Arnaldo della . . . *Storia dell'Accademia Platonica de Firenze*. Florence: Tip. G. Carnesecchi e figli, 1902. 858 pp.

Trever, Albert A. *History of Ancient Civilization*. New York: Harcourt, Brace & Co., 1939. 560 pp.

Tricotel, E. "Une satire inédite de Desportes," *Bulletin du Bibliophile* (1867), 177 ff.

Unamuno, Miguel de . . . *The Agony of Christianity*. Translation by Pierre Loving. New York: Payson & Clarke, Ltd., 1928. 183 pp.

Vaganay, H. "Du nouveau sur Desportes: Desportes et Malherbe," *Bulletin du Bibliophile* (1928), 502-6.

Villey, Pierre. *Sources d'idées au seizième siècle*. Paris: Plon-Nourrit et Cie, 1912. 278 pp.

———. *Les Sources italiennes de la Défense et illustration*. Paris: H. Champion, 1908. 162 pp.

Vossler, Karl. *Medieval Culture*. New York: Harcourt, Brace & Co., 1929. 2 vols.

INDEX

Académie de poésie et de musique, 16, 18, 127
Académie des derniers Valois, L' (Frémy), xv, 141, 149, 158
Académie du Palais, xv, 6, 9, 20, 51, 112, 131, 133, 136, 140, 141, 142, 149
Accademia Platonica, xi, 28, 35
Achilles, 5
Adams, Henry, 175
Aeneas, 153
Agathon, 28, 73, 84, 89, 90, 93, 94, 112, 123, 167
Albigensian Crusade, 61, 114
Alcaeus, 171
Alcibiades, 70
Al cor gentil ripara sempre Amore (Guinicelli), 166
Alexandria, viii
Alexandrian poets, 90, 95
All, 37
All-Love, 73
All-Soul, 44, 45, 73
Amboise, Bussy d', ix, 5
Amor, 91
Amor divinus, 63
Amores (Ovid), 90
Amours d'Hippolyte (Desportes), 157, 161, 162, 163, 164, 165, 166, 168, 169, 170, 171, 173, 174, 175, 177
Amyot, Jacques, 20, 146, 157
Anacreon, 171
Anacreontea, 90, 95
Anamnesis, 41, 48, 49, 50, 51
Anchises, 98, 152
Andalusia, 60
Andreas Capellanus, x, 12, 13, 59, 60
Androgyne, 50, 81, 82, 112
Angelic Mind, 54
Angels, 38
Anjou, duc d', 4, 5, 6, 146
Anteros, 95, 96
Aphrodite, 75, 88, 89, 92, 96, 98, 171
Apollo, 121, 127, 130, 131
Apology (Plato), 120, 164
Aquitaine, Guillaume d', 61
Arabian scholars, 60
Arabian poets, 61
Argonaut, 7
Argonautica, 91
Aristippus, Henricus, ix
Ariosto, 3, 92, 172
Aristophanes, 81, 167
Aristotle, 9, 26, 30, 33, 34, 35, 50, 51, 53, 58, 120, 121, 134, 135, 136, 141, 142, 152, 153, 158, 163

Aristotelianism, 32
Ars amatoria (Ovid), 59, 90
Art, 56, 57
Art of Courtly Love, The (Parry), 166
Art of Poetry, The (Aristotle), 175
Art poétique françoys (Sebillet), 121
Art poétique (Fresnaie), 9
Ascagne, 153
Asolani, Gli (Bembo), 13, 73
Astrology, 38
Atropos, 125
Atticus, 153
Aubigné, Agrippa d', 4, 8, 9, 136, 157
Augustine, Saint, ix, 19, 37, 53, 90, 113, 134, 135, 142, 151
Aultres inventions extraictes de Platon (Héroët), 95
Aventure première (Desportes), 158

Baïf, Jean Antoine de, 2, 8, 16, 17, 18, 127, 128
Baïf, Guillaume de, 15, 159
Baïf, Lazare, 16
Baldensperger, Fernand, 160, 173
Ballet comique de la Reine (Baïf), 127
Banquet (Plato), xiii
Bayle, Henri, 10
Beall, C. B., 161, 166, 169
Beatrice, 61, 62, 78, 98
Beauty, Beauté, the Beautiful, xiii, xiv, xv, 22, 33, 34, 36, 45, 46, 48, 52, 58, 60, 65, 68, 69, 71, 81, 84, 91, 97-105, 106, 111, 113, 114, 115, 133, 136, 141, 147
Being, 17
Belleau, Remy, 171
Bellière, Pomponne de, 21
Beloved, xii, 22, 59, 80, 85, 87, 106-118, 142, 147
Bembo, Cardinal, ix, 13, 54, 63, 64, 66, 68, 73, 74, 82, 148
Benivieni, Girolamo, 34, 63, 163
Bergeries et Masquarades (Desportes), 157, 169, 170, 172, 174
Bernard of Chartres, 2
Bertrand de Born, x
Bessarion, x, 63
Bibliographie et Prosographie des rois de France, 158
Bibliothèque d'Humanisme et de Renaissance, 158
Bibliothèque Nationale, xv, 141, 149, 177

INDEX

Bibliothèques françoises de La Croix du Maine et de Du Verdier Les, 161, 174
Bien, 36
Billings, Thomas H., 162
Bitter-sweet, 64, 65, 168
Blois, 14
Boccaccio, xv
Bodin, Jean, 9
Body, 41, 43, 45
Boethius, xvii, 2, 17, 34, 49, 62, 114, 136
Bologna, 61
Bonport, 21
Book of the Courtier, The (Castiglione), 168, 172
Bordeaux, 21
Borromeo, Carlo, 7, 19
Brantôme, 5
Bréhier, Emile, 36, 164
Briçonnet, Guillaume, xii, 35
Brigade, 127
Bruno, Giordano, 9
Brunot, Ferdinand, 16, 22, 160, 161, 179
Brutus, 142, 156
Budé, Guillaume, xi, xii
Bulletin de la Société de l'histoire du Protestantisme français, 160

Caesar, Julius, 142, 156
Caignet, 129
Callianthe, 123
Cameron, Alice, 161
Canso, xiii
Canzone dell'amore divino (Benivieni), 34, 163
Canzoni, 62
Carpe diem, 21, 124, 178
Carpenter, Nan C., 17
Cartels et Masquarades (Desportes), 176
Cassius, 142, 156
Castiglione, Baldassare, x, xii, xvii, 3, 13, 63, 64, 66, 73, 74, 80, 83, 99, 135, 136, 148, 168
Cathedral Schools, ix, 2
Catherine, *see* Medici
Cato, 142, 156
Cavalcanti, Guido, 61
Chalcidius, vii, 2, 32
Chamard, Henri, xviii
Champier, Symphorien, xi, 148
Champion, Pierre, 7, 9, 158
Chansons (Desportes), 30, 69
Chant d'Amour (Desportes), xiv, 27, 31, 72, 147
Chaos, 25, 26, 27, 28, 31, 85, 88, 92, 147, 172
Chariot, 40, 46, 72
Chariteo, 171

Charles VIII, xi
Charles IX, xii, 1, 2, 4, 6, 7, 16, 18, 66
Chartres, xii, 1, 2, 3, 12, 20, 39, 53, 67, 133, 145, 175
Chateauneuf, Mlle de, 8
Chrétien de Troyes, ix, 90
Christ, vii, 26, 34, 45
Christianity, viii, x, 19, 113, 114
Christians, 25, 34, 37, 40, 43, 45, 50, 51, 53, 103, 115, 134, 136, 140
Chrysolorus, x, 63
Church, Catholic, 50, 66, 113, 133
Church Fathers, ix, 24, 62
Cicero, vii, ix, 14, 32, 62, 141, 142, 153, 154, 163
Cioranescu, Al, 161
City of God, The (St. Augustine), 177
Civitas veri sive morum (Delbene), 9
Classical doctrine, 58
Classical Tradition, The (Highet), 178
Clements, Robert J., 23, 125, 130, 161, 162, 166, 175, 176, 177
Cléonice (Desportes), 101, 116, 157, 165, 166, 169, 170, 172, 174, 175, 176
Clerval, Jules Alexandre, 157, 166
Clotho, 125
Clytemnestra, 133
Colin, Jacques, xii, 157
Collège de Coqueret, 127
Collège de France, xv
Commentary on Cicero's Somnium Scipionis (Macrobius), 163
Commentary on the Symposium (Ficino), 11, 40, 41, 54, 63, 71, 74, 91, 99, 101, 112, 118, 126, 148, 163, 165, 168, 170, 171
Comparative Literature, 170
Complainte (Desportes), 38, 45, 106
Complete Works of Horace, The, 175
Confréries, 19, 20, 145, 160
Confrérie de Sainte Cécile, 160
Confrérie d'Hieronymites, 160
Congrégation de Notre Dame de la Vie Saine, 20, 160
Consolation of Philosophy (Boethius), xvii, 34, 49, 114
Constable, Henry, 22
Constantinople, ix, x
Contemplation, 73, 91, 97, 98, 105, 106, 133-40
Contre une nuict trop claire (Desportes), 3
Convivio (Dante), 54, 62, 135, 167, 177
Cooper, W. V., 163
Copetta, 162

Cordova, 60
Coreggi, 2, 112, 146
Corneille, Pierre xiv
Cortegiano, Il (Castiglione), xii, xvii, 3, 13, 66, 68, 74, 80, 136
Cosimo, *see* Medici
Cosmos, 22
Costanzo, 64, 165, 173, 174
Counter Reformation, 7
Courtly poets, 114
Courville, Joachim Thibault de, 18
Crainte, La, xiii, 83, 149-56, 177
Cratylus (Plato), 52, 167
Creation, 2, 24-39, 53, 60, 85, 147, 172
Creator, 25, 28, 30, 32, 33, 37, 39
Critical Theory and Practice of the Pléiade (Clements), 23, 175
Crito, 167
Cronos, 85, 86
Crusaders, 114
Cusa, Nicolas de, 35

Daedalus, 107
Dance, 119, 126, 127, 136
Daniel, Arnaut, x
Daniel, Samuel, 22
Daniello, 163, 173
Dante, x, xvii, 32, 43, 54, 61, 62, 65, 78, 79, 90, 98, 100, 101, 114, 115, 123, 135, 147, 164, 166, 177
Dante (Grandgent), 167
Dargan, F. Preston, 160
Darmesteter, A., 146
Dauphin, 21, 112
De amicitia (Cicero), viii
De amore (Ficino), 126
De arte honeste amandi (Andreas Capellanus), 59
Deffense et Illustration de la Langue Françoise, xii, 121
De institutione musica (Boethius), 17
De la vérité et du mensonge, 141
Delbene, Bartholomeo, 9
De l'envie et des mœurs contraires à icelle, 141
Délie (Scève), 55, 166
De l'ire et comme il la faut modérer, 141
Demiurge, 26
Démons, 37, 38, 85
Demos, Raphael, 88
Demosthenes, 142, 151
De mundo (Aristotle), 30
De musica (Plutarch), 163
De natura deorum (Cicero), viii
De republica (Cicero), 163
De rerum natura (Lucretius), viii
Dido, 113, 153
Diogenes, 142, 156

Dione, 75, 89
Dionysius the Areopagite, Saint, ix, 2, 19
Diotima, 69, 75, 89, 92, 102, 109, 113, 123
Discours de la cognoissance, 141
Discours de la crainte, 141
Discours de l'âme, 141
Discours de l'honneur et de l'ambition, 141
Diverses Amours (Desportes), 157, 158, 168, 169, 170, 172, 174, 176, 177
Diverses Œuvres de l'illustrissime cardinal Du Perron, Les, 159
Divina Commedia (Dante), 32, 176
Divine fury, 137
Divinus furor, 121
Dizains, 55
Doctrine de Malherbe d'après son Commentaire sur Desportes, La (Brunot), 160, 179
Dods, Marcus, 164
Dolce-amaro, 64
Dolce stil nuovo, x, 61, 62, 73, 90, 98, 99, 100
Donna mi prega (Cavalcanti), 61
Dorat, Jean, x, 7, 16, 17, 127
Dove's Neck-Ring, The (Ibn Hazm), 60, 61
Drummond, William, 22
Du Bartas, Guillaume de Saluste, 55
Du Bellay, Joachim, xii, 16, 43, 85, 121, 123, 131, 158, 163, 173
Du Faur de Pibrac, Guy, 6, 7, 10, 16, 18, 19, 127, 131, 176
"Du nouveau sur Desportes" (Vaganay), 161
Du Perron, Jacques Davy, 10, 14, 20, 122, 159
Durant, Will, xvii
Dernières poésies de Marguerite de Navarre, Les, 163, 165
Descartes, 144
Desire, 88, 92
Des passions de l'âme et de la joie, 141
Des passions humaines de la joie et de la tristesse et quelle est la plus véhémente, 141
Desportes, 20, 24, 27, 30, 32, 33, 35, 37, 38, 39, 41, 42, 43, 45, 46, 47, 48, 49, 50, 57, 59, 65, 67, 68, 70, 71, 74, 76, 77, 80, 81, 83, 84, 91, 92, 93, 94, 95, 96, 97, 101, 103, 105, 107, 108, 110, 111, 114, 116, 121, 122, 123, 124, 125, 127, 128, 129, 130, 132, 133, 136, 137, 138, 139, 140, 141, 142, 143, 145, 146, 147, 148, 149, 157, 158, 159, 160,

166; court poet, 6, 7, 8, 10, 11, 145, 146; churchman, 16, 20, 21, 133, 142, 146, 160; discourses of, xiii, 9, 19, 133, 140, 141-44; man of learning, 11, 146; patron of letters, 14, 15, 146; Platonic poet, x, xi, xii, 22, 23, 24-39 (creation), 40-51 (the soul), 52-57 (the Ideas), 59-87 (love), 88-96 (the God Love), 97-105 (beauty), 106-118 (the lover and the beloved), 119-131 (the poet and poetry), 145-148 (the virtues); the statesman, 21; youth and education of, 1, 3, 4, 5, 13, 14, 145, 146
"Desportes et Angelo di Costanzo" (Kastner), 161
"Desportes et Ariosto" (Cameron), 161
"Desportes et Guarini" (Kastner), 161
"Desportes et Petrarch" (Clements), 161
Desportes, Thibault, 15, 21
Destiny, 40
Dialoghi d'amore (Leone Ebreo), 115, 163, 165
Dialogues of Plato, xviii, 22, 32, 39, 52, 63, 85, 109, 133, 140, 144, 147, 162,
Diane, 6, 50, 102, 116, 166
Diane I, (Desportes), 12, 157, 162, 163, 168, 171, 172, 174, 175, 176, 177
Diane II, (Desportes), 157, 158, 159, 166, 169, 171, 172, 173, 176
Dictionaire historique (Bayle), 10

Ears, 81
Ecclesiastes, 103, 173
"Echo de Guinicelli dans Philippe Desportes, Un" (Beall), 161
Ecoles de Chartres au moyen âge, Les (Clerval), 166
Eleanor of Poitou, x
Elégies I (Desportes), 157, 164, 165, 166, 168, 169, 170, 171, 172, 173, 174
Elégies II (Desportes), 169
Elements—fire, water, air, earth, 27, 30, 37, 142
Elizabethan Sonnet Sequence, The (John), 171
Eloges des hommes illustres (Saint-Marthe), 160
Empedocles, vii
"Encore un imitateur de Desportes" (Scott), 161
England, 101
Enneads (Plotinus), 163, 165, 166, 168, 169, 170, 177

Entragues, 10
Epaminondas, 142, 156
Epernon, Jean-Louis de Nogarat de la Valette, dus d', 10, 11, 159
Ephors, 152
Epictetus, 142, 153
Epicureanism, 140
Epicurus, viii
Epitaphe de Claude de Bastarnay (Desportes), 38, 43
Epitaphes (Desportes), 157, 159, 163, 165, 173, 174
Eros, 88, 90, 92, 95, 96, 131
"Eros" (Demos), 171
"Eros et Anteros" (Merrill), 172
Eryximachus, 88, 167
Essay on the Vita Nuova (Singleton), 167, 171
Essence of Plotinus, The, 163
Estienne, Charles, xii
Estienne, Henri, 9, 15, 22, 146, 162, 171
Estienne, Robert II, 15
Estienne, Robert III, 15
Estrées, Françoise d', 8
Etaples, Lefèvre d', xii, 35
Eternity, 33
Ether, 30
Ethics (Aristotle), 9, 134, 163
Ethos, 18, 125, 126
"Etude sur les rapports de la littérature française et de la littérature espagnole au XVIIe siècle" (Lanson), 161
Eyes, 48, 78, 79, 80, 117

Fabricius, 142, 156
Faerie Queene (Spencer), 177
Faguet, Emile, 3, 27, 159
Faict du proces de Baïf, Le, 159
Fates—Lachesis, Clotho, Atropos, 121, 125
Fear, a passion of the soul, 51, 141, 144, 149, 156
Festugière, Jean, xiii, xiv
Ficino, Marsilio, ix, xi, 1, 2, 11, 13, 24, 35, 38, 40, 50, 54, 63, 66, 68, 70, 73, 80, 82, 85, 91, 99, 100, 101, 112, 115, 126, 135, 148, 163
Fiori delle rime, I, 168
Flamini, F., 161, 164
Florence, x, 63
Florentine Academy, ix, 2, 11, 35, 54
Flux, vii, 52
Forms, 53, 54
"Fortune du Tasse en France, La" (Beall), 161
France, 3, 4, 5, 6, 7, 8, 14, 16, 18, 20, 35, 50, 145
Francesca, 78

François I, xi, xii, 2
François II, xii
François, Michel, 163, 166
Frémy, Edouard, xv, 141, 149, 158, 160, 176, 177, 178
French Academies of the Sixteenth Century (Yates), 157
French Renaissance in England, The (Lee), 22
Friedländer, Paul, 162
Friendship, 28, 72
Fulbert, 2, 3
Fureur, love, poetic, 71, 72, 131, 169

Gaiffe, Felix, 175
Gargantua et Pantagruel (Rabelais), 76, 82
Garnier, Claude, 15
Genesis, 26
"Gil Polo, Desportes and Lyly's Cupid and my Campaspe" (Matthews), 161
Glaucon, 79, 144, 167
Glossary of Greek Birds, A (Thompson), 177
God, ix, 3, 11, 24, 25, 27, 28, 30, 33, 34, 35, 40, 54, 57, 85, 91, 97, 99, 107, 111, 113, 114, 115, 120, 130, 133, 134, 138, 151
Gods, 33, 37, 38, 39, 40
Gohin, Ferdinand, 165
Golden age, 85, 86, 87
Golden race, 85
Gombrich, E. H., 57
Gondi, Albert de, 5
Good, Goodness, 33, 34, 36, 37, 39, 42, 45, 68, 73, 91, 97, 99, 106, 115
Gorgias (Plato), 163, 165
Grace, 45
Grandgent, C. H., 167
Grands écrivains francais de la Renaissance (Lefranc), xviii, 163
Greek Anthology, 90, 95
Greek poets and philosophers of antiquity, 8, 16, 17, 59, 88, 97, 100, 113, 119, 121, 125, 126, 132
Greek scholars, viii, 63
Gregory, xiv
Guinicelli, 61, 166, 167, 169

Hadzsits, Geo. D., 178
Hair, 117
Harmony, 25, 26, 27, 28, 29, 30, 31, 39, 88, 126, 136, 142m 145, 147
Hatzfeld, Adolphe, 146
Hazm, Ibn, 60, 61
Headlam, Cecil, 3
Heaven, 41
Hebrews, viii
Helen of Troy, 113
Hélène (Ronsard's), 129

Henri II, xii
Henri III, xii, 1, 2, 4, 6, 8, 9, 10, 11, 15, 16, 18, 19, 20, 51, 133, 136, 140, 157, 158, 173
Henri IV, 1, 15, 20, 21, 112
Heptaméron (Marguerite de Navarre), 35, 55, 82
Heraclitus, vii, 30
Hermes Trismegistus, 19
Héroët, Antoine, xii, 39, 50, 55, 68, 70, 71, 74, 76, 84, 85, 95, 148,
Hesiod, 89, 172
Highet, Gilbert, 178
Hippolyte, 12, 101, 102, 116
Histoire de la civilization française (Lévêque), 159
Histoire de la poésie française (Faguet), 157
History of French Literature, A, (Nitze and Dargan), 160
History of Old French Literature (Holmes), 60
Hoby, Sir Thomas, 168
Holmes, Urban T., 60, 166, 168, 175
Holy Bible, 103, 162
Homer, vii, 88, 93, 97
Homeric Hymns and Homerica, The 172
Horace, 120, 123, 140, 142, 156, 178, 179
Huguenots, 4
Hutton, J., 161
Hymne de la surdité (Du Bellay), 163
Hymn to Aphrodite (Homeric), 98

Icarus, 22, 48, 107, 174
Ideas, xiv, xv, 2, 3, 22, 26, 28, 31, 36, 38, 49, 52-58, 55, 84, 91, 97, 101, 142, 147
Imitation, 65, 161
Imitations de l'Arioste de Philippe Desportes, Les (Cioranescu), 6, 157, 161, 176
"Imitatori stranieri di Jacopo Sannazaro, Gl'" (Torraca), 161
Immortality, 33
Influence de Ronsard sur la poésie L', (Raymond), 161
"Influence of Musique mesurée à l'antique, The" (Walker), 76
Innutrition, 23, 140
Inspiration, 22, 121, 122
Institution oratoria (Quintilianus), 17
Intelligence, 36, 42, 54, 139
Introduction to Saint Thomas Aquinas, 177
Intuition, 45
Ion (Plato), 120, 167
Isocrates, 142, 155

Italian Academies, xvii, 19
Italian city states, x
Italians, x, 23, 161
Italy, 3, 16, 61, 63, 66, 101

Jamyn, Amadis, 10
Jarnac, 5
Jason, 7
Jean, 53
John, Saint, 26
John, Lisle Cecil, 90, 171, 172
Jowett, Benjamin, xvi, 162, 178
Joyeuse, Anne duc de, 10, 15, 127, 159
Julian, ix
Justice, 127

Kastner, L. E., 161
Kristeller, Paul, 11, 126, 167, 177

Labé, Louise, xii
Lachesis, 125
La Croix du Maine, François Goudé, sr de, 161, 174
Lady, 61, 103, 104, 117
La Grotte, Nicolas de, 5, 176
Lanson, Gustave, 161
Lapp, John C., 158, 166
Latini, Brunetto, 123
Laubespine, Claude de, 4, 13, 14, 101, 168
Laubespine, Madeleine de, *see* Villeroy
Laumonier, Pierre, 158, 160, 176
Laura, 54, 62, 78, 79, 99, 164, 167
Lavaud, Jacques, xv, 6, 13, 157, 158, 159, 160, 161, 165, 168, 172, 173, 175, 176, 177, 178
Laws (Plato), 38, 42, 93, 119, 126, 142, 143, 171, 175
Lazarus, 113
Lee, Sidney, 22
Lefranc, Abel, xiv, 163, 165, 169
Guast, 5, 10
o X, *see* Medici
eone Ebreo, xiii, 9, 50, 54, 63, 82, 115, 148, 163
Le Roy, Louis, 158
L'Estoile, Pierre de, 8, 159
Lettres de Pomponne à Bevilliers sur la mort de son frère, 160
Lévêque, André, 159
Life of Michelangelo Buonarroti, The (Symonds), 172
Ligue, 4, 20
Lignerolles, Mme de, 136
Livre d'institution de l'Académie, 19, 136
Lodge, Thomas, 22
Logos, xvii, 26
Lombard, Peter, 135

Lorenzo, *see* Medici
Lorris, Guillaume, 171
Louis XII, xi
Love, x, xiv, 22, 27, 28, 36, 39, 45, 54, 59-87; creative force, 78; ennobling effects of, 73, 74, 75; flame of, 70; immortality of, 77, 78
Love, courtly, 60, 61, 64, 83
Love madness, 70
Love suffering, 60, 64, 65, 88, 100, 109, 147
Love, the God, 47, 51, 78, 84, 88-96, 102, 115, 171; blindness of, 93; inspiration of poets, 112, 122; winged, 93, 94
Lover, xiv, 22, 59, 61, 68, 71, 84, 85, 87, 106-118, 142, 147
Love's Labour's Lost (Shakespeare), 160
Loving, Pierre, xvii
Lucretia, 142, 156
Lucretius, viii
Lucretius and His Influence (Hadzsits), 178
Lyonese School, xii
Lyra Graeca, 171
Lysis (Plato), 97, 107, 119, 167, 171

Mackenna, Stephen, 163
Macrobius, 32, 163
Macrocosm, 79, 115
Madness, love, 107, 110; poetic, 119, 131
Maecenas, 14
Maison de la Charité, 160
Malherbe, François de, 15, 16, 147, 179
Marguerite de Navarre, xii, 2, 35, 36, 37, 39, 45, 50, 68, 82, 84, 99, 148, 160
Marie de Champagne, x, 12, 59
Marot, Clément, 158
Martha, sister of Lazarus, 113
Marty-Laveaux, 157, 173
Mary Magdalene, 113
Mary, Mother of Christ, 113, 114
Mary, sister of Lazarus, 113
Masquarade des chevaliers fidelles (Desportes), 127
Matthews, E. G., 161
Maugiron, 10
Medicis, viii, 1, 2, 11; Catherine de', xii, 2, 5, 7, 66; Cosimo de', x, 2; Leo X, xi; Lorenzo de', xi, 2, 54, 148; Piero de', xi
Mémoires (de Thou), 159
Meno (Plato), ix, 49, 167, 177
Mercury, 43

Merrill, Robert V., xiv, xvii, 34, 42, 82, 85, 114, 167, 168, 176, 172, 173, 176, 177
Michelangelo, xi, 47, 49, 54, 57, 100, 101, 108, 116, 148, 174
Michiels, Alfred, xv, 8, 14, 27, 157, 158, 159, 160, 161
Microcosm, 79, 115, 145
Middle Ages, 3, 17, 34, 87, 90, 113, 114
Mignons, 10, 70
Milan, 7
Mind, 42, 44
Mirandola, Pico della, xi, 63, 148
"Modèle de Desportes non-signalé encore: Pamphilo Sasso, Un" (Vianey), 161
Moitié, 112
Monica, Mother of St. Augustine, 113
Montaigne, 179
Montcontour, 5
Montereul, Jean de, 15, 20, 23
Mont-Saint-Michel and ...Chartres (Adams), 175
Monza, 7
Moon, 30
Mort de Rodomont (Desportes), 122
Motion, 29, 30, 39
Muses, 119, 120, 121, 123, 126
Music, 16, 17, 18, 119, 126, 136; effects of, 126, 127, 128, 129
Musica Disciplina, 178
"Music in the Medieval and Renaissance Universities" (Carpenter), 17
Mysticism, 68
Myth, of the Androgyne, 50, 81, 82; of the Cave, 65; of the Charioteer, 38, 46, 51, 72

Naïveté, 125, 162
Navarre, Marguerite de, *see* Marguerite de
Neoplatonism, viii, ix, x, 26, 35, 39, 40, 45, 54, 74, 99, 103, 161
Neoplatonism of the Italian Renaissance, The (Robb), 109, 174
Neoplatonists, ix, xi, 2, 19, 24, 33, 34, 36, 37, 51, 53, 62, 68, 71, 73, 91, 107, 110, 114, 115, 134, 140
Nérac, xii, 160
New Testament, 28, 40
Nitze, William A., 160, 177
Nominalists, 53
"Notes on Desportes and Du Bellay" (Dameron), 161
Notopoulos, James A., 63, 159
Nouvelles œuvres poétiques (Pontus de Tyard), 5
Nous, 26

Œuvres chrestiennes (Desportes), 25, 26, 30, 36, 132, 162, 163, 164, 165, 169, 173
Œuvres complètes de Maturin Régnier, 159
Œuvres complètes de Pierre Ronsard, 158, 176
Œuvres de Philippe Desportes, 157
Œuvres françoises de Du Bellay, 173
Œuvres poétiques d'Héroët, 165, 168, 170, 172
Œuvres poétiques de Pontus de Tyard, 157
Old Testament, 24, 40
Olive (Du Bellay), x, 158
One, 35, 37, 42
Order, 25, 26, 39
Ordre du Saint-Esprit, 160
Orlando, 92
Orpheus, vii, 7, 8, 17, 19, 91, 130
Ovid, 59, 60, 64, 90, 113

Palace Academy, xv, 6, 9, 19, 20
Pantheism, 37
Paolo, 78
Paradiso (Dante), 43, 163
Parfaicte Amye (Héroët), 55, 68, 70, 76, 84, 85, 165, 169, 170
Paris, 1, 3, 5, 9, 66
Parlement de Paris, 127
Parmenides, vii, 91, 167
Parnassus, 121
Parry, John Jay, 60, 166
Pascal, vii
Pasquils, 4, 159
Passions, 141-144
Pater, Walter, 172
Patterns, 55, 56
Pausanias, 75, 82, 89, 167
Pegasus, 121
Penia, 89
Père Pain et Vin, 131
Petrarch, ix, 34, 47, 54, 62, 63, 64, 78, 79, 80, 90, 91, 96, 99, 100, 101, 114, 115, 116, 123, 164, 165, 167, 174
Petrarchists, xii, 3, 5, 6, 23, 64, 65, 66, 68, 71, 80, 84, 86, 87, 90, 101, 106, 115, 130, 147, 148
Pétrarquisme en France au XVIe siècle (Vianey), 158, 161, 162, 163, 170, 171, 173, 175, 177
Phaedo (Plato), 33, 77, 130, 133, 164, 166, 178
Phaedra, 113
Phaedrus (Plato), xiii, 44, 46, 47, 49, 52, 70, 71, 84, 89, 91, 92, 93, 95, 101, 106, 110, 111, 119, 133, 164, 165, 167, 168, 172
Philebus (Plato), 178

INDEX

Philippe, King of Macedonia, 150
Philo, the Jew, viii, 26
Philosopher-king, 145
Philosophie de l'amour de Marsile Ficin et son influence sur la littérature française au XVIe siècle, La, xvi
Philosophy of Love, The (Leone Ebreo), 165
Philosophy of Marsilio Ficino, The (Kristeller), 159, 167
Phoebus, 131
Photiades, Constantin, 160
Physics (Aristotle), 177
Pibrac, see Du Faur de
Piero, see Medici
Plaintes (Desportes), 106
Plato, vii, viii, ix, x, xi, xiii, xv, xvi, 2, 8, 11, 17, 22, 23, 30, 31, 33, 34, 35, 36, 37, 38, 40, 42, 43, 45, 46, 48, 49, 50, 51, 52, 53, 54, 55, 56, 59, 60, 63, 65, 66, 67, 68, 69, 70, 71, 72, 73, 74, 76, 77, 79, 80, 82, 85, 87, 88, 89, 92, 93, 95, 97, 99, 100, 107, 112, 113, 115, 118, 119, 120, 121, 125, 126, 129, 131, 132, 133, 134, 137, 138, 140, 141, 142, 143, 144, 147, 155, 162
Platonic Academy, Athenian, viii
Platonic Love, iv, 13, 63, 97, 107, 110
Platonism, vii, ix, x, xi, xiii, xiv, 4, 5, 19, 22, 23, 24, 27, 40, 47, 65, 87, 91, 99, 103, 105, 111, 140, 141, 144, 145, 147, 161
Platonism of Joachim Du Bellay, The (Merrill), xviii, 164, 168, 171, 173, 175, 177
Platonism of Philo Judaeus, The (Billings), 162
"Platonism in Petrarch's Canzoniere" (Merrill), 167
"Platonism in Pontus de Tyard's Erreurs Amoureuses, The" (Merrill), 163
Platonism of Shelley, The (Notopoulos), 159, 167
Plautus, 142, 154
Pléiade, xii, 1, 7, 16, 17, 23, 55, 65, 74, 82, 91, 95, 121, 122, 123, 125, 147, 171
Plenty, 89
Plethon, Gemistus, x, 63
Plotinus, ix, 36, 37, 42, 44, 45, 53, 56, 57, 81, 114, 134
Plutarch, 141, 142, 157, 163
Poet, xiv, 22, 55, 90, 119-32, 145
Poète de cour au temps des derniers Valois, Philippe Desportes, Un (Lavaud), xviii
Poetica (Aristotle), 158, 175

Poetry, xiv, 22, 119-32, 141, 142; courtly poetry, 60, 61
Poland, 6, 7, 16, 146
Polyeucte (Corneille), 27
Polyhymnia, 126
Pompey, 153
Poncet, Didier, 129
Porphyry, 135
Porus, 89
Poverty, 89
Premier Curieux (Tyard), 24, 29
Premières œuvres (Desportes), 5, 179
Priam, 152
Prière en forme de confession (Desportes), 163
Prières et autres œuvres chrestiennes (Desportes), 157
Prisons (Marguerite de Navarre), 35, 45, 50, 82
Procez contre Amour (Desportes), xiv, 47
Protagoras (Plato), 177, 178
Prototypes, 54, 175
Protreptikos, 17
Provence, xv, 59, 61
Psalmist, 47
Psalms, 16, 20, 128, 129, 132, 146, 173
Pudeur, 22
Prugatorio (Dante), 166
Pythagoras, v, 17

Quelles sont les plus excellentes, les vertus intellectuelles ou les morales, xv, 136
Quélus, Jacques de Lévy, sr, 10, 70, 101, 102
Quintilianus, Marcus Fabius, 17

Rabelais, 13, 76, 77, 82, 131
Racan, le marquis de, 159
Racine, Jean, xiv
Ragnina, 169, 174
Rambouillet, la marquise de, 5
Ramée, Pierre de la, xii, 2
Raymond, Marcel, 161
Realists, 54
Reason, 42, 43, 47, 51, 52, 91, 94, 142
Recollection, 49, 50, 51, 52
Recueil de Dolce, 168
Régnier, Maturin, 15, 159
Regulus, Atilius, 142, 156
Remedia amoris (Ovid), 90
Renaissance, xii, 3, 24, 32, 35, 40, 66, 47, 48, 50, 54, 59, 64, 65, 67, 68, 73, 82, 83, 86, 87, 99, 100, 101, 106, 108, 112, 113, 115, 118, 121, 130, 131, 135, 136, 140, 146
Renaissance, The (Pater), 172

Rencontre des Muses de France et d' Italie, 161
Republic (Plato), 35, 42, 43, 79, 81, 119, 125, 126, 132, 133, 142, 143, 144, 162, 163, 165, 168, 175, 178
Retz, maréchale de, 5, 6, 22, 66, 136, 146, 159
Revelation, 53
Rien, 37
Rime de Fráncesco Petrarca, Le, 62, 79, 163, 165, 166, 167, 170, 172, 174, 175
Rime diverse di molti eccellentiss. autori, 168
Rime di diversi nobili poeti toscani, 168
Rime di gli illustrissimi sig. Accademi Eterei, 168
Rime di Michelangelo Buonarroti, 165
Rime scelte, 168
Rival, Jean de, 20
Robb, Nesca, 109, 174
Roland, 92
Roland furieux (Desportes), 172
Roman de la Rose, Le (Lorris & Meung), 90
Romans, 17, 62, 131
Rome, viii
Ronsard, xiii, xiv, 1, 4, 6, 10, 12, 14, 16, 19, 22, 121, 123, 124, 127, 129, 136, 137, 174, 178
Ronsard et son luth (Photiades), 160
Roscelin, 53
Rouen, 15, 21
Royale Bibliothèque, 149

Saint Bartholomew Massacre, 4
Sainte-Chapelle, 20, 21
Sainte-Beuve, Charles-Augustin, 160
Sainte-Marthe, Scévole de, 21, 124, 125, 160, 176
Saint-Gelais, Mellin de, 158
Saint-Luc, 10
Saint-Mégrin, 10
Sannazaro, 64, 174
Sappho, 64, 88, 168
Sasso, 64, 171
Saulnier, V.-L, 166
Scaevola, Mucius, 156
Scaliger, Joseph, 10
Scève, Maurice, xii, 55, 148, 166
Science, 139
Scott, J. G., 161
Scotus Erigena, John, ix, 2
Scriptures, 24, 141
Sebillet, Thomas, 121
Seconde Semaine, La (Du Bartas), 55

Seizième siècle en France (Darmesteter & Hatzfeld), 146
Semaine, La (Du Bartas), 55
Seneca, 140, 141, 142, 178
Senecterre, Antoine de, 3, 66
Sextus, 142, 156
Shakespeare, 101, 160
"Siège de Rouen (1591-92) et son importance pour l'information de Shakespeare" (Baldensperger), 160
Singleton, Charles S., 167, 171
Six livres de la république (Bodin), 9
Socrates, vii, 11, 24, 25, 37, 42, 45, 53, 65, 70, 71, 73, 77, 88, 91, 95, 97, 102, 106, 110, 113, 119, 130, 133, 135, 138, 139, 142, 144, 156, 167
Solitaire premier (Tyard), 121
Solitaire second (Tyard), 17
Solon, 142, 152
Sommo Ben, 34
Somnium Scipionis (Cicero), viii, 32
Sonnets à Hélène (Ronsard), 6, 124
Sonnets de Shakespeare, Les (trans. by Baldensperger), 173
Sonnets spirituels (Desportes), 25, 72, 103
Sophia, 115
Sophists, vii
Soul, xiv, 11, 22, 33, 38, 39, 40-51, 99, 142, 137; appetitive, 134; dwelling place in star, 43, 49, 51; effects of music on, 126; immortality of, 41, 48, 49, 51, 70; intellectual, 134; passions of, 141-44; preexistence of, 50, 51; prison of, 44, 45, 46, 51; recollection of, 49, 50, 51; role of love, 60; two souls, mortal and immortal, 142; wings of, 44, 47, 51
Souverain bien, 35, 36, 39, 45
Spain, 60
Spencer, Herbert, 177
Sphere, 28, 29, 39
Stars, 38, 42
Statesman (Plato), 164, 171
Stephanus, *see* Henri Estienne, 162
Stoics & stoicism, viii, 53, 140, 142, 155
Story of Art, The (Gombrich), 57
Story of Chartres, The (Headlam), 3
Studi di storia letteraria italiana e straniera (Flamini), 161
Summa Theologica (Thomas Aquinas), 42, 135
Summum bonum, 33, 34, 35, 51, 103
Sun, 99

Sur la mort de Jacques de Lévy, sieur Quélus (Desportes), 70
Swan, 130, 131, 132
Symonds, John A., 172
Symposium (Plato), 11, 28, 39, 42, 66, 68, 69, 73, 75, 77, 81, 82, 83, 84, 89, 91, 96, 99, 109, 113, 123, 168, 171, 172, 173, 174, 175, 176, 177

Tansillo, 164
Tasso, Bernardo, 165, 170
Tasso, Torquato, 170, 175
Tebaldeo, 64, 171, 173, 174
Tertullian, 142, 155
Thélème, Abbey of, 77
Theologia platonica de immortalitate animarum (Ficino), xi, 19
Thibulle, 166
Thomas Aquinas, Saint, ix, 19, 42, 53, 135
Thompson, D'Arcy, 177
Thou, Augustin de, 15
Thou, Jacques-Auguste de, 15, 159
"Three Notes on French Authors: Desportes, Guéroul, Ronsard" (Hutton), 161
Timaeus (Plato), viii, ix, 2, 3, 24, 25, 26, 27, 28, 29, 32, 37, 38, 39, 40, 41, 42, 53, 79, 126, 161, 162, 164, 166, 167, 168
Tombeau (Montereul), 15
Torraca, F., 161
Tout, 37, 117
Traité des passions de l'âme (Descartes), 144
Translations, 23
Trilingue et noble académie, xii
Trinity, 26
Trionfi (Petrarch), 123
Trojan War, 88, 113
Troubadours, x, 59, 60, 61, 62, 85, 99
Truth, 17, 33, 34, 45, 49, 91, 97, 99, 106, 112, 115
Turks, ix
Turnbull, Grace H., 163
Tusculan Disputations (Cicero), vi

Tusson, xii
Tutte le opere di Dante Alighieri, 167, 170, 172
Tyard, Pontus de, xii, 9, 17, 24, 29, 34, 121, 148, 157

Unamuno, Miguel de, vii, xiii
Universe, 39, 40, 145
Universe of Pontus de Tyard, The, 158, 160, 162
Uomo di virtù, 16, 64, 136
Uomo universale, 16
Urania, 126
Uranus, 75, 89

Vaganay, H., 161
Vanvres, 21, 146
Vaudemont, Louise de, 7
Vaugelas, 22
Veniero, 174
Ventadorn, Ebles II de, 61
Venus, 92, 93, 96, 131, 171
Vianey, J., 158, 161, 162, 163, 165, 169, 170, 171, 173, 174, 175, 177
Vices, xv
Vie de Malherbe, La (Racan), 159
Villeroy, Madeleine de, 4, 44
Villeroy, Nicolas de Neufville, seigneur de, 4, 5, 14
Vincennes, 20
Virgil, 142, 166
Virtues, xiv, 22, 49, 51, 81, 99, 133-40, 142, 147; Christian, 135; intellectual, 134 ff; moral, 134 ff.; Platonic, 134-35
Vita nuova (Dante), 62, 64, 65, 79, 90

Walker, D. P., 145, 176
Wharton, H. T., 168
Wisdom, 91, 112, 134
Word, 26
Works of Aristotle, The, 175, 177
Works of Guillaume de Salluste sieur Du Bartas, The, 166
World-Soul, 40, 55, 78

Yates, Frances, 2, 18, 127, 145, 157, 158, 160, 175, 176, 177

www.ingramcontent.com/pod-product-compliance
Lightning Source LLC
Chambersburg PA
CBHW021841220426
43663CB00005B/358